UNITED NATIONS PEACE OPERATIONS IN AFRICA

This book provides a comprehensive overview of the United Nations peace operations in Africa with a focus on civil-military coordination and state-building. With case studies from Sudan, South Sudan, and Congo, it examines themes like the colonization of Africa and long-term conflicts; United Nations peace operations in Africa from 1956–1964; and United Nations' return to Africa in the 1990s and 2000s. The author investigates how modern civil-military coordination gradually becomes an effective tool to assist in national-level state-building in conflict-ridden countries. The volume also discusses the organizational culture of civilian and military entities as well as civil-military cooperation in health, agriculture, energy, sports, and education to showcase the strategic direction for long-term peace in the region. Rich in ethnographic analysis, this book will be an essential read for scholars and researchers of African Studies, UN studies, peace and conflict studies, defence and strategic studies, international relations, and military studies.

Brigadier General Saleem Ahmad Khan (Retired) earned his PhD from the University of New Brunswick, Canada and became a historian. His other academic credentials are Masters of Philosophy, Strategy & Development Studies, War Studies and Defence Studies. He obtained Bachelor of Technology from the Jawaharlal Nehru University, India. He has wide range of experience in Bangladesh army including international peacekeeping experience. General Saleem served in the UN missions in Sierra Leone and Sudan. He chaired the 2014 Triennial Review Meeting of Contingent Owned Equipment at the UNHQ and served as the Director Overseas Operations and Director Information Technology of Bangladesh Army. He authored three books, one chapter of a book and several articles. He is a Community of Expert of Pearson Peacekeeping Centre Canada, and a member of the Academic Council on the United Nations System. The author facilitated seminars and panels on UN peace operations-related matters organized by Canadian Defence Academy, International Association of Peacekeeping Training Centres, Rotary International, and ACUNS in Bangladesh, Indonesia,

Uruguay, and the US. He presented conference papers at the Dalhousie University and University of New Brunswick in Canada, Central Michigan University and University of Maine in the US. He established a telecommunication and Information Technology firm "Trust Innovation Ltd" under the Bangladesh Army Welfare Trust and was its founder managing director. The author's academic awards are first prize in oral presentation, Graduate Research Conference, University of New Brunswick, Canada; Milton Gregg United Nations Internship Award; Henry Harvey Stuart Research Award; President's Doctoral Tuition Award; Second Best thesis in Master of War Studies, and one of the best theses in Master of Defence Studies.

UNITED NATIONS PEACE OPERATIONS IN AFRICA

Civil-Military Coordination and State-Building

Saleem Ahmad Khan

LONDON AND NEW YORK

Designed cover image: Saleem Ahmad Khan

First published 2023
by Routledge
4 Park Square, Milton Park, Abingdon, Oxon OX14 4RN

and by Routledge
605 Third Avenue, New York, NY 10158

Routledge is an imprint of the Taylor & Francis Group, an informa business

© 2023 Saleem Ahmad Khan

The right of Saleem Ahmad Khan to be identified as author of this work has been asserted in accordance with sections 77 and 78 of the Copyright, Designs and Patents Act 1988.

All rights reserved. No part of this book may be reprinted or reproduced or utilised in any form or by any electronic, mechanical, or other means, now known or hereafter invented, including photocopying and recording, or in any information storage or retrieval system, without permission in writing from the publishers.

Trademark notice: Product or corporate names may be trademarks or registered trademarks, and are used only for identification and explanation without intent to infringe.

Disclaimer: Maps used in this book are for representational purposes only. The international boundaries, coastlines, denominations, and other information shown in the maps in this work do not necessarily imply any judgement concerning the legal status of any territory or the endorsement or acceptance of such information. For current boundaries please refer to Survey of India maps.

British Library Cataloguing-in-Publication Data
A catalogue record for this book is available from the British Library

Library of Congress Cataloging-in-Publication Data
A catalog record has been requested for this book

ISBN: 978-1-032-22270-7 (hbk)
ISBN: 978-1-032-23046-7 (pbk)
ISBN: 978-1-003-27540-4 (ebk)

DOI: 10.4324/9781003275404

Typeset in Bembo
by Taylor & Francis Books

This book is dedicated to all peacekeepers, who sacrificed their lives for world peace.

CONTENTS

List of Tables	*ix*
List of Figures	*x*
List of Abbreviations	*xii*
Foreword	*xv*
Preface	*xvii*
Acknowledgements	*xix*

	Introduction	1
1	Modern African Conflict, Evolution of Civil Affairs and Civil-Military Coordination in United Nations Peace Operations	18
2	The Emergence of Modern Civil-Military Coordination in United Nations Peace Operations	39
3	United Nations peace operations in the Democratic Republic of Congo: State-Building vis-à-vis Civil-Military Coordination	61
4	The United Nations Peace Operations in Sudan: State-Building vis-à-vis Civil-Military Coordination	102
	Conclusion	145
	Glossary	167

Appendix 1	*172*

viii Contents

Appendix 2	*173*
Appendix 3	*174*
Appendix 4	*175*
Appendix 5	*176*
Appendix 6	*177*
References	*178*
Index	*192*

TABLES

1.1	Civil affairs and CIMIC in different periods	32
2.1	Development of policies/guidelines related to CIMIC	47
3.1	QIPs undertaken by TCCs in the DRC (2004–10)	92
4.1	QIPs undertaken by TCCs through CIMIC in Sudan (2005–09)	122
4.2	Location and number of schools in Southern Sudan states	129
4.3	Areas and beneficiaries by providing mechanical ploughing in Southern Sudan	133

FIGURES

0.1	Quick Impact Projects (QIPs) by category in all UN peace operations in 2017–18	11
2.1	Relationship between UN Mission and Development, Humanitarian Actors through UN-CIMIC and UN-CMCoord	50
2.2	Coordination between UN Mission Headquarters (Deputy Special Representative of the Secretary General/Resident Coordinator/Humanitarian Coordinator), UN Country Team, and Humanitarian Country Team with entities at the UN Headquarters	54
2.3	Coordination structure in an integrated UN peace operation	55
3.1	ONUC Civilian Operations' Organization Chart	74
4.1	A glimpse of CIMIC activities in 2009–10: Agro-based project in Southern Sudan by Bangladesh military unit	116
4.2	Assistance to Child Survival Initiative (ACSI) programme, Yei, Southern Sudan, January 21–26, 2010	118
4.3	QIP coordination flow chart in the UNMIS	121
4.4	A glimpse of the Wau Eye Clinic before renovation	123
4.5	Wau Eye Clinic after renovation and furniture provided	124
4.6	Solar power system for the hospital and the secretariat of social services in Abyei	125
4.7	Solar power system for schools in Abyei	126
4.8	Handing over ceremony of the project: Sports for Peace	128
4.9	A glimpse of a few completed schools of the project	130

4.10	Conditions of classrooms before starting the project	131
4.11	A glimpse of furniture upon completion of the project	132
4.12	BRAC official handing over tractor to the local community in Southern Sudan	134
4.13	Images showing state of slaughterhouse, water point and school complex	136
5.1	A glimpse of the Wau Eye Clinic, South Sudan as of February 2019	157
5.2	Suggested coordination mechanism for QIPs management in UN peace operations	159
5.3	Establishment of CIMIC cell at UN headquarters and coordination link with different departments and offices	161
A.1	Map of Africa as of 2011	172
A.2	Map of the Democratic Republic of Congo as of 1998	173
A.3	Map of Sudan as of 2007	174
A.4	A history of the Abyei border agreements	175
A.5	Map of Sudan, encircled areas were the locations of UN deployment and CIMIC activities from 2005 to June 2010	176
A.6	Map of South Sudan (Erstwhile Southern Sudan)-encircled areas were the locations of UN deployment and CIMIC activities from 2005 to June 2010	177

LIST OF ABBREVIATIONS

ABC	Abyei Boundaries Commission
ACSI	Assistance to Child Survival Initiative
AFDL	Alliance of Democratic Forces for the Liberation of the Congo
BRAC	Building Resources Across Communities
CIA	Central Intelligence Agency
CIMIC	Civil-Military Coordination
CJMC	Ceasefire Joint Military Committee
CMF	Commonwealth Monitoring Force
CPA	Comprehensive Peace Agreement
CPC	Ceasefire Political Commission
DDR	Demobilization, Disarmament, and Reintegration
DDRR	Demobilization, Disarmament, Resettlement, and Reintegration
DDRRR	Demobilization, Disarmament, Repatriation, Resettlement, and Reintegration
DFS	Department of Field Support
DOCO	Development Operations Coordination Office
DOS	Department of Operational Support
DPA	Department of Political Affairs
DPKO	Department of Peacekeeping Operations
DPO	Department of Peace Operations
DPPA	Department of Political and Peacebuilding Affairs
DRC	Democratic Republic of Congo
DSRS	Deputy Special Representative of the Secretary-General
ECOWAS	Economic Community of West African States
ECOMOG	ECOWAS Military Observer Group
ERC	Emergency Relief Coordinator
FAO	Food and Agricultural Organization

FARDC	Forces Armees de la Republique Democratique du Congo
FDLR	Forces for the Democratic Liberation of Rwanda
FLN	Front de libération nationale
FRPI	Front de Resistance Patriotique d' Ituri
EU	European Union
GNP	Gross National Product
GOS	Government of Sudan
GOSS	Government of South Sudan
GPA	General Peace Agreement
HC	Humanitarian Coordinator
HCT	Humanitarian Country Team
HIPPO	High-Level Independent Panel on Peace Operations
IGAD	Inter-Governmental Authority on Development
IFI	International Financial Institute
ISS	Integrated Support Services
JDB	Joint Defence Board
JIU	Joint/Integrated Unit
JLOC	Joint Logistics Operations Centre
JMAC	Joint Mission Analysis Centre
JMC	Joint Monitoring Committee
JMT	Joint Military Team
JOC	Joint Operation Centre
LRA	Lord Resistance Army
MCD	Military and Civil Defence Assets
MDG	Millennium Development Goal
MLT	Mission Leadership Team
MONUA	United Nations Observer Mission in Angola
MONUC	United Nations Organization Mission in the DRC
MONUSCO	UN Organization Stabilization Mission in the DRC
MPLA	Movement of Popular Liberation of Angola
MSF	Médecins Sans Frontières (Doctors without Borders)
NAM	Non-Aligned Movement
NATO	North Atlantic Treaty Organization
NCP	National Congress Party
NGO	Non-Governmental Organization
OAU	Organization of African Union
OCHA	Office for the Coordination of Humanitarian Affairs
ONUC	United Nations Operations in the Congo
ONUMOZ	United Nations Operations in Mozambique
PCA	Permanent Court of Arbitration
PCC	Police Contributing Country
QIP	Quick Impact Project
RC	Resident Coordinator
RCD	Congolese Rally for Democracy

xiv List of Abbreviations

RCSO	Resident Coordinator's Support Office
RENAMO	Mozambican National Resistance
RPF	Rwanda Patriotic Front
RUF	Revolutionary United Front
SADC	Southern African Development Community
SAF	Sudan Armed Forces
SDG	Sustainable Development Goal
SPLA	Sudan Peoples' Liberation Army
SPLM	Sudan Peoples' Liberation Movement
SRSG	Special Representative of the Secretary General
SSR	Security Sector Reform
SWAPO	South-West Africa People's Organization
TCC	Troop Contributing Country
UN	United Nations
UNAMIR	United Nations Assistance Mission in Rwanda
UNAVEM	United Nations Verification Mission in Angola
UN-CIMIC	UN military CIMIC component
UN-CMCoord	UN humanitarian CIMIC component
UNCT	United Nations Country Team
UNDAF	United Nations Development Assistance Framework
UNDP	United Nations Development Programme
UNEF	United Nations Emergency Force
UNICEF	United Nations Children's Fund
UNITA	Union National Independence of Total Angola
UNITAF	Unified Task Force
UNHCR	United Nations High Commission for Refugees
UNISFA	United Nations Interim Security Force in Abyei
UNAMSIL	United Nations Assistance Mission in Sierra Leone
UNMEE	United Nations Mission in Ethiopia-Eritrea
UNMIL	United Nations Mission in Liberia
UNMIS	United Nations Mission in Sudan
UNMISS	United Nations Mission in South Sudan
UNOCI	United Nations Operations in Ivory Coast
UNOL	United Nations Operations in Liberia
UNOMIL	United Nations Observer Mission in Liberia
UNOMSIL	United Nations Observer Mission in Sierra Leone
UPDF	Ugandan People's Defence Forces
UNTAG	United Nations Transition Assistance Group
US	United States
USSR	Union of Soviet Socialist Republics
WFP	World Food Programme
WHO	World Health Organization

FOREWORD

by Nobel Laureate Professor Muhammad Yunus

The author Dr. Saleem Ahmad Khan gained valuable experiences in the United Nations peacekeeping operations over more than twenty years. He played an instrumental role in bringing professionalism by designing policies for peacekeeping which are now in practice. He contributed his skill and understanding around the world as an expert of the Pearson Peacekeeping Centre and the Canadian Defence Academy. Now he is sharing his experiences through this book. I am happy that he decided to take the initiative to produce this book on the basis of his PhD dissertation and his field experiences.

In this book, he analyses the history of civil conflicts, civil-military coordination during the conflicts and the involvement of the United Nations in support of state-building through peacekeeping. He brings the results of his in-depth research on civil-military coordination during the United Nations peace operations in Sudan, South Sudan, and the Democratic Republic of Congo. His personal experience in Sudan and South Sudan immensely enriches the narrative in the book.

He presents the unique coordination among the different stakeholders: host government, the UN agencies, the UN peace operations components, and local community. He analyzed challenges of bringing various stakeholders with different cultural background under one umbrella to undertake projects covering health, education, agriculture, energy, and sports sector. I am delighted to see his endeavour to integrate sports in the peace process. I believe his contributions will serve as examples for future operations.

Through his research Saleem brings out how United Nations-Civil Military Coordination have delivered positive contributions towards state-building at different levels. Additionally, how it has emerged as one of the "bottom-up" approach tools which assisted in building trust and confidence of local populations through a peace process.

Saleem's work is a pioneering and timely study. This study will be very useful for practitioners and students of history, political science, and international relations. This book will certainly help design a platform of sustainable development in any conflict-ridden scenarios.

I hope readers will be inspired by reading this book in dedicating themselves in various nation-building efforts.

Professor Muhammad Yunus, Nobel Peace Prize Laureate 2006

PREFACE

The main themes and objectives of the book are that United Nations Civil-Military Coordination (UN-CIMIC) teams can and have assisted in national-level state-building and build trust and confidence of local populations in a peace process. The book identifies that strategic direction to CIMIC activities at the national level was missing due to lack of a dedicated CIMIC structure at the UN headquarters in New York. However, in country- and community-level practice, the bottom-up approach of UN-CIMIC activities and projects especially in Sudan can contribute to national-level state-building and helps to build trust and confidence of the host government and local populations that is vital to long term peace and stability.

The author had the opportunity to observe and participate in CIMIC efforts in Sudan while serving as the Chief of UN-CIMIC section (2009–10) in the mission headquarters. Additionally, the author has extensive UN operational, training, and professional development experience. He served on the UN Mission in Sierra Leone (2000–01) as Contingent Owned Equipment Officer; as peacekeeping affairs officer at the army headquarters Bangladesh (2002–2005); on a reconnaissance visit to the DRC (2003) and Central African Republic (2014); in the triannual review of the contingent owned equipment working group meeting at the UN head-quarters (as a member in 2004, as a vice chairman in 2014); in negotiations at the UN headquarters on closed and ongoing peace operations (2001, 2003, 2004); in negotiations of Memorandum of Understanding with the UN (Liberia 2002, Ivory Coast 2004, DR Congo 2003, Sudan 2005); as Director Overseas operation of the Bangladesh army (2013–15); on an operational visit to UN Missions in 2014 (the DRC, Western Sahara, and Mali); and in the force generation and launching of Bangladeshi military units in Liberia (2002), DR Congo (2003), Sudan (2005), Ivory Coast (2004), Mali (2014), and Central African Republic (2014). Since his overseas deployments he has also presented papers on peace operations on UN peacekeepers Day (2014), at the joint UK-Bangladesh UN logistics seminar (2014),

xviii Preface

the Rotary Peace Conference (2015), the UN High-level Independent Panel's Asia Pacific Regional Consultation (2015). He likewise facilitated UN peace operations modules at the Pearson Peacekeeping Centre in Canada in 2010, the Canadian Defence Academy sessions offered in Uruguay in 2012, in Indonesia in 2013, in the US in 2014, 2019.

These experiences provided access to substantial collections of primary evidence for this book. Professional familiarity with those collections and policies have added much to this book. Especially the period as the Chief of UN-CIMIC Section in Sudan from 2009–10 saw the establishment of unique nation-wide medical support coordination, a national-level state-building effort, as well as the identification, supervision, and implementation of a number of QIPs in the fields of education, agriculture, health, sports, and energy. These contributed to local capacity as part of national/state level plans. These observations along with other evidence serves to build a case-study of what CIMIC in UN peace operations looks like in practice to illuminate how UN CIMIC sections contribute to national-level state-building.

The main audience for the work includes students of history, political science and international relations, and practitioners of United Nations Peace Operations-related studies. The book will be appealing covering areas/fields related to Civil-Military coordination in national-level state-building in UN peace operations. This book will be useful for the Undergraduate courses and modules including Masters' courses related to students of history, political science, and international relations. Additionally, the secondary market for the project is likely to be the United Nations, its agencies and systems, and NGOs.

ACKNOWLEDGEMENTS

This book is an outcome of my PhD dissertation, which I undertook at the University of New Brunswick, Fredericton, Canada in 2017–20. I took interest in the PhD programme for continued persuasion of my beloved mother (Arefa Billah), who dreamt her son to be a Doctor of Philosophy. She always inspired me to think big and do the best of the best.

I thank Dr. Lee Windsor, my supervisor, who gave his full efforts to nurture me and to put me in the right direction during the PhD programme. He had always high hopes on my ability and inspired me to achieve the goal. He was forthcoming and steered me to take the next step(s) always including transforming the dissertation into a book project. Dr. Marc Milner, one of the reading fields supervisor on colonization and decolonization studies and a mentor, guided me throughout my journey. Dr. Sean Kennedy assisted me in the reading field on decolonization studies in general and Sudan and the Congo in particular. Dr. Gary Waite and Dr. Erin Morton supported me during the PhD studies on Writing History and Thinking History respectively. Dr. David Emelifeonwu of Royal Military College/Canadian Defence Academy was instrumental in providing scholarly guidance with respect to dimensions of political science and United Nations peace operations, based on his vast experience. The University of New Brunswick (UNB) library, the United Nations Archives (New York), and National Archives (Ottawa) reinforced me with great assistance during my research work. The assistance of the Writing Centre of the UNB; Valerie Gallant, Administrative Assistant, Gregg Centre; Elizabeth Arnold, Graduate Administrative Assistant in the Department of History was invaluable. Valerie was very prompt and supportive in her approach.

I thank my wife Dr. Nawshin Shabnam, a Child Specialist for sacrificing her full time to look after our children during my PhD study. My two lovely daughters (Saiha Nawar Khan and Manha Surur Khan) were excited and encouraged me too.

xx Acknowledgements

My father and mother in laws rendered valuable assistance. My brother and sisters, paternal and maternal uncles, including other family members all supported me. Especially my brother-in-law Syed Nurul Basir (Shahed) and younger sister Tanyeema Khan, who live in Toronto supported me in all ways possible which included but not limited to rendering lessons on cooking.

INTRODUCTION

Over five centuries modern Africa was colonized, decolonized, and embroiled in a Cold War rivalry[1] imposed by external imperial powers. The United Nations (UN) first stepped in to maintain peace and stability in Africa during the era of decolonization beginning in the 1950s. During the earliest efforts in Africa, state-building became part of the role of the UN, especially in the Congo from 1960 to 1967. State-building includes good governance, public administration, the rule of law, education, health, political inclusion of the people, and other endeavours to ensure peace and prosperity, as well as the wellbeing of its populations. These components of state-building mostly apply to national level top-down activities involving the host government and assistance from international community. Scott Straus also opined the same by saying that the responsibility of making nations is ultimately the purview of domestic leaders and external actors may not be able to engineer such narratives, but they can look for ways to encourage or support them.[2]

This book is premised on the reality that one of the root causes of persistent conflict in some African states has been the failure to engage in state-building. In response to this problem, early peacekeeping developed into more long-term state-building programs because, as one analyst said, "the reality of state weakness means that peacekeepers need to foster state-building if there is to be any hope for exit without a return to considerable violence."[3] State-building is "a truly inter-disciplinary activity involving social sciences, international relations, political studies, anthropology, economics, international development and security studies."[4] Therefore, according to Zoe Scott, many security and conflict experts see peacebuilding as the same as state-building, while for other disciplines, peacebuilding is viewed as a sub-set of state-building. This book employs the term peacebuilding as the "UN's politically sensitive way of discussing the controversial topic of state-building from the outside and it is the need for an 'exit strategy' and for 'sustainability' that turns peacebuilding into state-building."[5] In UN peace operations, terms such as Demobilization, Disarmament, and

DOI: 10.4324/9781003275404-1

2 Introduction

Reintegration (DDR), Security Sector Reform (SSR), and the protection of civilians (POC), were coined in the late twentieth century as a part of state-building.[6] The peacebuilding approach is generally employed by the UN Peacebuilding Support Office under the Department of Political and Peacebuilding Affairs in post conflict regions in the absence of or upon the termination of a UN operation to establish peace in the immediate aftermath of conflict. During recent UN peace and stability operations, civil-military coordination (CIMIC) efforts have emerged as a mechanism to deliver early post-conflict state-building efforts at the national and local levels. According to UN policy, CIMIC refers to the "coordination mechanisms and procedures used by civilian partners and the UN military within the UN System."[7] UN-CIMIC officers undertake socio-economic activities including Quick Impact Projects (QIPs) as tools to reach out to populations and assist in community-level state-building. According to the UN Department of Peace Operations and Department of Field Support, QIPs are small-scale, low-cost projects, funded by UN missions, that are planned and implemented within a short timeframe to address the needs of local communities.

The main argument here is that UN-CIMIC can and have assisted in national-level state-building as well as build trust and confidence of local populations through a "bottom-up" approach in a peace process. Therefore, this book examines broad short-term causes of conflicts in Africa leading to the consequences for local state capacity. This context reveals the colonial era linkage to modern African conflicts, the role of the UN from 1956 to 2011, and the individual African state-building requirements. The book also focuses on the evolution of UN involvement in Africa and the evolution of civil affairs and CIMIC practices to provide international community assistance for national-level state-building, delivered in consultation with the peoples and governments in need.

The on-going conflicts in Africa have origins dating back to the era of modern European and Arab colonization. Although external interventions are not the only cause, colonization and often-violent decolonization are the primary roots of conflict in today's Africa. Their legacy – economic exploitation, socio-ethnic and ideological differences among them – have made state-building extremely challenging, if not impossible. Other sources of conflict included – but were not limited to – Cold War rivalry in addition to internal conflicts and struggles for power, such as the communal violence in Sudan, and the unresolved land issues in the eastern Democratic Republic of Congo.[8] The influx and migration of refugees fleeing violence became a by-product of conflict.

The Great War heightened the desire for self-determination in many African nations. After the First World War, there was the sense of a new order emerging. Margaret Macmillan argued that "Borders suddenly shifted, and new economic and political ideas were in the air."[9] The League of Nations, founded after the First World War, unfortunately was influenced by the unfair exercise of power by its permanent members and the frequent exit – as well as entry – of member states. However, the League was involved in fields such as health, education, agriculture, aviation, economics, law, nutrition, prisoner- and refugee-related affairs, and international commerce.[10] These efforts marked the beginning of state-building by an international organization. Though the League was a failure, its idea and structure became the outline for the creation of the United Nations.

During the Second World War, the world powers decided that they needed a replacement for the dysfunctional League of Nations and thus created the UN to maintain international peace and security. In 1943, the UN Relief and Rehabilitation Administration (UNRRA), established to deal with human catastrophes resulting from the Second World War, assisted with state-building affairs in war affected countries and contributed humanitarian aid for survivors.[11] From the time of its establishment on October 24, 1945, the UN assisted with state-building affairs: it provided technical assistance, steered trust territories toward independence, and helped settle a number of African boundary disputes including Togo, Cameroon, Rwanda, and Burundi. Therefore, in the immediate aftermath of the Second World War, the UN took its first steps towards addressing the roots of conflict related to the failure of state-building and the partitioning of Africa. UNRRA closed its operations in 1947[12] for many reasons, including the emerging Cold War rivalry, and transferred its responsibilities to different international organizations, which later became UN agencies.[13]

Maintaining international peace and security was the first purpose listed in the first chapter of the UN Charter.[14] Peacekeeping, in a broader sense, "refers to the various means that the UN employs on the spot to prevent disputes from arising, or to stabilize a situation where trouble has arisen."[15] The League of Nations had introduced peacekeeping by sending a small force to occupy an area disputed by Colombia and Peru in 1933–34 that secured withdrawal of Peruvian forces.[16] However, the UN Charter did not provide a definition for peace operations, nor did it provide guidelines for when or how to establish peace operations. As early as 1945, Chapter VI and VII of the UN Charters articulated "the measures for the settlement of disputes as well as actions related to threats on international peace and security."[17] Norrie Macqueen argued "Article 39 of Chapter VII ...made the Security Council responsible for deciding when a situation required collective security action and what form that action should take."[18] Article 55 of Chapter IX[19] related to "International Economic and Social Cooperation," which laid the foundation for assistance with state-building affairs and connected to sustained peace and development – requisites for a successful UN peace operation. However, it was not clear yet how to promote these state-building affairs in peace operations through UN Security Council Resolutions. To put these policies and ideas into practice, the UN General Assembly established funds and programmes, including specialized agencies.[20] These have become crucial components to deal with state-building affairs, for both developing the capacity of the state to serve its people, and helping sustain peace and development.

During its first decade, the UN also had to deal with conflicts in Africa resulting from the process of decolonization. According to Raymond Betts, "African countries were not decolonized by means of a systematic approach to state-building. Instead, processes were often hurried, insensitive to people's needs, and subject to demands

4 Introduction

for self-determination."[21] As a result, many newly independent countries experienced state collapse during the 1980s and 90s. However, since 1956, UN involvement became critical in number of African countries to ensure peace and security.

Modern UN peace operations (known as peacekeeping) came about as a result of the foresight and creative employment of the UN Charter by Canada's foreign minister, Lester B. Pearson and UN Secretary-General Dag Hammarskjold in 1956.[22] However, peace operations have evolved considerably since then. In 1992, the UN Agenda for Peace defined peace operations as a "field mission, usually involving military, police, and civilian personnel, deployed with the consent of the belligerent parties to monitor and facilitate the implementation of ceasefires, separation of forces or other peace agreements."[23] International conflict management has undergone significant change since the end of Cold War especially by adding humanitarian assistance and development efforts of UN agencies to diplomatic and military efforts.

The period of 1956–1964 also brought the Cold War and the UN into Africa. The UN experienced two different dimensions of peacekeeping in the Suez and Congo. Both peace operations occurred in a context of Cold War tensions and the pursuance of the economic interests by the major world powers. The major UN operation came in the Congo crisis from 1960–1964, when through the Opération des Nations Unies au Congo (ONUC) state-building was initiated. The ONUC mission in the Congo was the outcome of Europe's economic interest as well as a failure to develop state-building during the long colonial era.[24] ONUC marked the first operation where the UN was authorized to use force to fulfill its mandate to maintain peace and security in the newly decolonized, independent nation. The UN also undertook massive state-building activities through its civilian operations in the Congo. This approach involved a considerable body of experts from the UN and its specialized agencies to help build a stable society and government. Arguably, state-building efforts in the Congo followed the Second World War concepts and examples employed by the UN Relief and Rehabilitation Administration (UNRRA). The civilian operations employed an integrated approach to maintaining security alongside state-building programmes – creating a new dimension in UN peace operations. However, these efforts resulted in the "top-down" creation of state institutions which bore similarities to foreign imposed colonial methods of state-building.[25]

After the departure of UN peacekeeping forces from the Congo in 1964, no new UN peace operations were undertaken in Africa until the end of Cold War in 1989. The UN's experience in the Congo was also marred by enduring controversy surrounding the death of Prime Minister Patrice Lumumba, the loss of the UN Secretary-General Dag Hammarskjold, and the costs associated with operations.[26] In any case, according to Norrie Macqueen, "a new wave of foreign intervention began as Africa became a Cold War battleground"[27] by the 1960s. From 1965 to 1989, the Cold War rivalry there was at its peak. Although Africa experienced widespread internal conflicts, the international community did not intervene since many of those conflicts became proxy wars between the Cold War superpowers.[28] Many conflicts in Africa were civil wars, especially in Somalia, Chad, Sudan, Ethiopia, Eritrea, Uganda, Guinea Bissau, Southern Rhodesia, and the Democratic Republic of Congo (DRC). Namibia, Mozambique, and Angola fought wars of independence against their former colonial overlords that later evolved into civil wars in Mozambique and Angola.

The end of the Cold War changed international relations and opened avenues for the UN to assist with resolving long-standing regional crises in nations that had largely been the victims of superpowers' influence, in Africa and other parts of the world. With the end of the Cold War in the early 1990s, the UN's agenda for peace and security rapidly expanded. Peacebuilding or stabilization missions within fragile states became part and parcel of peace operations.[29] The UN also had to establish a separate entity, the Department of Peacekeeping Operations, to manage the gamut of new peacekeeping scenarios in 1992.[30]

During the 1990s and 2000s, Africa experienced thirteen major armed conflicts – the highest total for any region of the world.[31] The UN then stepped-in in Namibia, Angola, Mozambique, Western Sahara, Somalia, Rwanda, Liberia, Sierra Leone, Ethiopia, Eritrea, the Central African Republic, the DRC, Burundi, Ivory Coast, Sudan, and Chad. The UN had a variety of mandates in these countries, ranging from verification of ceasefires and the protection of civilians to assistance in state-building, and peace enforcement.

During this period the UN faced some of its toughest challenges and suffered infamous failures in Somalia and Rwanda. The UN also struggled with the realities of colonial underdevelopment and exploitation while dealing with state-building endeavours.[32] The colonial era left behind a weak state capacity to govern and to deliver public services including education and healthcare, along with extreme poverty that remain sources of many African conflicts. Somalia and Rwanda represented a turning point in the history of the UN and international community's involvement in Africa. In trying to meet many of the peacekeeping challenges in the mid-1990s, the UN experienced some dramatic failures in these two countries. Most scholars and commentators are critical on the role of UN for its failure in Somalia and Rwanda. In Somalia, the UN confronted the challenges of providing humanitarian relief on a massive scale in chaotic, unsecure conditions. In Rwanda, the genocide that killed hundreds of thousands of minority Tutsi along with moderate Hutus, also resulted in two million Rwandese, generally Hutus refugees fleeing to neighbouring countries, mostly in the Democratic Republic of Congo (DRC). Amy Sayward and Jeanna Kinnebrew argued that "the Rwandan genocide caused shock waves that forced the international community to review its ability to intervene."[33] After these failures, the UN reviewed its role in peacekeeping. It evaluated its successes, for instance, in Namibia and Mozambique versus its failures in Angola in 1991 and 1997, Somalia in 1993, Rwanda in 1994, and Bosnia in 1995,[34] the nature of the conflicts, and the lessons of the peace operations of the 1990s. When the demand for peace operations surged again at the end of the decade, UN Secretary-General Kofi Annan asked a high-level group of experts to assess the UN system's shortcomings, so as not to repeat that experience.[35] The Report of the Panel, known as the "Brahimi Report" after the Panel chair, UN Under-Secretary-General Lakhdar Brahimi, was issued in August 2000. It offered an in-depth critique of UN operations to date and made specific recommendations for change. The panel recommended multidimensional peacekeeping and the integration of all UN entities in one system, in manner similar to the Congo mission of the early 1960s.[36] This marked a major paradigm shift, from "traditional peacekeeping" to "multidimensional peacekeeping," and was a requirement of the time. Traditional peacekeeping operations are "model of a military operation deployed in support of a political activity. These operations involve military tasks such as monitoring ceasefires and patrolling buffer zones between hostile parties and are carried out by UN peacekeepers who may or may not be armed."[37] In contrast, multidimensional peace operations are "composed of a range of components, including military, civilian police, political affairs, the rule of law, human rights, humanitarian, reconstruction, public information, and gender."[38] The UN later developed corresponding principles and guidelines to address the recommendations of the Brahimi panel. Therefore, in the "integrated missions," coherence was established between the aid and development partners, known as UN Country Teams; humanitarian agencies, known as Humanitarian Country Teams; and components of the UN peace operation.[39] Making these efforts work in concert required massive coordination, involving the UN military forces from Troop Contributing Countries (TCCs) and other development and humanitarian partners. It resulted from ten to fifteen years of difficult trial and error efforts around the world.

Sustainable peace is the best measure of successful peacekeeping,[40] and many would argue that state-building is a crucial component of that success. The new multidimensional approach called for peacebuilding to commence simultaneously with other mandated tasks in UN peace operations in order to properly utilize the time and resources, and to bring the aid and development partners into a coordinated platform for a long-lasting gain.[41] Arguably, the UN civilian operation in the Congo (ONUC: 1960–64) served as a model in this regard. ONUC's mandate to provide technical assistance contributed to Congolese state-building in a major way. The UN taught the Congolese government and public service how to run their country by involving them in different fields of state-building. From the beginning of the civilian operations, UN got involved in different state-building fields – security, public administration, finance, economics, foreign trade, judiciary, natural resources, public works, health, education, agriculture and food supply, communications, labour, and social affairs.[42] After the long Cold War pause, by the 1990s, mandates for subsequent UN peace operations started to include aspects of state-building. UN missions sought to partner and assist state-building efforts rather than to lead it.[43] This demanded greater coordination in UN peace operations between the military and civilian components. Thus, the study of two key components of UN peace operations – civil affairs and civil-military coordination – becomes pertinent.

The practice of Civil affairs emerged during the Second World War. At that time, the Military Government of the Allied Forces was responsible for the effective functioning of civil affairs inside war-ravaged nations.[44] Afterwards, in the UN, the role of civil affairs is to engage and assist local civilian authorities and communities in efforts to consolidate peace by restoring the political, legal, economic and social infrastructures that support democratic governance and economic development."[45] UN civil affairs teams have evolved over seventy-five years. They assist in national-level state-building through their support of local government machineries and political processes.

Modern Civil-Military Coordination (CIMIC) also dates back to the Second World War and the period thereafter. The military involvement in civilian efforts were sometimes referred to as "in aid to civil administration" or "pacification" by the different armies in different environments, with different end goals. However, in the UN setting, in recent decades, such efforts are known as "CIMIC activities", which not only include liaising and information-sharing, but also the providing of assistance to local populations affected by armed conflict. In the 1990s and 2000s, the UN faced major challenges in fragile, conflict-affected states. The UN recognized that if peace was to be achieved all humanitarian and development partners, and UN missions' components needed to be involved. In this regard, the UN established Peacebuilding Commission in 2005 to support peace efforts in conflict affected countries.[46] The approach was followed by establishing the Peacebuilding Support Office to assist and support this commission and the office was mandated to administer the Peacebuilding Fund. However, such peacebuilding components generally operate after the termination of a UN peace operation. To bridge the gap between these peacebuilding partner agencies and UN military peacekeepers, CIMIC emerged as vital to sustain peace.[47] Thus, CIMIC became one of the tools to assist in national-level state-building.

Civil-Military coordination/cooperation is used by different organizations and countries to suit their requirements. For instance, in the North Atlantic Treaty Organization (NATO), the European Union (EU), and countries in Europe and Canada, it is known as "Civil-Military Cooperation."[48] In the US, "the terms 'Civil Affairs' and 'Civil Military Operations (CMO)' address civil-military cooperation indirectly or implicitly."[49] In UN peace operations, it is known as "UN-Civil-Military Coordination (UN-CIMIC)[50]" and within the UN system for the humanitarian community, it is termed "Humanitarian CIMIC (CMCoord)." CIMIC in the UN context follows a different approach from NATO, the EU, the US, and Canada, which are coalition type operations and deployed in a more contested environment as peace enforcement operations.[51] A UN peace operation is generally a consent-based operation, based on core principles, consent of the parties in conflict and involve operations that are civilian led. Not all UN-led peace operations had the consent of all the parties in conflict such as in UN operation in the DR Congo employed Force Intervention Brigade to eliminate a militia outfit in 2013. Additionally, UN peace operations in Mali is operating without taking consent of all the parties. However, CIMIC in UN peace operation scenario operates taking consent of all the parties involved in an event/project. NATO developed its own concept for civil-military cooperation in the 1990s and used it when its troops replaced UN forces in the Former Yugoslavia.[52] There are

8 Introduction

differences between the functioning of CIMIC in NATO versus UN peace operations. These differences are related to the organization and tasks of CIMIC in an operating environment. For instance, in NATO, military units have dedicated CIMIC elements and doctrine. In contrast, in UN peace operations, most of the TCCs from the Asia and the Africa do not have dedicated CIMIC elements in their units.

Nonetheless, by the 2000s, CIMIC in the UN became a critically important element to engage in the larger coordination process at all strategic, country and community levels. CIMIC staff linked the security dimensions and military components with the rest of the UN system.[53] UN Policy on CIMIC was developed in 2002, practiced for seven years, and reviewed in 2010 – the review created a clear division of functions between the UN military and other partners in the field of development and humanitarian assistance.[54] This change demanded more engagement from CIMIC sections to reach out to populations and assist with capacity-building activities ranging from agriculture, education, and healthcare, to energy.

Modern CIMIC gradually became a key tool in the 2000s to assist with country- and community-level state-building in conflict-ridden countries. At the beginning of the 2000s, CIMIC policies and practice were just emerging during the multi-dimensional or integrated UN Mission in the DRC (MONUC) and the UN Mission in Sudan (UNMIS). This book examines how CIMIC sections played a crucial role at the country- and community-level state-building in these missions.

In both operations CIMIC activities and projects were not outlined through a well-orchestrated plan or applied evenly by Troop Contributing Countries (TCCs). Nevertheless, they offered a flexible and "bottom-up" solution to delivering state-building programmes at the country- and community-level. CIMIC activities – as a tool of the mission leadership in different levels – assisted in national-level state-building, and thereby contributed to achieving overall UN peace mission tasks in the 2000s. CIMIC sections also assisted in addressing other roots of conflict in Sudan. They undertook projects to assist local populations and internally displaced persons (IDPs) designed to minimize socio-ethnic difference. Additionally, CIMIC activities contributed to preventing conflict in areas of operation by engaging people in different fields like education, agriculture, health, energy, and sports. However, TCCs from Asian countries mostly engaged in CIMIC activities, therefore, efforts were applied unevenly on these missions.

The uneven application of civil-military coordination activities in Sudan and the DRC was further challenged by the lack of strategic direction at the country level due to absence of a dedicated structure for CIMIC at the strategic level at UN headquarters in New York. CIMIC activities and challenges emerging from UN peace operations therefore remain unaccounted for at the strategic level.[55] In practice, CIMIC-related issues were reported by the force commander to the Department of Peace Operations at the UN headquarters. Although CIMIC issues remain the responsibility of the Deputy Military Adviser of the Department of Peace Operations, there was no staffing.[56] As a result these issues were not followed up subsequently due to the absence of a dedicated entity at the Department of Peace Operations.

Despite these limitations the UN Mission in Sudan (UNMIS) undertook CIMIC activities to support the peace mission's mandate from 2005 to 2011. CIMIC activities promoted the presence of the UN through a wide range of activities and Quick Impact Projects (QIPs) in different parts of Sudan which assisted with alleviating the sufferings of its people. It may be mentioned here that the QIPs discussed here on UN peace operations are civilian-led projects to support local populations in post-conflict areas and implemented by partners ranging from NGOs, UN agencies, and TCCs military units as part of the wider peace building plan. In contrast, QIPs undertaken by the NATO forces are military-led projects, which are often less connected to peace-building strategy and more usually undertaken by combat commanders to assist in attaining military objectives in counter-terrorism or counter-insurgency operations, for instance in Iraq and Afghanistan.[57]

The author had the opportunity to observe and participate in CIMIC efforts in Sudan while serving as the Chief of UN-CIMIC section (2009–10) in the mission headquarters.[58] Additionally, the author has extensive UN operational, training, and professional development experience. He served on the UN Mission in Sierra Leone (2000–01) as Contingent Owned Equipment Officer; as peacekeeping affairs officer at the army headquarters Bangladesh (2002–2005); on a reconnaissance visit to the DRC (2003) and Central African Republic (2014); in the triannual review of the contingent owned equipment working group meeting at the UN headquarters (as a member in 2004, as a vice chairman in 2014); in negotiations at the UN headquarters on closed and ongoing peace operations (2001, 2003, 2004); in negotiations of Memorandum of Understanding with the UN (Liberia 2002, Ivory Coast 2004, DR Congo 2003, Sudan 2005); as Director Overseas operation of the Bangladesh army (2013–15); on an operational visit to UN Missions in 2014 (the DRC, Western Sahara, and Mali); and in the force generation and launching of Bangladeshi military units in Liberia (2002), DR Congo (2003), Sudan (2005), Ivory Coast (2004), Mali (2014), and Central African Republic (2014). Since his overseas deployments he has also presented papers on peace operations on UN peacekeepers Day (2014), at the joint UK-Bangladesh UN logistics seminar (2014), the Rotary Peace Conference (2015), the UN High-level Independent Panel's Asia Pacific Regional Consultation (2015). He likewise facilitated UN peace operations modules at the Pearson Peacekeeping Centre in Canada in 2010, the Canadian Defence Academy sessions offered in Uruguay in 2012, in Indonesia in 2013, in the US in 2014, 2019.

These experiences provided access to substantial collections of primary evidence for this book. Professional familiarity with those collections and policies have added much to this book. Especially the period as the Chief of UN-CIMIC Section in Sudan from 2009–10 saw the establishment of unique nation-wide medical support coordination, a national-level state-building effort, as well as the identification, supervision, and implementation of several QIPs in the fields of education, agriculture, health, sports, and energy. These contributed to local capacity as part of national/state level plans. These observations along with other evidence serves to

10 Introduction

build a case-study of what CIMIC in UN peace operations looks like in practice to illuminate how UN-CIMIC sections contribute to national-level state-building.

In contrast to Sudan, the UN Operation in the Democratic Republic of Congo (Mission de l'Organisation de Nations Unies en Republique Democratique du Congo, MONUC: 1999–2010) struggled to manage internal conflict and a wider regional crisis in south central Africa,[59] and at the same time was mandated to assist in state-building endeavours from 2004. In contrast to the UN mission in Sudan, the scale of the conflict and geography in the DRC meant that UN CIMIC personnel in MONUC had difficulties due to the security situation and was confined initially within small areas, but with the improvement of the security situation extended its horizon to undertake QIPs.[60]

The 2015 High-Level Independent Panel on Peace Operations (HIPPO)[61] recommended that there be "more people-centric UN peace operations." This demanded "more focused attention on community-related activities and support for national initiatives to enable rural and local development."[62] In this regard, through CIMIC and civil affairs teams, all UN peace operations reach out to people and engage with local communities. However, these practices of the Troop Contributing Countries (TCCs) military forces usually take the form of ad hoc activities without enough strategic focus or clear intent. Such ad hoc community assistance activities also remained specific to a mission to "win the hearts and minds" of local populations by delivering QIPs.[63] These ad hoc activities demand a well-articulated strategy for CIMIC as part of broader national/state level plans at the country- and community-level, and with the UN "Sustainable Development Goals 2030."

CIMIC experience in Sudan and the DRC illustrated the UN approach towards integrating security, peace, and development efforts. The sixteenth of the Sustainable Development Goals, to "Promote peaceful and inclusive societies for sustainable development, provide access to justice for all and build effective, accountable and inclusive institutions at all levels"[64] – covered the aspects of assistance with state-building. In line with the requirement of SDGs, HIPPO also advocated for "one mandate-one mission-one concept."[65] Therefore, many now argue that a well-articulated strategy is essential to link CIMIC sections' community driven activities in UN peace operations with plans at the national-level, and thus the CIMIC plan attaches with SDGs 2030 at the strategic level.

Successful post-conflict state-building also depends on leadership. The High-Level Independent Panel on Peace Operations (HIPPO) identified quality of leadership as one of the most vital factors in the success or failure of UN peace operations. The HIPPO report argued that "the best UN leaders are remembered for their courage, vision, integrity, humility and ability to inspire others."[66] Additionally, the role of leadership is crucial at the different tiers of a mission to make CIMIC activities effective. As Kenzo Oshima, the Emergency Relief Coordinator, Office for the Coordination of Humanitarian Affairs in 2004, once pointed out, "Coordination is all about your personality, all about everything that you bring to the business, nothing else. That means your personal character, knowledge, energy – everything that you have, that you bring to bear – that to me is coordination, nothing more, nothing less."[67] Therefore, the skillful leadership of CIMIC personnel, who serve as soldier-diplomats, will always matter in different tiers of UN peace operations. Sudan is an excellent case study to consider how CIMIC officers can deliver programmes in support of the wider country- and community-level peacebuilding mission. The author's Sudan experience underscores how effective coordination depended on initiative, interest in leadership, *focused* commitment, and a great deal of knowledge about the missions' stakeholders.[68]

Sudan was thus the ground to demonstrate how different leaders approached CIMIC activities at the country- and community-level. According to the statistics of the UN Intranet Global, CIMIC entities as a whole undertook twelve QIPs out of two hundred forty-seven QIPs in all eight UN peace operations during 2017–18 (as shown in Figure 0.1).[69]

In contrast, the CIMIC section completed seven QIPs within three to eight months in a single UN peace operation in Sudan in 2009–10. This accomplishment demonstrates how the practice of appropriate leadership skills leads to successful QIPs. A number of CIMIC activities and projects were linked to apparatuses of state-building – agriculture, education, health, sports, and energy sectors – and contributed to sustainability as well as to instilling "local ownership." Additionally, medical support coordination to provide basic medical services to local populations involved all relevant stakeholders – TCCs, government ministries, UN agencies, NGOs – was another example of leadership acumen as well as assistance with national-level state-building in a UN peace operation.

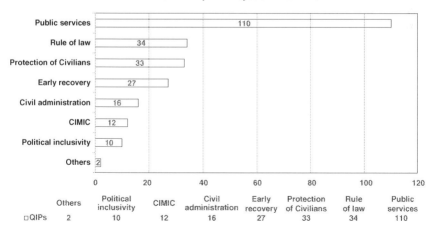

FIGURE 0.1 Quick Impact Projects (QIPs) by category in all UN peace operations in 2017–18.
The UN Intranet Global, 'Quick Impact Projects (QIPs) | Iseek-External.Un.Org', Quick Impact Projects 2017-18, 10 December 2018, https://iseek-external.un.org/departmental_page/quick-impact-projects-qips. (Developed by the author)

12 Introduction

CIMIC requires well developed policies, doctrines, and concepts for appropriate application on the ground. Before the introduction of CIMIC, civil affairs teams played a minor role in peacekeeping missions. For that reason, there is limited scholarship on how civil-military relationships function in practice. More importantly, the literature does not examine how these relationships affect national-level state-building and the outcomes for populations in order to sustain peace and development in unique African conflicts. This book seeks to address these historiographical gaps.

CIMIC is applied according to the situation, the TCCs involved, the operation mandate, the leaders involved, and the nature of the conflict. The book addresses the main argument by investigating three broad issues in four chapters. First, it identifies a broad range of short-term causes of conflict in Africa, specifically in Sudan and the DRC, that created unique crises, and ultimately drew in the international community and the UN. Second, it considers the evolution of civil affairs and role of the UN in restoring peace in Africa through an approach of state-building. Third, it examines the emergence of modern CIMIC in UN peace operations to assist in national-level state-building efforts, and outreach to populations in Sudan and the DRC.

Chapter one reviews the broad short-term causes of modern African conflicts through the periods of decolonization and armed conflicts that led the UN to undertake peace operations there until the 2000s. It focuses on Africa before concentrating on Sudan and the Congo as case studies. This chapter discusses the origin and establishment of the UN Relief and Rehabilitation Administration (UNRRA) and the evolution of civil affairs, as a key function related to assisting in state-building. Thereafter, it covers the evolution of the civil-military coordination in the UN setting.

Chapter two traces the modern emergence of CIMIC in UN peace operations. It covers the organizational culture of civilian and military entities, and the development of concepts, doctrine, and policy formulation for employing CIMIC. It also discusses the complex structure of a UN peace operation and how the CIMIC section works within the complex integrated mission.

Chapter three reviews the first complex UN operation as a case study of the book: UN peace operations in the Congo – with the mandates of peace enforcements as well as assistance with state-building. It focuses on both the military as well as civilian peace operations from 1960–1964 that employed a "top-down" approach to state-building. This chapter makes a bridge between UN operation in the Congo (1960–64) and the launching of the second UN operation in the DRC in 1999. Thereafter, it discusses the management of UN, covering its role to improve security situations and to assist with state-building. It discusses the CIMIC practices in the DRC.

Chapter four focuses on another complex UN operations as the second case study of the book: UN peace operations in Sudan, which had the mandates of peace enforcements as well as assistance with state-building. The chapter also analyzes the civil war in Sudan as a background study, and efforts undertaken by the international community to reach the peace agreement. The chapter excludes the issues and conflicts in Darfur due to the different dimensions of that conflict, which would require a separate study. This chapter delves into the CIMIC practices in Sudan in order to understand their contribution to national-level state-building efforts in both war-torn places and how CIMIC efforts offered a "bottom-up" solution to delivering national-level state-building programmes. Additionally, it examines the effectiveness and impact of CIMIC over the population in Sudan. A substantial portion of the chapter is based on observations, experience, and data gathered by the author while serving in the UN Mission in Sudan as the Chief of CIMIC section. Perhaps the most important observation from this practical CIMIC examination is that UN security building and CIMIC worked best when delivered side by side in order to effectively rebuild viable and stable post-conflict state.

Overall, this book illuminates the UN involvement in Sudan and DRC to sustain long-term peace and development by practice of civil-military coordination to assist in state-building. Furthermore, it reveals how UN-CIMIC emerged as one tool to address the roots of conflict, by providing assistance with national-level state-building through a "bottom-up" approach and helping to build trust and confidence of local populations in the peace process.

Notes

1 "Cold War was largely a post-colonial phenomenon which was a competitive enterprise during the Cold War i.e. newly independent states were supported strategically as part of a Western strategy for containing socialism and the Soviet Union in the third world.", Zoe Scott, "Literature Review on State-Building," *Governance and Social Development Resource Centre*, May 2007, 13.
2 Scott Straus, *Making and Unmaking Nations: War, Leadership, and Genocide in Modern Africa* (Ithaca, UNITED STATES: Cornell University Press, 2015), 13, http://ebookcentral. proquest.com/lib/unb/detail.action?docID=3138725.
3 Zoe Scott, "Literature Review on State-Building," *Governance and Social Development Resource Centre*, May 2007, 18.
4 Zoe Scott, "Literature Review on State-Building."
5 "Peacebuilding is just the UN"s politically sensitive way of discussing the controversial topic of state-building from the outside. It is the need for an "exit strategy" and for "sustainability" that turns peacebuilding into state-building; realistically, UN can only withdraw when effective institutions have been built.", Zoe Scott, "Literature Review on State-Building," *Governance and Social Development Resource Centre*, May 2007, 3, 6, 32.
6 Hideaki Shinoda, "Peace-Building and State-Building from the Perspective of the Historical Development of International Society", *International Relations of the Asia-Pacific* 18, no. 1 (31 January 2018): 25–43, https://doi.org/10.1093/irap/lcx025.
7 Department of Peacekeeping Operations and Department of Field Support, "Policy: Civil-Military Coordination in UN Integrated Peacekeeping Missions (UN-CIMIC)" (United Nations, 1 November 2010).
8 Channel Research, Belgium, "Joint Evaluation of Conflict Evaluation and Peacebuilding in the Democratic Republic of Congo", Synthesis Report (Ohain, Belgium, June 2011), 48, https://www.oecd.org/countries/congo/48859543.pdf.
9 Margaret MacMillan, *Paris 1919: Six Months That Changed the World* (Random House Publishing Group, 2007), xxviii.
10 Amy L Sayward, *The United Nations in International History* (New York: Bloomsbury, 2017), 18.
11 George Woodbridge, *UNRRA: The History of the United Nations Relief and Rehabilitation Administration*, vol. II, 3 vols (New York: Columbia University Press, 1950).

14 Introduction

12 George Woodbridge, *UNRRA: The History of the United Nations Relief and Rehabilitation Administration*, vol. I (New York: Columbia University Press, 1950), 303.

13 "Funds, Programmes, Specialized Agencies and Others", 18 November 2014, http://www.un.org/en/sections/about-un/funds-programmes-specialized-agencies-and-others/index.html.

14 Stephen Buzdugan and Anthony Payne, *The Long Battle for Global Governance* (Routledge, 2016), 40.

15 Clarke M. Eichelberger, *UN: The First Twenty Years* (New York: Harper & Row, 1955), 28.

16 Gibbons and Morican, *The League of Nations and UNO*, 38.

17 UN Department of Public Information, "UN Yearbook: 1946–47," The Yearbook of the United Nations: The authoritative reference work on the UN System, 47 1946, 835, https://www.unmultimedia.org/searchers/yearbook/page.jsp?bookpage=180&volume=1946–47.

18 Norrie Macqueen, *United Nations Peacekeeping in Africa Since 1960* (London, United Kingdom: Routledge, 2014), 4.

19 UN Department of Public Information, "UN Yearbook: 1946–47", 837.

20 "UN Funds, Programmes, Specialized Agencies and Others", 18 November 2014, http://www.un.org/en/sections/about-un/funds-programmes-specialized-agencies-and-others/index.html.

21 Raymond Betts, *Decolonization* (London: Taylor and Francis, ProQuest Ebook Central, 2004), 1.

22 Eichelberger, *UN: The First Twenty Years*, 29; Kevin A. Spooner, *Canada, the Congo Crisis, and UN Peacekeeping, 1960–64* (Vancouver, Canada: UBC Press, 2009), 5.

23 Boutros-Ghali, Boutros, "An Agenda for Peace: Preventive Diplomacy, Peacemaking and Peace-keeping," *International Relations*, 1992, 201–18; Cedric De Coning, "Civil-Military Coordination in United Nations and African Peace Operations," *The African Centre for the Constructive Resolution of Disputes (ACCORD)*, UN Complex Peace Operations, n.d., 48; "The 2015 High-level Independent Panel on Peace Operations (HIPPO) report strongly urged the UN to embrace the term "peace operations" to signify the full spectrum of responses required. Thus, in 2019, the UN changed the name of the Department of Peacekeeping Operations to the Department of Peace Operations.", Cedric De Coning and Mateja Peter, *United Nations Peace Operations in a Changing Global Order* (Springer, 2018), 11.

24 Ruth Slade, *The Belgian Congo*, Second edition (Ely House, London: Oxford University Press, 1961), 6–7.

25 Jean-Pierre Lacroix, Interview with the UN Under Secretary-General of the Department of Peace Operations on "The United Nations Peace Operations in Africa", Dhaka, 24 May 2018. During the interview, the Under-Secretary-General mentioned that, the Congo example was a "top-down approach" of state-building. Not all host governments would accept this colonial method of state-building. Therefore, the approach of UN towards state-building demands the consent of the host government.

26 James Dobbins, *The UN"s Role in Nation-Building: From the Congo to Iraq* (Santa Monica, CA: RAND Corp., 2004), 31, http://catdir.loc.gov/catdir/toc/ecip054/2004027669.html.

27 Norrie Macqueen, *United Nations Peacekeeping in Africa Since 1960* (London, United Kingdom: Routledge, 2014), 14–16, 111; John MacKinlay, "The Commonwealth Monitoring Force in Zimbabwe/Rhodesia, 1979–80", in *Humanitarian Emergencies and Military Help in Africa*, ed. Thomas G. Weiss, Issues in Peacekeeping and Peacemaking (London: Palgrave Macmillan UK, 1990), 38–39, https://doi.org/10.1007/978-1-349-11582-2_3; "Commonwealth Monitoring Force, Rhodesia", accessed 15 February 2019, http://www.peacekeepers.asn.au/operations/OpAGILA.htm. The international community got involved in a crisis associated with Rhodesia (a former colony of the UK) in 1979—not by the UN, but by the Commonwealth led by the UK.

28 Rose Ngomba-Roth, "Multinational Companies and Conflicts in Africa: The Case of the Niger Delta", 1, accessed 28 June 2019, https://books.google.com.bd/books?id=9c5oVTu lYwcC&pg=PA1&dq=internal+conflict+in+Africa+1965+to+1989&hl=en&sa=X&ved= 0ahUKEwjYrf78p4vjAhXCvo8KHZcWBxcQ6AEIMzAC#v=onepage&q=internal%20conflict%20in%20Africa%201965%20to%201989&f=false.

Introduction **15**

29 Joshua S. Goldstein, *Winning the War on War: The Decline of Armed Conflict Worldwide* (New York: Plume, 2012), 74.

30 Goldstein, 115.; Department of Peacekeeping Operations, "United Nations Peacekeeping", United Nations Peacekeeping, accessed 13 February 2019, https://peacekeeping.un.org/en/node.

31 Paul D. Williams, *War & Conflict in Africa*, 2nd ed. (Cambridge UK and Maiden, USA: Polity Press, 2016), 5.

32 United Nations Security Council, "Special Report of the Secretary-General on the United Nations Mission in Liberia", Final Report (New York, 15 November 2016), 7, https://unmil.unmissions.org/sites/default/files/special_unmil_sg_report_15_november_2016.pdf.; United Nations Security Council, "Final Report of the Secretary-General on the UN Operation in Mozambique", Final Report (New York, 23 December 1994), 4, https://documents-dds-ny.un.org/doc/UNDOC/GEN/N94/515/76/PDF/N9451576.pdf?OpenElement. For instance, in Sierra Leone, a former British colony, the British were steering the affairs in the UN Security Council and were involved in the training of Sierra Leone Armed Forces through bilateral arrangements. Similarly, the French were extensively involved in the political and security affairs of Ivory Coast. The US was engaged with Liberian affairs, including screening and the training Liberian Armed Forces. South Africa was also engaged frequently in Namibian affairs. Portugal assisted with the training of Mozambique military. However, former colonial powers assisted in bringing the parties of the conflicts to the negotiation table in order to sign peace agreements.

33 Amy L Sayward and Jeanna Kinnebrew, "Making and Keeping the Peace: U.N. Peacekeeping and Refugee Assistance Operations", in *The United Nations in International History* (London, Oxford, New York, New Delhi, Sydney: Bloomsbury, 2017), 139.

34 Goldstein, *Winning the War on War*, 75.

35 William J. Durch et al., *The Brahimi Report and the Future of UN Peace Operations* (Washington, D.C.: The Henry L. Stimson Center, 2003), https://www.stimson.org/sites/default/files/file-attachments/BR-CompleteVersion-Dec03_1.pdf.

36 Goldstein, *Winning the War on War*, 115.

37 UN Peacekeeping Best Practices Unit, "Handbook on United Nations Multi-dimensional Peacekeeping Operations" (Department of Peacekeeping Operations and Department of Field Support, December 2003), 1, https://peacekeeping.un.org/sites/default/files/peacekeeping-handbook_un_dec2003_0.pdf.

38 UN Peacekeeping Best Practices Unit, "Handbook on United Nations Multidimensional Peacekeeping Operations".

39 Cedric De Coning, "Civil-Military Coordination in United Nations and African Peace Operations", *The African Centre for the Constructive Resolution of Disputes (ACCORD)*, UN Complex Peace Operations, n.d., 53.

40 UN Department of Peacekeeping Operations, "United Nations Peacekeeping Operations: Principles and Guidelines" (United Nations, 2008), https://peacekeeping.un.org/sites/default/files/capstone_eng_0.pdf.

41 UN Department of Public Information, "United Nations Peace Operations 2009: Year in the Review", January 2010, 42.

42 Library and Archives Canada, ONUC Staff New York, "Report of the United Nations Operation in the Congo as on May 1, 1963", Yearly (New York: United Nations, 1 May 1963), MG 30, C241, Volume 32, Personal stuffs of John King Gordon, Senior Information Officer, United Nations, Library and Archives Canada, Government of Canada.

43 Lacroix, Interview with the UN Under-Secretary-General of the Department of Peace Operations on "The United Nations Peace Operations in Africa". During the interview, the Under-Secretary-General mentioned that, the Congo example in the 1960s was a "top-down approach" of state-building. Not all host governments would accept this colonial method of state-building. Therefore, the approach of UN towards state-building demands partnership with the host government.

16 Introduction

44 Thijs Brocades Zaalberg, *Soldiers and Civil Power: Supporting or Substituting Civil Authorities in Modern Peace Operations* (Amsterdam University Press, 2005), 31–40, https://doi.org/10.5117/9789053567920.

45 UN Peacekeeping Best Practices Unit, "Handbook on United Nations Multidimensional Peacekeeping Operations", 35.

46 United Nations, "United Nations Peacebuilding", Official, United Nations Peacebuilding, accessed 26 March 2020, https://www.un.org/peacebuilding/.

47 Cedric De Coning, "Civil-Military Coordination in United Nations and African Peace Operations", *The African Centre for the Constructive Resolution of Disputes (ACCORD)*, UN Complex Peace Operations, n.d., 53.

48 Coning, "Civil-Military Coordination and UN Peacebuilding Operations", 97–98.

49 Stijn van Weezel, "CIMIC Concepts & Capabilities: Research into the CIMIC Operationalization of Nations", *Civil-Military Co-Operation Centre of Excellence, The Hague, The Netherlands*, no. August, 2011 (2011): 14.

50 Cedric de Coning, "Civil-Military Coordination Practices and Approaches Within United Nations Peace Operations", *Journal of Military and Strategic Studies* 10, no. 1 (1 September 2007): 12, https://jmss.org/article/view/57636.

51 Coning, "Civil-Military Coordination and UN Peacebuilding Operations", 99; Coning, "Civil-Military Coordination Practices and Approaches Within United Nations Peace Operations", 5.

52 African Centre for the Constructive Resolution of Disputes (ACCORD), "The African Civil-Military Coordination Programme 2006", 2006.

53 Christopher Ankersen, *Civil-Military Cooperation in Post-Conflict Operations: Emerging Theory and Practice* (Routledge, 2007), 70.

54 UN Department of Peacekeeping Operations and Department of Field Support, "Policy: Civil-Military Coordination in UN Integrated Peacekeeping Missions (UN-CIMIC)".

55 Lacroix, Interview with the UN Under Secretary-General of the Department of Peace Operations on "The United Nations Peace Operations in Africa", 24 May 2018, Dhaka. During the interview, the issue of CIMIC at the strategic level was mentioned by the author. Under-Secretary-General acknowledged and mentioned that, "CIMIC relies on leadership on the ground and thus, its success depends on application of CIMIC policies by leaders at the different tiers in UN peace operations."

56 Chief Current Military Operations Service Colonel Alexander Senchilin Department of Peace Operations, UN Headquarters, Civil-Military Coordination arrangements in UN Headquarters, One to one meeting, 30 August 2018.

57 Chiyuki Aoi, "Legitimacy and the Use of Armed Force: Stability Missions in the Post-Cold War Era", 126–27, accessed 28 June 2019, https://books.google.com.bd/books?id=lbeNA gAAQBAJ&pg=PA126&dq=quick+impact+projects+by+US+forces&hl=en&sa=X&ved=0ahUKEwily9CHtYvjAhVGi3AKHbQDA_8Q6AEIJjAA#v=onepage&q=quick%20impact%20projects%20by%20US%20forces&f=false.

58 "The author (then Lieutenant Colonel from the Bangladesh Army) worked as the Chief of CIMIC section in UNMIS headquarters from June 9, 2009 to July 8, 2010."

59 Channel Research, Belgium, "Joint Evaluation of Conflict Evaluation and Peacebuilding in the Democratic Republic of Congo", 15.

60 United Nations, "United Nations Organization Mission in the Democratic Republic of the Congo (MONUC)", MONUC, accessed 15 November 2018, https://peacekeeping.un.org/sites/default/files/past/monuc/index.shtml. The entire electoral process represented one of the most complex votes the UN had ever helped organize.

61 United Nations, "Report of the High-Level Independent Panel on Peace Operations", Review on Peace Operations (New York, 16 June 2015), 14, https://peaceoperationsreview.org/wp-content/uploads/2015/08/HIPPO_Report_1_June_2015.pdf. The HIPPO held its Regional Consultation for Asia Pacific in Bangladesh in January 2015. The author was the Director Overseas Operations at the Army Headquarters. He took personal initiative to organize the forum and presented a keynote paper, "Challenges and Way

Ahead for UN peace operations: Experience of Bangladesh." A few issues were addressed in the final report of the HIPPO from the paper.

62 United Nations, HIPPO, 39.

63 Youssef Mahmoud, "People-Centric Approaches to Peace: At Cross Roads Between Geopolitics, Norms, & Practices", in *United Nations Peace Operations in a Changing Global World* (Springer, 2018), 94–95.

64 *SIPRI Searchlight: Towards Peace, Justice and Inclusive Governance by 2030*, Video file, 2018, https://www.youtube.com/watch?v=xZkaORxlksI.

65 Coning and Peter, *United Nations Peace Operations in a Changing Global Order*; United Nations, "Report of the High-Level Independent Panel on Peace Operations", 120.

66 United Nations, "Report of the High-Level Independent Panel on Peace Operations", 70.

67 *The Humanitarian Decade: Challenges for Humanitarian Assistance in the Last Decade and into the Future*, vol. I (New York: United Nations, 2004), 59.

68 "The authors' personal experience in UN peace operations in Sudan (2009–10) as Chief of CIMIC section assisted to use relevant materials as primary sources in this book."

69 The UN Intranet Global, "Quick Impact Projects (QIPs) | Iseek-External.Un.Org", Quick Impact Projects 2017–18, 10 December 2018, https://iseek-external.un.org/departmental_page/quick-impact-projects-qips. (Data obtained from this intranet and developed by the author)

1

MODERN AFRICAN CONFLICT, EVOLUTION OF CIVIL AFFAIRS AND CIVIL-MILITARY COORDINATION IN UNITED NATIONS PEACE OPERATIONS

Introduction

In recent decades, Africa became the focus of much of the United Nations' (UN) peacekeeping efforts. Between 1999 and 2008 alone Africa experienced thirteen major armed conflicts, the highest for any region of the world.[1] Many of those conflicts involved deployment of UN peacekeeping forces to maintain peace and security, although there are differences of opinion as to whether UN efforts worked or not. The first wave of UN peace operations was launched in Africa during the Suez crisis in 1956 and in the Congo in 1960. The second wave commenced in 1989 and UN peace operations continue in Africa to this day.

In her 2018 article "The Crisis of Peacekeeping: Why the UN Can't End Wars," Séverine Autesserre argued that the UN often "organizes elections and declares victory, but without having fixed the root causes that brought them there."[2] The sources of modern conflict in Africa today are vast and involve local and external factors. Of the later, the most prominent is the legacy of over five centuries of colonization and the process of decolonization that laid the grounds for the enduring conflicts on the continent. Local factors also contributed, K. J. Holsti analyzed armed conflict in Africa in the period c. 1945–1995 and concluded that sixty-six percent conflicts were related to internal dynamics.[3]

The period of Arab and European colonization in Africa introduced the conflict and instability that plagues the continent even today, while widespread enslavement resulted in an identity crisis as well as in massive displacement of people. European economic penetration into Africa initially targeted products like spices, gold, diamonds, ivory, and rubber for the benefit of the European nations and businesses.[4] The European states partitioned Africa without consideration for regional demography, ethnicity, or culture. The introduction of European settlers and the systematic seizure of land further marginalized indigenous people. Finally, the failure of colonial

DOI: 10.4324/9781003275404-2

processes to address state-building[5] became a source of conflict during decolonization and the period after independence.

By the 1960s the world had rejected European colonialism, which led to a wave of African decolonization and subsequent violence. Martin Shipway's 2008 book, *Decolonization and Its Impact: A Comparative Approach to the End of the Colonial Empires,* identified the Second World War as having had catastrophic and costly consequences for both the African colonies and the colonizers.[6] The war became a catalyst for Europe's withdrawal from Africa. Decolonization was not planned and thus done too hastily.[7] As a consequence, a good number of countries in Africa erupted in armed violence resulting in short-term conflicts, civil wars, political disorders, and wars of independence. At the same time, Cold War ideological warfare became a part and parcel of African conflict.

Cold War ideological warfare between the West and the Soviet Union compounded the difficulties of decolonization in Africa. The West was apprehensive about the rise of communism, while the Communist powers saw the potential for cultivating African allies. As a result, the United States (US) and the Soviet Union gathered allies among dependent states (e.g., the Democratic Republic of Congo, Angola, and Somalia), then engaged in providing economic and military assistance to them during the Cold War.[8]

The United Nations (UN), created in the aftermath of the Second World War, was established "...to save the succeeding generations from scourge of war...."[9] The League of Nations was a product of the First World War; with unsuitably the same mandate of the later UN. The League's successes were relatively few, mainly limited to technical assistance, which were to assist in state-building of war-torn countries. The concept of the UN developed as a result of 1941's Atlantic Conference between Britain and the US, during which were declared common principles for nation-states, principles designed to secure a better future for the world as a whole. In 1942, fifty-eight Allied countries agreed on principles that resulted in the Declaration by United Nations, the basis for the UN itself.

In 1943, the UN Relief and Rehabilitation Administration (UNRRA) was established to deal with human catastrophes resulting from the war, assist with state-building affairs in affected countries and contribute positively to the lives of survivors.[10] From the time of its establishment on October 24, 1945, the United Nations assisted with state-building affairs. It provided technical assistance, steered trust territories toward independence, and helped settle a number of African boundary disputes, thus partly addressing the roots of conflict related to failure of state-building and the partitioning issues. UNRRA closed its operations in 1947 for many reasons, including the emerging Cold War rivalry, and transferred its responsibilities to different international organizations, which later became UN agencies.

The UN Funds and programmes, including specialized agencies (referred to as UN agencies) have remained crucial components of state-building affairs, both developing the capacity of a state to serve its people, and helping sustain peace and development. These agencies work along with the respective host government to

20 United Nations Peace Operations

render assistance with state-building. Key agencies include the Food Agriculture Organization, the UN High Commission for Refugees, the World Health Organization, the UN Children's Fund, the World Food Programme, and the UN Development Programme. These agencies established their presence in Africa after the Second World War to render assistance to provide food security, to handle refugee crises, to provide health care, to support children's education and health, and to undertake development projects in support of governments.

Like all UN agencies, UN civil affairs teams have evolved over seventy-five years to assist in state-building through supporting local government as well as developing political mechanisms. Civil Affairs involvement includes political components as well as the "machinery" of government. Civil Affairs had its origins during the Second World War, when the Military Government of the Allied Forces was responsible for the effective functioning of public service affairs in newly liberated areas. There is evidence, during the war, of coordination between respective military governments and the UNRRA concerning the handling of refugees and displaced persons. UN interest in civil affairs surfaced officially in the 1990s, though it was practiced in the UN civilian operations in the Congo from 1960–64.

Like civil affairs, modern Civil-Military Coordination (CIMIC) dates back to the Second World War, when military involvement in civilian efforts was known as an "in aid to civil administration" or "pacification." These efforts were used in different scenarios with varied objectives after the Second World War by the colonial powers to "win the hearts and minds" of local populations agitating for independence. After the Cold War, the UN and other stakeholders, including Non-Governmental Organizations (NGOs), began to operate in conflict-ridden countries in the 1990s. This proliferation demanded greater coordination between the civilian and military stakeholders operating in the same environment. It was only in the 2000s when CIMIC appeared in UN settings, involving UN military forces to participate in meeting humanitarian needs for local populations.

This chapter briefly introduces the short-term causes of modern African conflicts as a background study. Thereafter, it focuses on the evolution of civil affairs as a key function related to assisting in state-building in the context of the emergence of Second World War Allied Military Government and its subsequent adoption by the UN. The evolution of Civil-Military Coordination (CIMIC) in the UN setting is brought in as a tool to assist in state-building in the UN peace operations. Therefore, the combined study of the evolution of civil affairs and CIMIC functioning forms the background to the study of modern civil-military coordination in UN peace operations.

Decolonization from 1919, issues of short-term conflicts, and UN involvement in Africa

A study of the decolonization period in Africa reveals several short-term causes of conflict, new kinds of international involvement, and eventually UN engagement there to manage and contain conflicts. The period of decolonization and the Cold

War partially overlap. The first period, c. 1919–1939, highlights the new expectations of Africans vis-à-vis the realities of decolonization. The second period, c. 1940–1945, is dominated by the Second World War and the rise of the United States (US) as a major global player, which sped up decolonization. Additionally, the establishment of the UN to maintain international peace and security is also considered as a significant event in the subsequent decolonization process. The third period, c. 1946–1989, covers the era of decolonization until the end of the Cold War. It involved significant change in international politics resulting from the rise of new nation-states either through bloodshed or smooth decolonization, and an increased role for the UN as well as the aftermath of decolonization. The Cold War, struggle between the US and the Soviet Union for political and economic domination affected decolonization in some African countries.

The sources of short-term conflict considered during decolonization included the Cold War rivalry and issue of the failure to address state-building. However, failure to address state-building remains both as a long- and short-term source of conflict in Africa. The case studies of Sudan and the Congo are the focus to examine how decolonization contributed to the armed conflicts that broke out in those parts of Africa. These conflicts prompted the involvement of the UN to Africa in an effort to manage the conflicts.

Issues of short-term conflict: Cold War Rivalry in Africa

Some conflicts during the period of decolonization led to the involvement of the international community in Africa mainly out of Cold War rivalry. The Cold War was not triggered by decolonization. Rather the ideological warfare between the West and the Soviet Union for political and economic domination affected decolonization in Africa. Jan C. Jansen and Jurgen Osterhammel argued that "decolonization can be situated at the intersection of the East-West conflict and the North-South antagonism."[11] The West was apprehensive about the spread of communism from the East either within nationalist movements or when the newly independent nation-states were formed. According to Michael Howard, "[The West] encouraged 'Wars of liberation' when these weakened the adversary, but not if they undermined the stability or threatened the existence of friendly states."[12]

After the Second World War European financial constraints meant that US aid became a key factor for the colonizers and the colonies. Historians are of the opinion that the rise of the US played a major role in shaping decolonization. Such an opinion of the US was based on the fate of the French in Indo-China.[13] The 1954 First Indo-China War resulted in influencing and supporting independence movements by the US. Concurrently, the anti-communist policy of the US sped up the independence of some former colonies.

During the Cold War "the US and the Soviet Union gathered allies of dependent states based on ideological commonalities, where the liberal and capitalist West confronted an authoritarian and socialist East."[14] The picture of East-West confrontation was complicated by the fact that many states were not linked to either

22 United Nations Peace Operations

of the two powers, whether by treaty or by informal affinity. This third group, non-aligned, then organized the 1955 Asian-African Conference in Bandung and "proclaimed its neutrality in its East-West confrontation."[15] Arguably, some new leaders of Africa often turned to socialism for rebuilding their countries after the end of colonial occupation. In some cases, "their ideological inclination led them to an alliance with the Soviet Union."[16] The superpowers were also engaged in providing economic and military assistance to the newly emerging nation-states during the Cold War.[17]

There are examples of direct interference of these superpowers as well as consequent UN involvement during the 1960s in the decolonization of Africa. For instance, in the Congo, President Patrice Lumumba turned towards the Soviet Union during the crisis of 1960, initiating Cold War rivalry in Africa. Lumumba once said, "I want to work with everybody…and if it is the United States, Ok, but if it's the Soviet Union, that's also Ok."[18] Thus westerners worried that Lumumba would not allow them to continue exploiting the vast resources of his country. Lumumba's appeal for aid from the Soviet Union resulted in the arrival of arms and personnel.[19] However, Jeanne Haskin in his 2005 book, *The Tragic State of the Congo: From Decolonization to Dictatorship,* notes that "The Congolese government initially requested the United States to send 3000 troops and with the advice of the United States appealed the UN for assistance."[20] But later it was clear that Lumumba sought assistance from the Soviet Union, too. The UN force deployment took place within a very short time. This was simply due to Cold War influence in Africa immediately upon decolonization "to prevent rising socialism."[21] Lumumba was a victim of Cold War rivalry and his assassination later resulted in the establishment of US influence in the Congo.

The Congo continues to experience instability to this day. In the 1980s and 90s, the local Congolese resorted to smuggling of gold and coffee, and established a reign of terror, which resulted in massive displacement of populations. These displaced people formed their own militias and by 2002 a complete militarization of society was in place.[22] Therefore, the Congo turned into a new dynamic of conflict and resulted to second UN involvement in 1999.

Similarly, "the Angolan crisis of 1975 was both a cause and an early symptom of the unravelling of the superpowers' detente in the later 1970s."[23] The three largest tribal groups of Angola allied with the Soviet Union, South Africa, Cuba, or the US.[24] Additionally, two major contenders for power, the Movement of Popular Liberation of Angola and the Union National Independence of Total Angola, were supported by the Soviet Union and the US, respectively.

Like the Congo and Angola, Somalia became entangled in the politics of the Cold War because of its strategic location on the Horn of Africa. In 1977, Somalian leader General Said Barre, a revolutionary socialist, annexed the disputed Ogaden territory in Ethiopia. This annexation was repulsed by Ethiopia, which was supported by the Soviets and the Cubans. This event resulted in a refugee crisis, food shortage and a massive famine.[25] However, due to the support of the US, Somalia survived the crisis, thereafter, aligning itself with Washington.

Decolonization and involvement of the UN

The UN played a role in the process of decolonization in Africa, not least in managing and containing conflicts during the Cold War. In those decades, tensions rose in the UN between the General Assembly, dominated by emerging nation states and to some extent the Non-Aligned Movement, and the Security Council which was controlled by the Great Powers.[26] This situation effectively crippled the UN during the Cold War.

The UN started its role by supervising the administration of Trust territories, inherited from the League of Nations and intended to promote the advancement of their people towards self-government and independence.[27] In addition, the smaller nations at the UN promoted anti-colonial views. A major UN resolution was adopted through the Declaration on the granting of independence to colonial countries and peoples by the General Assembly on December 14, 1960, which envisioned a free world by 2000. Later a UN resolution was adopted on immediate decolonization in 1961. Thus, a Special Committee on Decolonization was formed to examine applications from the member states and to make recommendations for implementing the Declaration. The Security Council was mandated to intervene when developments in colonial territories threatened international peace and security, to call for a ceasefire between a national liberation movement and the colonial power or, if necessary, form a peacekeeping operation to supervise the transition to independence.[28]

The UN Trusteeship Council was especially involved in the independence process of the former colonies. The main function of the Trusteeship Council was to examine the administration of each territory and to supervise the transition towards independence. The League's interwar system of mandates was converted into the UN system of trust territories, to be administered by Allied former colonial powers. In 1946, those administrative powers presented respective draft agreements of concerning the trust territories to the UN and obtained approval – Britain presented agreements covering Tanganyika, British Togoland, and the Cameroon; France for its Togoland and Cameroon; and Belgium for Ruanda-Urundi.[29] An investigation of the process of independence of the trust territories concluded that the UN assisted in obtaining independence of all African trust territories by 1962.

There are cases where the influence of the Trusteeship Council was relatively marginal in the quest for independence, as in Togoland, Cameroon, and Tanganyika. The UN also handled the independence of the former Italian colonies of Libya, Somaliland, and Eritrea. The Trusteeship Council intervened actively in Ruanda-Urundi.[30] In Ruanda-Urundi, the Council resisted Belgian resistance to merge these two territories.

By 1962 all the trust territories in Africa were independent. The administrative powers of the trust territories dealt with the functioning of state-building affairs following indirect rule from the period of the colonial era. Mahmoud Mamdani argued that direct and indirect rule evolved into complementary ways of native control in the early colonial period.[31] This indirect rule was applied to the civil

24 United Nations Peace Operations

affairs functioning of the government machineries, where the key positions were controlled by the colonial powers and the lower-level positions were given to indigenous people and the European dominated populace of a particular colony.

Issue of the failure to address state-building: a key source of conflict

The failure of state-building in Africa during colonization and after decolonization remains as the most important source of conflict there. The 2005 Tony Blair's Commission for Africa suggested that Africa's fundamental problem was its lack of "good governance," which was the root cause for its wars and underdevelopment.[32] State-building includes good governance, the establishment of law and order in the absence of government authority, the construction of infrastructure and security forces, and facilitation of smooth transfer of power.[33] Amin Saikal's chapter "The Dimensions of State Disruption" in *From Civil Strife to Civil Society: Civil and Military Responsibilities in Disrupted States* lays out different forms of state failure:

(1) due to fragmentation of the national elite and breakdown of social order, e.g., Somalia, (2) driven by ethnic antagonisms, which in the absence of a robust state and corrective processes lead to open social conflict, e.g., Rwanda, (3) can be a product of ideological struggle, e.g., the Congo, (4) due to confessional or sectarian roots, e.g., Sudan, (5) due to collapse of the revenue base of the state, e.g., Iraq upon enforcement of UN sanctions, (6) internal disruption from a specific legitimacy crisis especially due to loss of charismatic leader, e.g., Ivory Coast, Ethiopia, and (7) from separatism on regional, ethnic and religious grounds, e.g., Sudan.[34]

African countries were not decolonized through a systematic approach of state-building leading to transition problems. After the First World War, the plague in West Africa due to poor hygiene and sleeping sickness in the Congo in 1919 drew attention to the failures of colonial health and hygiene policies in Africa.[35] As a norm, security was not guaranteed, political institutions had decayed, and public services declined rapidly. Alex Thomson in his 2016 book *An Introduction to African Politics* argued, "African states, by contrast, were relatively weak at independence. African political managers had been left with neither suitable state capacity, nor established institutional tools, to do this job."[36] After the Second World War Africans achieved their independence hurriedly during the 1950s and 60s without a formal approach of establishing state-building, which is very fundamental problem for many African countries. As a result, during the 1980s and 90s, several African countries experienced state collapse. In short, a majority of African governments were soon struggling to sustain even the most basic functions of a modern state.

Moreover, during the Cold War, African rulers hardly paid attention to state-building and according to Alex Thomson, "gained greater rewards for servicing the interests of the international community than they did for representing their own people."[37] This is especially true for Sudan and the Congo. Sudan has borne the weight of its colonial legacy. The Turks, Egyptians and British did not pay much attention to its southern territories, which were dependent on the north for economic and educational support. Southern Sudan hardly received any resource for development.[38] This legacy of underdevelopment persisted for decades even after independence. In his 2007 book, *Southern Sudan: Colonialism, Resistance and Autonomy*, Lam Akol argued, "the first three decades of British rule in the south were mostly to control local opposition by force of arms and to impose law and order... the education had been largely left to Christian missionaries."[39]

The Ottomans, Egyptians and the British all got involved in the state-building process in Sudan, but their focus was mostly on the north. The Turks and Egyptians were involved through limited economic development and administration. After Turco-Egyptian rule, the British paid attention to state-building endeavours, which remained insignificant over their fifty-six-years of rule. After independence, Sudan concentrated state-building efforts again on the North. Therefore, the South continued to remain underdeveloped and lacked state-building endeavours due to civil war from 1964.

Neither Sudan or the Congo created the apparatuses of a modern state, like development of military and police forces. Maintaining territorial integrity remains a prime responsibility of a nation-state. Paul D. Williams in his 2016 book *War & Conflict in Africa* argued, "by failing to control their territory, encouraging unprofessional security forces, and weakening traditional dispute resolution mechanisms, these regime strategies also encouraged the other, non-state world of armed conflicts in Africa."[40] Therefore, porous borders, for instance, due to lack of border management force and skill, as well as exerting authority within own territory, remain one of the key factors for failure to address state-building.

The history and dynamics of colonization of the Congo also reveals a failure to address state-building. During the 1870s, the Belgian King Leopold II planned a private venture to colonize the Congo. The Congo's governor general had far less power than other colonial governors and the Congo used to be governed from Belgium by the king directly. The Congolese were given no political responsibilities or higher positions in the colonial administration.[41] As such, socio-ethnic discrimination existed in all the key social welfare indicators. The Belgians extracted resources like ivory, rubber and diamonds from the Congo, which brought Belgium's economy to new heights, but in return it did nothing significant for the Congo other than building a small railway network to facilitate the easy transfer of resources outside the country.

The Belgians provided limited healthcare and primary education in the Congo and the Congolese had extremely limited secondary education, no established political processes or parties, no trade unions, and no intelligentsia. Only in 1953 were the Congolese allowed to become landowners for the first time. By 1958, a few Congolese had been accepted by Belgian universities. Thus, upon independence, the Congo could not stand on its own, resulting in anarchy and chaos. A UN peacekeeping force was deployed in 1960 to stabilize the situation and withdrew in 1964 after completion of its mandate.[42] In the meantime, the national government created in 1961 ultimately collapsed and was replaced by a military regime that took over power in 1965 after the withdrawal of the UN forces.[43]

26 United Nations Peace Operations

The Congo is an example of a gradual state failure upon departure of the UN in 1964. The UN civilian operations in the Congo (1960–64) focused on state building, starting from with government machineries at the different tiers, financial institutions, civilian operations, and socio-economic development. These were classical components of state-building efforts. Later, upon departure of the UN, Joseph Mobutu took power and in his thirty-two-year rule as president (1965–97), the Congo oversaw a systematic state failure of the highest order.[44] Within the first ten years of his leadership, the Congo started its journey of state collapse. The Congo's state institutions collapsed gradually, and led to civil war, which resulted in UN involvement in 1999.

Establishment of the UN Relief and Rehabilitation Administration (UNRRA)

UNRRA was the first organized operating entity of the international community to deal with the tragic human sufferings of the Second World War. The organization laid the foundation for UN operations and services in the field in war-destabilized places. In fact, the concept of UNRRA led in part to the emergence of modern civil-military coordination and assistance with state-building endeavours in the UN system.

UNRRA was established in 1943 to deal with healthcare and food supplies for refugees and displaced persons, and to supply aid to countries in poor economic shape as a result of the war.[45] UNRRA was run by a council that assigned one delegate from each of the forty-four signatories; its Central Committee consisted of members from the US, Britain, the Soviet Union, and China (which collectively provided seventy-five percent of UNRRA's budget). It had four working committees: Financial Control, Technical Advisory, Advisory, and Administration – all located in Washington D.C.[46] UNRRA began rehabilitating refugees and displaced persons (DPs), and administered refugee camps located all over the Mediterranean, Africa, and the Middle East from May 1944.

UNRRA was, of course, limited in what it could accomplish until the war ended. After the war, the organization dealt with millions of refugees and DPs in Europe alone.[47] In order to fulfill its mandate, it worked with the Allied military, and UNRRA established the Military Liaison Office under the administration of its European Regional Office in November, 1944.[48] The Liaison Office was responsible for coordinating the efforts of its Allied counterparts operating in Allied-occupied territories – a beginning of classic civil-military coordination.

Effective coordination between UNRRA and the Allied military occurred during their operations in liberated territories. As a result of an agreement with the US, British, and French authorities in Europe, UNRRA was placed, during field operations in occupied zones, under the control of each country's military command. The military command and UNRRA divided responsibilities: the military took care of housing, maintenance of peace and security, and provision of basic supplies; UNRRA accepted responsibility for running DP camps; for providing health and welfare services,[49] entertainment, and job training, and for contributing supplies that the military could not. UNRRA also provided food, clothing, raw materials, medical supplies, farming machinery, livestock, fishery infrastructure, and more to various recovering regions and countries.

UNRRA mainly assisted in state-building affairs such as economic development and the provision of technical assistance to countries affected by the Second World War. It provided supplies for industrial rehabilitation in four broad categories: highway, railway, and water supply equipment; coal, other fuels, and lubricants; materials for the restoration of public utilities, provision of shelter, and repair of highways; plus materials and equipment needed for restoration of essential industries.[50] The Agricultural Rehabilitation programme helped toward developing agro-based economies in recipient countries.[51] The programme, which covered deliveries related to seeds, fertilizers, harrows, ploughs, pesticides, and harvesting equipment, posed challenges for UNRRA,[52] because crop timing varied so much. Nevertheless, it played a key role in economic development, which was essential for successful state-building.

Apart from economic initiatives, UNRRA offered fellowship programmes for recipient countries to facilitate development of technical expertise in fields related to health, social welfare, and agricultural/industrial rehabilitation. From 1944, 165 fellowships were provided from UNRRA's budget. It negotiated bilateral programmes elsewhere, which permitted another 155 fellows to receive training. UNRRA's fellowship programme concept was subsequently embedded in the UN Children's Fund and the World Health Organization for subsequent follow up.[53]

UNRRA was also involved in state-building affairs for countries including Albania, Austria, Belarus, China, Czechoslovakia, Ethiopia, Finland, Germany, Greece, Hungary, Italy, Korea, the Philippines, Poland, the Soviet Socialist Republic, the Ukraine Soviet Socialist Republic, and Yugoslavia. Ethiopia suffered six years of Italian occupation until its liberation by British forces in 1941. Here, UNRRA's efforts were concentrated on developing training projects that involved health, welfare, transport, and agricultural rehabilitation.[54] Such initiatives proved to be pioneer programmes in state-building for countries negatively affected by the Second World War. Once its footprint was established in affected areas, UNRRA withdrew gradually, to facilitate smooth transitions.[55]

UNRRA's role in Europe was gradually dissolved from 1947 and its responsibilities transferred to other organizations. Health functions were taken over by the World Health Organization's Interim Commission in 1947.[56] The International Children's Emergency Fund assumed responsibility for child welfare; the Food and Agriculture Organization took over agricultural rehabilitation-related affairs. Displaced persons were initially handled by the Intergovernmental Committee on Refugees; subsequently, by the International Refugee Organization. By 1948, UNRRA had closed down its offices around the world[57] – the US, which provided over seventy percent of UNRRA funds and whose nationals occupied most of the organization's senior management positions, was deeply critical of its repatriation policies and decided to terminate the organization.[58]

The Cold War began while UNRRA was in operation. The US preferred bilateral agreements and developed the Marshall Plan to support war-affected countries as well as to promote cooperation between different European states. UNRRA also became involved in controversies related to lack of detailed policies, procurement, graft, and illegal diversion of relief goods. Differences between national government(s) and UNRRA were often the result of failure of alignment of UNRRA activities with the government plans/policies of recipient countries and, most importantly, of Cold War rivalry.[59] That said, UNRRA was sorely needed; it brought positive contributions to many lives.

Above all, UNRRA had shown the way to involvement in state-building and civil-military coordination by a UN entity immediately after the Second World War. The organization brought positive contributions to the life of those whose lives were disrupted by the war. It was a bridge and that gave time for the process of creation of the UN. UNRRA was the platform from where the UN funds, programmes, and specialized agencies were established; they worked together to support state-building in war-torn and developing countries.

Evolution of Civil Affairs

During the Second World War civil affairs was primarily under military control, but after 1945 UN agencies gradually took on this function in developing countries. The term "civil affairs" relates to assisting with state-building through significant involvement in ensuring that the machinery of local governments functions. According to the *Handbook on United Nations Multidimensional Peacekeeping Operations*,

> The role of civil affairs is to engage and assist local civilian authorities and communities in efforts to consolidate peace by restoring the political, legal, economic and social infrastructures that support democratic governance and economic development. Because of the range of specialized expertise required, whether in a civil affairs, civil administration or other multidimensional mandate, there is a broad range of professional backgrounds among civil affairs officers. These include political science, law, international relations, business administration, engineering, economics or a specific sectoral area pertinent to the needs of a mission, such as education, health and finance. Civil affairs officers are the civilian face of the mission to the local population.[60]

The functions expanded to handling the affairs of the refugees and displaced persons during the Second World War, relieving combat soldiers of some of their traditional security duties. These functions were originally handled by the Allied Military Government, of which civil affairs were a key component. After the Second World War, NGOs were deeply involved in socio-economic development as well as civil affairs related activities in developing countries.[61] However, in the UN setting, civil affairs officially appeared in the 1990s in UN peace operations and its function was different from the Military Governments' civil affairs. This study of civil affairs will develop understanding of the civil-military coordination in UN peace operations in following chapters.

The development of civil affairs, especially in the African context, was shaped by the British colonial practice of engaging local personnel to assist in governance. Finding the personnel to impose direct rule in colonized territories was always difficult, hence more indirect methods of administration were the option of governance. British military administration in Africa was clearly another example of a huge operation run with a minimum of resources, where the avoidance of direct rule was a major issue. During the First World War, a form of Military Government was adopted in Palestine by the British to control all political matters through appointing political officers under the Chief Political Officer.[62]

The British introduced the Military Government in Italian East Africa, covering Ethiopia, Eritrea, and Italian Somaliland, during the Second World War. The British also established Political Branch Headquarters in Cairo by Major-General Sir Philip Mitchell at the end of January 1941.[63] In 1944, it moved to Europe, however, some portions remained to administer East Africa, which in May 1943 turned into Civil Affairs Branch.[64] During the Second World War, civil affairs operations in a liberated or conquered country denoted the operation of administration through a Military Government.[65] Civil affairs were therefore taken into consideration by the Allied forces when planning to capture territories in Europe and administer them, in part to keep refugees and displaced persons away from impending military operations.[66] For instance, the British zone in Germany in 1945 had approximately 2.5 million displaced persons from different nationalities that the civil affairs of the Allied Military Government of Occupied Territories handled.

The British Military Government involved civil affairs officers in state-building activities through pacification programmes, including public works, maintenance works, medical and veterinary services, agriculture, forestry, and education for the local population in Italian Somaliland (Somalia). While operating in Ethiopia, the staff were known as political officers but while in Eritrea in 1943, they became civil affairs officers.

During the 1943 Operation Husky in Italy, the duty of civil affairs officers was to relieve the fighting troops from the challenge of delivering humanitarian aid or dealing with a hostile population. The concept was that the occupying power would avoid formulating plans for the reform of Italy, and instead leave space for the Italians to shape their own political future[67] – in present terminology, what is called "local ownership." Civil affairs officers were also responsible for determining if existing administrators, including mayors, prefects, and even teachers, were suitable to remain in their posts.[68] This model was later developed for civil affairs operation in France, Belgium, and the Netherlands as well as for future Allied operations. Such types of operations were also undertaken through coordinated efforts by the Allied Military Government of Occupied Territories and the UNRRA.[69]

The US followed the British approach to civil affairs when the US War Department established a Civil Affairs Division in March 1943 and the Combined

30 United Nations Peace Operations

Chiefs of Staff established a Combined Civil Affairs Committee in July 1943. This arrangement was made by the US to undertake the civil affairs job by the military in the liberated territories in absence of UNRRA for the military period of responsibility. Later UNRRA also used the committees' resources for distribution in the affected areas.[70] The committee also negotiated dealing with displaced persons operations related to Northwest Europe and Germany.[71] UNRRA worked closely with the Combined Civil Affairs Committee for functioning related to food, agriculture, health care, supply, infrastructure development, and child welfare.[72] Such assistance with state-building affairs was also prominent in the civil affairs functioning under the UN.

The functioning of civil affairs under the Allied Military Government and civil affairs in UN peace operations/missions is quite different. However, the UN Trusteeship Council had assisted with the functioning of civil affairs in the trust territories in Africa during 1950s to 1960s. Civil affairs officers in UN missions – the primary interface between the mission and local authorities and communities – oversee governance, public administration and economic development as well as assist in developing state apparatus through training and monitoring during the implementation of the UN mandate.[73] In the UN setting, civil affairs became one of the key functions in 1992, when it was embodied in the mandate of the UN Protection Force in the former Yugoslavia.[74] However, prior to that – though not much pronounced – the functions of civil affairs surfaced in the UN Civilian Operations in the Congo (1960–64), where before June 1964 the Civilian Operations personnel were assigned under a Civilian Affairs Officer with regional responsibility.[75] Thereafter, such functions were visible in UN peacekeeping in Cyprus, Tajikistan, Georgia, Central America, Namibia, and in Cambodia (1991–1993). The UN approach to civil affairs continued to evolve in the 2000s, resulting in actively supporting the implementation of the UN mandate in different conflict-ridden countries.

Evolution of Civil-Military Coordination in the UN setting

Civil-Military Relations has existed as long as soldiers have come into contact with civilians in the course of military operations.[76] Simone Haysom urged that there was a long history of militaries participating in the humanitarian crisis, including during the Abyssinian Crisis in 1935.[77]

The modern conception of CIMIC dates back to the Second World War, where military involvement in civilian efforts was known as civil affairs and functioned with a view to restoring services after the war in the Military Government of the Allied Forces. Such assistance or functions were also known as, "in aid to civil administration." The term "pacification" was also used widely in different scenarios with varied aims and objectives after the Second World War by the colonial powers to "win the hearts and minds" of local populations agitating for independence. European military forces were thus engaged in the functions of civil affairs as well as providing humanitarian assistance to the population. The British adopted "pacification" in Kenya (1952–60) while operating against Mau Mau insurgents, targeting pro-British cross section of population only.[78] However, many innocent people were affected by British operations. After 1945, colonial rule continued in Algeria in the face of a growing and increasingly militant independence movement. During the subsequent Algerian War (1956–62), the French undertook "pacification" activities as part of the function of civil affairs but targeted only pro-French populations against the Algerian National Liberation Front (*Front de libération nationale*, FLN).[79] In contrast, the FLN, who were fighting for self-determination, targeted the entire population to deliver their own "pacification" efforts.[80]

After the Cold War, the UN, and other stakeholders, including NGOs, began to operate in conflict-ridden countries in the 1990s. This proliferation demanded greater coordination between the civilian and military stakeholders operating in the same environment. As discussed, civil affairs were introduced in the UN setting in the 1990s, where entire populations were targeted to deliver humanitarian assistance and to attain the UN objective, which was to maintain peace and stability. It was only in the 2000s when civil-military coordination (CIMIC) appeared in UN peace operation scenarios in integrated missions. Thus, the military became officially involved to provide humanitarian assistance in UN peace operations. The evolution of civil affairs since the Second World War and the emergence of CIMIC in the 2000s are appended in table 1.1.

There is a distinct difference between the functioning of civil affairs and CIMIC. The main function of military forces engaged in UN peace operations is to help create a secure environment for others to work. Civil Affairs personnel at the local level provide advice concerning civilian issues in the broader context of a mandate's implementation. They assist in managing any misunderstanding or conflict between communities and other stakeholders. Civil affairs officers assist in the planning and implementation of joint civil-military initiatives, including protection of civilians.[81] When CIMIC came into the scene in the UN setting, it became a bridge between civil affairs and UN military forces. CIMIC policy evolved in the 1990s and 2000s, in response to experiences during UN peace operations in the Democratic Republic of Congo (1999–2010) and Sudan (2005–11).

Modern Civil-Military Coordination in UN peace operations

Modern civil military coordination (CIMIC) emerged in UN peace operations in the 2000s and gradually became an effective tool to assist in national-level state-building in conflict-ridden countries. Cedric De Coning argued that although CIMIC "has not been used as an overall operational level coordination tool, the concept has often been used to suggest multidimensional cohesion and coordination."[82] Coning emphasized that CIMIC is mainly applied in a coordination role. However, the author's field experience in Sudan (2009–10) suggests that CIMIC's crucial involvement has been in assisting national-level state-building efforts. Arguably, CIMIC teams can play an important role in national-level state-building, but they are not the only solution to post conflict state-building. At the beginning of the 2000s, the practice of CIMIC

TABLE 1.1. Civil affairs and CIMIC in different periods.

	Second World War	French in Algeria (1956–62)	Algerian National Liberation Front (FLN) 1956–62	British in Kenya (1952–1960)	UN Mission in the 1990s	UN Mission from 2000
Known as	Civil Affairs by Allied Forces	Pacification	Pacification	Pacification	Introduction of civil affairs and humanitarian affairs.	Introduction of Civil-Military Coordination.
Objective	To assist restoration of services.	To maintain colony and reduce the popularity of anti-colonial insurgent forces.	Self-determination	To eliminate Mau Mau.	To attain UN objectives related to peace support and conflict resolution.	To attain UN objectives related to peace support and conflict resolution.
Target audience	Entire populations	Sympathizers (pro-French populations)	Entire population	Sympathizers (pro-British populations)	Affected population	Affected population
Type of operations	In aid to civil administration	French Counter Insurgency operations	Algerian Nationalist movement	British Counter Insurgency operations	Peacekeeping	Peacekeeping and introduction of peacebuilding
Implementing outfits	Allied Civil Affairs units	French military	Algerian nationalists	British military	UN Agencies, NGOs	Military becomes a stakeholder along with UN agencies and NGOs.

Source: Developed by the author.

policies were shaping up through multidimensional or integrated UN peace operations, such as the UN Organization Mission in Democratic Republic of Congo (MONUC: 1999–2010) and the UN Mission in Sudan (UNMIS: 2005–11). In both the missions, CIMIC entities played their part in different fields targeting country- and community-level activities. In Sudan, CIMIC played a significant role assisting in the implementation of the 2005 Comprehensive Peace Agreement (CPA), though not one that was fully acknowledged. In the Democratic Republic of Congo (DRC), the overall security situation, especially during the first few years, was not as conducive as Sudan to facilitate the wider role of CIMIC in assisting in the implementation of the 1999 Lusaka Peace Agreement.

In both peace operations, CIMIC activities, although not outlined through a well-orchestrated plan by the Troop Contributing Countries (TCCs), contributed through involvement in projects (e.g., Quick Impact Projects – QIPs). CIMIC activities therefore can assist in national-level state-building and thereby help achieving mandated tasks. In both missions, concerned UN agencies assisted with the coordination mechanisms as and when necessary. Apart from addressing difficulties in state-building as a source of conflict, CIMIC entities also addressed the root of conflict in Sudan, rendering community-driven projects for populations and internally displaced persons (IDPs). Additionally, CIMIC activities played their part in preventing conflict in areas of operation by engaging people in different fields of state-building such as agriculture, sports, and education.

CIMIC in Sudan mostly followed the established principles and core tasks in integrating humanitarian assistance from 2005. Workable liaison arrangements and functional lines of communication were established at all levels for the exchange of information. The UN mission in Sudan faced challenges upon its establishment in 2005 with respect to CIMIC due to a lack of understanding by various stakeholders and also due to lack of capacity of CIMIC personnel.[83] As the mission moved on, these challenges were overcome through the training of personnel in CIMIC. However, such challenges remained throughout the duration of the mission.

The UN mission in Sudan undertook a wide range of CIMIC activities to support the peace mission mandate. CIMIC activities displayed the presence of the UN through a varied range of events and QIPs in different parts of Sudan to assist local populations. The author had the opportunity to see the effects of the initial CIMIC efforts and expand them by his role as Chief of UN-CIMIC section (2009–10) in the mission headquarters. That time saw the establishment of a unique nation-wide medical support coordination, as well as the identification, supervision, and implementation of a significant number of QIPs in the fields of education, agriculture, health, sports, and energy. Together these serve as a case-study of what CIMIC in UN peace operations looks like in practice in order to evaluate its contribution to national-level state-building.[84]

Unlike Sudan, the mission in the Democratic Republic of Congo (DRC) handled both the volatile internal conflict and a regional crisis and was mandated to assist in state-building endeavours from 2004. CIMIC in the DRC had difficulties due to the security situation and was confined initially within small areas, but with the

34 United Nations Peace Operations

improvement of the security situation extended its horizon to undertake QIPs all over the area of operation. When a Bangladeshi infantry battalion was deployed in eastern DRC in August 2004, the security situation was so fluid that during the first year the unit was occupied in its role to ensure a secured environment and hardly got any chance of undertaking CIMIC activities.[85] Thereafter, the CIMIC section's key task was liaising with different stakeholders, including the Congolese armed force (Forces Armées de la République Démocratique du Congo, FARDC). Military contingents of the mission were involved in CIMIC activities and implemented a variety of QIPs. Details of these missions including their practice of CIMIC are discussed in subsequent chapters.

Conclusions

The period of decolonization and the Cold War overlapped, amplifying the problem. After the Second World War, African initiatives through different events, forums, and the OAU played a key role in achieving self-determination. The conflicts during the period of decolonization led to the involvement of the international community and engagement of the UN in Africa. During the Cold War, the West was apprehensive about the influence of communism upon the nationalist movements and the newly independent nation-states. Thus, the low-intensity warfare between the West and the Soviet Union affected decolonization in some African countries.

Failure to address state-building in Africa during colonization and after decolonization remained as a critical source of instability and conflict. The colonizers did not pay much attention to state-building and African countries were decolonized quickly without a systematic approach to state-building. Further, after independence some of the African rulers hardly paid attention to state-building, resulting in state collapse. For instance, Sudan and the Congo soon became conflict-ridden after independence and could not handle or administer state institutions. This led to the involvement of the international community and UN to provide assistance to state-building, as well as ensuring peace and security. These roots of conflict shaped the subsequent evolution of the UN, its peacekeeping operations (now known as peace operations) along with civil affairs and civil military coordination functions, as explored in the following chapters.

The UN was established to save the world from the scourge of war as well as to maintain peace and stability. Though its predecessor the League of Nations achieved little, it provided a precedent for the establishment of the UN. UNRRA was created at the time of need to assist states and peoples affected by war. UNRRA also provided foundations for assisting in state-building affairs and civil-military coordination in different countries affected by the Second World War through its efforts in economic development. UNRRA's success gave all nations a fresh assurance that they could work together for the humanity and achieve a common goal. However, UNRRA suffered from Cold War rivalry and was not fully credited for its achievements; instead, arguably it was accused of failing to not align its functions with the receiving countries' governments. The UN achieved a lot during its initial two decades of operations especially through its trusteeship council in obtaining the independence of all African trust territories by 1962.

The nature of civil affairs as established through the Allied Military Governments during the Second World War remains a guideline to civil-military coordination, but there have also been important changes. Being a key interface between the UN mission component and the local authorities as well as communities, civil affairs play a significant role in accomplishing the mandate of the UN. This was proven in the former Yugoslavia, Cambodia, Sierra Leone, Democratic Republic of Congo, Liberia, Ivory Coast, Burundi, Sudan, Chad, and the Central African Republic. This background study of the short-term African conflict, tracing the evolution of the UNRRA, the development of civil affairs operations and civil-military coordination provides a context to embark into the modern Civil-Military Coordination in UN peace operations.

Notes

1 Paul D. Williams, *War & Conflict in Africa*, 2nd ed. (Cambridge UK and Maiden, USA: Polity Press, 2016), 5.
2 Séverine Autesserre, "The Crisis of Peacekeeping: Why the UN Can't End Wars", *Foreign Affairs*, 11 December 2018, 101–2.
3 KJ. Holsti, "War, Peace, and the State of the State", *International Political Science Review* 16, no. 4 (1995): 321.
4 Stephen Luscombe, "The British Empire", accessed 28 January 2018, http://www.britishempire.co.uk/.
5 "State-Building includes good governance, public administration, the Rule of Law, education, health, political inclusion of the people, and other endeavours to ensure peace and prosperity, as well as the wellbeing of its populations."
6 Martin Shipway, *Decolonization and Its Impact: A Comparative Approach to the End of the Colonial Empires* (Malden, MA: Blackwell Publishing, 2008), 235.
7 Raymond Betts, *Decolonization* (London: Taylor and Francis, ProQuest Ebook Central, 2004), 1.
8 Jan C. Jansen, Jurgen Osterhammel, *Decolonization A Short History*, trans. Jeremiah Riemer (New Jersey: Princeton University Press, 2017), 142.
9 Department of Public Information, "UN Yearbook: 1946–47", The Yearbook of the United Nations: The authoritative reference work on the UN System, 47 1946, 831, https://www.unmultimedia.org/searchers/yearbook/page.jsp?bookpage=180&volume=1946-47.
10 George Woodbridge, *UNRRA: The History of the United Nations Relief and Rehabilitation Administration*, vol. II, 3 vols (New York: Columbia University Press, 1950).
11 Jan C. Jansen, Jurgen Osterhammel, *Decolonization A Short History*, 144.
12 Michael Howard, *War and the Liberal Conscience* (New Brunswick, New Jersey: Rutgers University Press, 1999), 5–6.
13 John D. Kelly and Martha Kaplan, "My Ambition Is Much Higher Than Independence: US Power, the UN World, the Nation-State and Their Critics", by Prasenjit Duara (London: Taylor and Francis, ProQuest Ebook Central, 2003), 145.
14 Jan C. Jansen, Jurgen Osterhammel, *Decolonization A Short History*, 139.
15 John Darwin, *After Tamerlane: The Rise & Fall of Global Empires, 1400–2000* (Penguin Group, 2007), 444.
16 Jussi M Hanhimäki and Odd Arne Westad, eds., "Decolonization and the Cold War", in *The Cold War: A History in Documents and Eyewitness Accounts* (New York: Oxford University Press, 2003), 347.
17 Jan C. Jansen, Jurgen Osterhammel, *Decolonization A Short History*, 142.

36 United Nations Peace Operations

18 *King Leopold's Ghost*, Video file, 2016, https://digital-films-com.proxy.hil.unb.ca/Porta lPlaylists.aspx?wID=106437&xtid=118372.

19 Darwin, *After Tamerlane: The Rise & Fall of Global Empires, 1400–2000*, 467.

20 Jeanne M. Haskin, *The Tragic State of the Congo: From Decolonization to Dictatorship* (New York: Algora Publishing, 2005), 24.

21 Hanhimäki and Westad, "Decolonization and the Cold War," 348.

22 *King Leopold's Ghost*.

23 Norrie Macqueen, *United Nations Peacekeeping in Africa Since 1960* (London, United Kingdom: Routledge, 2014), 27.

24 Christopher D O'Sullivan, *The United Nations: A Concise History* (Malabar, Fla.: Krieger Pub. Co., 2005), 75.

25 Macqueen, *United Nations Peacekeeping in Africa Since 1960*, 201.

26 Gordon Martel, *A Companion to International History 1900–2001* (John Wiley & Sons, 2008), 323.

27 United Nations, "Teaching about Decolonization" (Department of Public Information, 1991), 14.

28 United Nations, "Teaching about Decolonization" (Department of Public Information, 1991), 6–14.

29 "After the First World War Rwanda was governed by Belgium as Ruanda-Urundi. After independence Urundi became Burundi on July 1, 1962".

30 Evan Luard, *A History of the United Nations, Volume 2: The Age of Decolonization, 1955–1965* (London: Macmillan, 1989), 130.

31 Mahmood Mamdani, *Citizen and Subject: Contemporary Africa and the Legacy of Late Colonialism* (Princeton: Princeton University Press, 2018), 18.

32 Williams, *War & Conflict in Africa*, 8.

33 Paul F. Diehl, "The International Community and Disrupted States", in *From Civil Strife to Civil Society: Civil and Military Responsibilities in Disrupted States* (New York: United Nations University Press, 2003), 42.

34 Amin Saikal, "The Dimensions of State Disruption", in *From Civil Strife to Civil Society: Civil and Military Responsibilities in Disrupted States* (New York: United Nations University Press, 2003), 20–22.

35 Thomas, *Fight or Flight: Britain, France, and Their Roads from Empire*, 15–20.

36 Thomson, *An Introduction to African Politics*.

37 Thomson, 275.

38 Shipway, *Decolonization and Its Impact: A Comparative Approach to the End of the Colonial Empires*, 181.

39 Lam Akol, *Southern Sudan: Colonialism, Resistance and Autonomy* (Trenton, Asmara: The Red Sea Press Inc., 2007), 21.

40 Williams, *War & Conflict in Africa*, 3.

41 Ruth Slade, *The Belgian Congo*, Second edition (Ely House, London: Oxford University Press, 1961), 6–7.

42 "ONUC", accessed 30 January 2018, https://peacekeeping.un.org/sites/default/files/pa st/onucB.htm.

43 Shipway, *Decolonization and Its Impact: A Comparative Approach to the End of the Colonial Empires*, 218.

44 Thomson, *An Introduction to African Politics*, 205.

45 Woodbridge, *UNRRA: The History of the United Nations Relief and Rehabilitation Administration*, 1950, I: xxv; "United Nations Relief and Rehabilitation Administration - UNARMS", accessed 11 October 2018, https://search.archives.un.org/united-nations-re lief-and-rehabilitation-administration-1947; Kelley Lee, *The World Health Organization (WHO)* (Routledge, 2008), 13.

46 Division of Public Information UNRRA, *Fifty Facts About UNRRA* (Washington, D.C., 1946), 3.

47 Alexander Betts, Gil Loescher, and James Milner, *The United Nations High Commissioner for Refugees (UNHCR): The Politics and Practice of Refugee Protection* (Routledge, 2013).

48 Evan Luard, *A History of the United Nations, Volume 1: The Years of Western Domination, 1945–1955* (London: Macmillan, 1982), 77; Woodbridge, *UNRRA: The History of the United Nations Relief and Rehabilitation Administration*, 1950, I:165.

49 Jessica Reinisch, *The Perils of Peace: The Public Health Crisis in Occupied Germany* (OUP Oxford, 2013), 33.

50 Woodbridge, *UNRRA: The History of the United Nations Relief and Rehabilitation Administration*, 1950, I:457.

51 Reinisch, *The Perils of Peace,*19, 280; Woodbridge, I:506.

52 Woodbridge, *UNRRA: The History of the United Nations Relief and Rehabilitation Administration*, 1950, I:478.

53 Woodbridge, *UNRRA: The History of the United Nations Relief and Rehabilitation Administration*, 1950, II:35–38; Lee, *The World Health Organization (WHO)*, 12–24.

54 UNRRA, *Fifty Facts About UNRRA*, 7; Woodbridge, *UNRRA: The History of the United Nations Relief and Rehabilitation Administration*, 1950, II:334–41.

55 Reinisch, *The Perils of Peace*, 196.

56 Woodbridge, *UNRRA: The History of the United Nations Relief and Rehabilitation Administration*, 1950, I:303.

57 Reinisch, *The Perils of Peace*, 140,196; Woodbridge, I:301–20.

58 Betts, Loescher, and Milner, *The United Nations High Commissioner for Refugees (UNHCR)*; Y. Beigbeder, *New Challenges for UNICEF: Children, Women and Human Rights* (Springer, 2001), 8.

59 Beigbeder, *New Challenges for UNICEF*, 8; Jefferson Ray, "UNRRA in China" (Institute of Pacific Relations, New York, 1947), 1–10.

60 UN Peacekeeping Best Practices Unit, "Handbook on United Nations Multidimensional Peacekeeping Operations" (Department of Peacekeeping Operations and Department of Field Support, December 2003), 35, https://peacekeeping.un.org/sites/default/files/peacekeeping-handbook_un_dec2003_0.pdf.

61 Daniel Evans, *Journal of the International Relations and Affairs Group, Volume II, Issue II* (Lulu.com, 2013), 13.

62 Philip Boobbyer, "Lord Rennell, Chief of AMGOT: A Study of His Approach to Politics and Military Government (c.1940–43)", *SAGE*, War in History, 2017, 5, https://doi.org/10.1177/0968344516671737; Francis James Rennell of Rodd, *British Military Administration of Occupied Territories in Africa during the Years 1941–1947* (Westport, Conn.: Greenwood Press, 1970), 16.

63 Rennell of Rodd, *British Military Administration of Occupied Territories in Africa during the Years 1941–1947*, 295.

64 Rennell of Rodd, 475.

65 Harry Lewis Coles; Albert Katz Weinberg, *Civil Affairs: Soldiers Become Governors*, First (Washington: Office of the Chief of Military History, Dept. of the Army, 1964), IX.

66 F. S. V. Donnison, *Civil Affairs and Military Government: North-West Europe, 1944–1946*, History of the Second World War. United Kingdom Military Series (London: H.M.S. O., 1961), 341.

67 Boobbyer, "Lord Rennell, Chief of AMGOT: A Study of His Approach to Politics and Military Government (c.1940–43)", 3.

68 Cindy Brown, ""To Bury the Dead and to Feed the Living": Allied Military Government in Sicily, 1943", *Canadian Military History*, Special Edition, The Sicily Campaign, 22, no. 3 (Summer 2013): 35–37.

69 Donnison, *Civil Affairs and Military Government*, 342–46.

70 Woodbridge, *UNRRA: The History of the United Nations Relief and Rehabilitation Administration*, 1950, I:23,445–46.

71 Woodbridge, *UNRRA: The History of the United Nations Relief and Rehabilitation Administration*, 1950, II:477.

72 UN Archives, Combined Civil Affairs Committee, "United Nations Relief and Rehabilitation Administration", 11 August 1944, Series 0805, Box 2 and 4, File 2 and 14, United Nations Archive Records Management Section.

38 United Nations Peace Operations

73 Joanna Harvey, Cedric de, ed., *Civil Affairs Handbook* (New York, NJ: United Nations, 2012), 22.

74 Joanna Harvey, Cedric de, 30.

75 UN Archives, Acting Civilian Affairs Officer H. Kaufman ONUC Stanleyville, "Police Advisory Services and Training", Letter to S. Habib Ahmed, Chief Civilian Operations, ONUC Leopoldville, 5 June 1963, S-0728, Box 30, File 2, United Nations Archives Records Management Section; Arthur H. House, *The U.N. in the Congo: The Political and Civilian Efforts* (Washington: University Press of America, 1978), 178.

76 UN Department of Peacekeeping Operations & Department of Field Support, *United Nations Civil-Military Coordination (UN-CIMIC) Specialized Training Materials* (New York: Department of Peacekeeping Operations and Department of Field Support, 2014).

77 Simone Haysom, "Civil-Military Coordination: The State of the Debate", ODI HPN, 1 January 2013, https://odihpn.org/magazine/civil%c2%96military-coordination-the-sta te-of-the-debate/.

78 Shipway, *Decolonization and Its Impact: A Comparative Approach to the End of the Colonial Empires*, 147–50.

79 Jennifer Johnson, *The Battle for Algeria: Sovereignty, Health Care, and Humanitarianism* (University of Pennsylvania Press: University of Pennsylvania Press, 2016), 4,12, http://unb.worldcat.org. proxy.hil.unb.ca/title/battle-for-algeria-sovereignty-health-care-and-humanitar ianism/oclc/932050741&referer=brief_results.

80 Jennifer Johnson, *The Battle for Algeria: Sovereignty, Health Care, and Humanitarianism* (University of Pennsylvania Press: University of Pennsylvania Press, 2016), 40–41, http://unb.worldcat. org.proxy.hil.unb.ca/title/battle-for-algeria-sovereignty-health-care-and-humanitarianism/oc lc/932050741&referer=brief_results.

81 Joanna Harvey, Cedric de, *Civil Affairs Handbook*, 41–42.

82 Cedric De Coning, "Civil-Military Coordination Practices and Approaches Within United Nations Peace Operations," *Journal of Military and Strategic Studies* 10, no. 1 (September 1, 2007): 30, https://jmss.org/article/view/57636.

83 UNMIS, Khartoum, "UNMIS Military Update: The Force Commander's Six Monthly Military Report: March–September 2005", Six monthly report (Khartoum, 30 October 2005).

84 "The author (a Lieutenant Colonel from Bangladesh Army) worked as Chief of CIMIC section in UNMIS headquarters from June 9, 2009 to July 8, 2010."

85 "The author was the Staff Officer of Military Operations Directorate at the Army Headquarters, Bangladesh Army, December 2002 to April 2005." During this period, he oversaw the activities of the unit. When this unit was relieved after one year, the second unit got involved in CIMIC activities in 2005.

2

THE EMERGENCE OF MODERN CIVIL-MILITARY COORDINATION IN UNITED NATIONS PEACE OPERATIONS

Introduction

The increase in United Nations peace and stability missions in Africa at the turn of the millennium coincided with emerging trends in multidimensional peacekeeping. In the 1990s, the strategic context for UN peacekeeping transformed to encourage "multidimensional" peace operations. According to the UN, "Multidimensional peace operations are composed of a range of components, including military, civilian police, political affairs, rule of law, human rights, humanitarian, reconstruction, public information and gender. There are also a number of areas, such as mission support and security and safety of personnel, that remain essential to peacekeeping regardless of a particular mission's mandate."[1] In his 2007 article, "Civil-Military Coordination Practices and Approaches Within United Nations Peace Operations," Cedric De Coning argued that "Peacekeeping used to be a military affair, but more and more civilian roles were added after the end of the Cold War when UN peace operations started to change from being ceasefire observation operations to becoming multidimensional missions."[2] Therefore, different types of stakeholders, including NGOs started operating in conflict-ridden countries. After all, "no single agency can deal with recovery efforts alone."[3] According to the 2008 *United Nations Peacekeeping Operations: Principles and Guidelines*, "UN peace operations involved the employment of a mix of military, police and civilian capabilities to support the implementation of a mandate."[4] These principles and guidelines for UN peace operations were the outcome of challenges and difficulties faced by the UN in the 1990s. Thus, massive coordination efforts involving Troop Contributing Countries (TCCs), Police Contributing Countries (PCCs), and other stakeholders resulted from ten to fifteen years of difficult trial and error efforts around the world.

Modern UN Civil-Military Relations has historical context and several precedents. According to Christopher Ankersen, "like human security, the notion of civilian and

DOI: 10.4324/9781003275404-3

40 The Emergence of Modern Civil-Military Coordination

military cooperation is not completely new."[5] Such coordination was part of the Allied military strategy during the Second World War as discussed in Chapter I. The civil-military functions or assistance were sometimes referred to as "in aid to civil administration" or "pacification" by the different armies in different environments, with different objectives. After the Second World War, especially in the 1990s, a variety of development and humanitarian organizations, including the UN and NGOs, began to proliferate in conflict-ridden countries. This proliferation demanded appropriate coordination between the civilian and military stakeholders operating in the multidimensional environment.

By the 2000s, the concept Civil-Military Coordination (CIMIC) appeared in UN peace operations. According to the UN, "CIMIC refers to the coordination mechanisms and procedures used by civilian partners and the UN military within the UN System."[6] Thus CIMIC was integrated with missions and thereby the military from TCCs became involved in community assistance activities in a coordinated method. CIMIC has an important role to play in the coordination process at all levels: strategic, operational (country-level), and tactical (community-level). This demands CIMIC entities to associate the military component with the rest of the components in the UN system.[7] Thus, the CIMIC policy was developed by the UN in 2002, and its subsequent review in 2010.[8] This review clearly differentiated CIMIC in UN peace operations as "UN-CIMIC" and CIMIC in humanitarian assistance as "UN-CMCoord." In the context of a peace operation, "UN-CIMIC refers to the coordination mechanisms between the civilian partners and the UN military and UN-CMCoord refers to interaction or coordination for humanitarian purposes through the Office for the Coordination of Humanitarian Affairs (OCHA)."[9] In summary, OCHA remains responsible in organizing humanitarian partners for the coordinated delivery of humanitarian action. At the country-level, OCHA works in coordination with the UN Resident Coordinators/Humanitarian Coordinators on matters related to humanitarian assistance. Thus, in both UN-CIMIC and UN-CMCoord contexts, "CIMIC acts as facilitator, enabler and coordinator of human security type projects."[10]

The organizational culture of civil and military in UN peace operations are important as they operate in the same multidimensional environment. It is therefore critical on UN peacekeepers as well as the civilians to understand each other's organizational culture. Apart from the organizational culture, the national interpretation of Civil-Military Relations in TCCs matters in peacekeeping scenarios. For instance, Third World armies – in Asia and Africa – during the Cold War were often involved with military coups, countercoups, and internal instability. After the Cold War, military coups decreased, and Third World armies gradually deployed in peace operations. These Third World countries, under civilian governments, were developing democracy and state institutions. These armies utilized their experience of counter-insurgency operations and internal instability in UN peace operations context in the 1990s to help maintain peace and stability.

Sustainable peace is required as an end state for any successful peace operation. Michael W. Doyle and Nicholas Sambanis argued that "the deeper the hostility,

The Emergence of Modern Civil-Military Coordination   41

the more damaged local capacities, and the more international assistance are necessary to succeed in establishing a stable peace."[11] State-building is a crucial component for attaining sustainable peace. The UN recognized that "this phase needs to commence concurrently in UN peace operations in order to utilize the time and resources to bring the stakeholders into a coordinated programme for a long-lasting gain."[12] However, in the UN civilian operation in the Congo (ONUC: 1960–64), the mandate of technical assistance with state-building, was implemented through a "top-down" approach, directed by UN headquarters. Mandates for subsequent UN peace operations in the 1990s started to include aspects of social reconstruction to address state-building as involving a more "bottom-up" approach and partnership with host governments. This demanded greater coordination between the civilian and military stakeholders in UN peace operations. Therefore, the policy on CIMIC was developed in 2002, practiced for seven years, and then reviewed in 2010 in order to delineate a clear division of functions between the UN military component and other components in the field of development and humanitarian assistance for working with local populations.

The 2015 High-Level Independent Panel on Peace Operations (HIPPO) recommended "More people-centric UN peace operations" – for an essential shift with respect to peace operations.[13] Therefore, the HIPPO report stated that, "peace operations must pay focused attention to community-related activities, such as maintaining the closest possible interaction with the communities and supporting national initiatives regarding rural and local development."[14] In this regard, TCCs and civil affairs personnel often reach out to local populations in peace operations by CIMIC activities – facilitating a "bottom-up" approach to national-level state-building. However, according to Youssef Mahmoud, "these practices tended to take the form of ad hoc activities without enough strategic focus and such ad hoc community engagement activities also remain mission-centric."[15] These activities included any "local confidence building projects," including Quick Impact Projects. Therefore, a well-articulated strategy is essential to link community driven activities in UN peace operations with national/state level plans at the community/country level, and with Sustainable Development Goals (SDGs) 2030 at the strategic level.

The objective of this chapter is to trace the emergence of modern CIMIC in UN peace operations through examining the organizational culture of civilian and military entities, and the development of concepts, doctrine, and policy formulation for employing CIMIC. Therefore, the study of the concepts and policies of CIMIC will help develop a clear understanding of the application of CIMIC to assist with national-level state-building in UN peace operations.

Organizational culture of civilian and military entities

Historically the organizational culture of civilian and military entities operating together in the same conflict area varied. According to a study by the African Centre for the Constructive Resolution of Disputes (ACCORD), "In a multinational setting like UN peace operations, understanding an organization's cultural practices of civil

42 The Emergence of Modern Civil-Military Coordination

and military outfits remains a vital tool for effectively integrating within a working environment."[16] The organizational culture affects UN peace operations as soldiers from a variety of cultural backgrounds work together in the same area of operation. Joshua Goldstein opined that the military culture of different countries was not the same. He also argued that a "cultural problem for UN peacekeepers was that in coordinating with NGOs working in the same territory, there is a mismatch of cultural expectations."[17] It is therefore important for peacekeepers of a country to understand the cultural norms of peacekeepers from other nations. Additionally, they need to understand and adjust to the local culture in areas of operation.

In the military soldiers follow a chain of command to implement a decision. According to James V. Arbuckle, "It is commonly apprehended that the military is an authoritarian organization, that the authority of individual members is severely limited."[18] In UN peace operations scenario, the military operates within a limited authority with vast responsibilities. For instance, "Major-General Romeo Dallaire as a force commander faced severely limited authority with unlimited responsibilities in the UN Assistance Mission in Rwanda."[19] In contrast, the organizational culture of UN agencies and NGOs differ significantly from the military. There, according to the ACCORD, "coordination within an outfit is very common in nature and demands more decentralization to achieve a goal."[20] Ashraf Ghani and Clare Lockhart in their 2008 book, *Fixing Failed States: A Framework for Rebuilding a Fractured World* argued, "Often responsibilities and lines of authority of [NGOs] are unclear, which creates competing agendas and overly complex sets of relationships. These stakeholders affect the state's ability to set rules, access resources (information, knowledge, trade systems, credit, aid), and determine the way its citizens are perceived from abroad."[21] Simone Haysom also opined the same argument regarding the humanitarian community;

> The humanitarian community also needs to recognize and address its own deficiencies when it comes to adherence to humanitarian principles. Organizations have a poor track record in following existing guidelines, ... different mandates, philosophies and approaches, makes it very difficult to achieve a consensus view on the appropriate level and form of interaction with the military. The heterogeneous and loosely aligned nature of the humanitarian sector also makes it difficult for militaries to know how to interact, and whom to interact with.[22]

However, NGOs contribute greatly to humanitarian assistance to alleviate the suffering of populations in conflict-ridden countries and resist the involvement of military in humanitarian space. Military forces are, by comparison, often deployed on a short-term basis – Western military personnel for three to six to nine to twelve months, Asian and African military generally for one year. UN agencies (e.g., UN High Commission for Refugees deploys personnel for two years) and NGOs (generally deploy personnel for a minimum of one year) remain in the missions on a long-term basis.[23] Therefore, due to the varied tours of duty of both the military personnel and UN agencies/NGOs, need to understand each

The Emergence of Modern Civil-Military Coordination **43**

other's culture while working in the same location. Author's personal experience in UN peace operations supports such variations of tour of duty and it affected overall functioning of a mission.

Military and humanitarian organizations are not much aware of each other's responsibilities in a UN setting. Thus, "Organizational culture clashes occur when they do not know each other's duties and responsibilities."[24] Therefore, coordination becomes complicated in any UN peace operations.[25] Additionally, each of the components have their own mandate and policies, which may not have been articulated taking the organizational culture into consideration. Nevertheless, by "training together," all such organizations can be encouraged to work together more harmoniously.

The UN recognized in the 2000s that coordination is a shared responsibility facilitated by liaison and common training.[26] The Chief of the Civil Military Coordination section in UN Mission in Sudan (2009–10)[27] underwent a five day UN Civil-Military Coordination Course, run by the Office for the Coordination of Humanitarian Affairs (OCHA) in 2009 in Nairobi, Kenya.[28] There, all stakeholders from various peace operations organizations participated: military, police, UN agencies, civil affairs, and NGOs. The participants were not only together during training hours but were socializing after training hours as part of the programme. On the first two days of the training there were differences of opinion between the participants about the role of the military and of civilians in a peace operation, in the context of humanitarian domain, and most of the participants remained on their respective sides. From the third day onward, the mindset changed because they began to understand each other's jobs and responsibilities, and on the last day they developed a well-orchestrated plan to support a peace operation through consensus. Thus, training together remains the key to breaking the barrier of organizational culture. Specific training is also required for CIMIC personnel related to the contemporary operating environment, the several stakeholders with respect to their roles in the conflict, and how they interact with the military.[29] David Curran argued that

> through joint training between the military and the civilian organizations, [remained]… a key component to improving relations between military and humanitarian organizations. Referring to study of non-traditional techniques of training for military forces, the study recommended that the Canadian military receive training 'on dealing with other military and civilian field partners, so as to increase Canadian ability to play a role in enhancing unity of effort by all civilian-military components of a UN field operation.'[30]

Arguably, Troop Contributing Countries (TCCs) receive more training in this regard than other stakeholders, but all stakeholders need to train together and know each other to deliver their tasks effectively in a UN setting. For instance, several CIMIC training programmes were organized in Sudan (2009–10), where military observers, contingent members and staff officers attended. It is difficult to get personnel from UN agencies and NGOs to share training and experience

44 The Emergence of Modern Civil-Military Coordination

related to UN peacekeeping or CIMIC in a field mission. In a conflict-ridden area, it may not be practical to train personnel from NGOs, and, moreover, NGOs as a rule do not do mission-specific training. Instead, they hire qualified personnel for a specific field according to the requirement of service.[31] However, the Office for the Coordination of Humanitarian Affairs/Inter Agency Standing Committee needs to arrange training for NGOs including military personnel in UN peace operations. In absence of training, NGOs remain ignorant about the functioning of components of UN peace operations, thus organizational clashes will continue.

Apart from the organizational culture, the Civil-Military Relations situation in TCCs matters in peacekeeping scenarios. A congenial Civil-Military Relationship that develops in its own country first, and then in its military, and then upon deployment in a peacekeeping, can successfully apply the Civil-Military Relations doctrine in a UN setting. Any military with coup experience is likely to adopt a dictatorship role in peace operations. Any military with combat experience is likely to follow a robust approach in peacekeeping. A military with counter-insurgency experience is likely to adopt a different attitude while dealing with local populations. Soldiers who were rebels and were absorbed into the military through a reintegration programme will have a different culture. Therefore, it is important that regardless of background, the training of peacekeepers in the organizational culture of the stakeholders, including the recent history of the conflict area(s), remains a prerequisite before deployment in UN peace operations. The Civil-Military Relationship must also be built between UN military forces and civilian agencies.

The key UN agencies – UN Children's Fund, UN High Commission for Refugees, World Food Programme, UN Development Programme, and World Health Organization – contribute to the long-term construction of sustainable peace in conflict-ridden countries. According to Lorraine Elliott, "They have no official mandate of peacekeeping, but functionally and organizationally become involved in peace operations in the broader sense."[32] These agencies form the UN Country Team (UNCT) as development partners, or Humanitarian Country Team (HCT) as humanitarian partners, in any UN peace operation. In UN peace operations, the Humanitarian Country Team works in parallel while the UN peace operations are ongoing, and UN Country Team continues as a development partner after withdrawal of the peacekeeping components. In the UN Operation in the Congo (ONUC, 1960–64), these agencies took the lead to coordinate state-building tasks from the beginning of the peace operation. However, in most other operations, state-building is generally undertaken as a peacebuilding task only when the scale of conflict is reduced substantially.

The UN agencies have organizational differences with other peacekeeping components. This difference was especially evident among the personnel of different UN agencies in Sudan (2009–10).[33] The UN agencies were known as "Blue UN" for the colour of their emblem, while the peacekeeping component was known as "Black UN" for the colour of their emblem. Such differences exist in the mind and in the working environment also. UN agencies treat themselves as superior to the peacekeeping components, as "Blue UN" is permanent and usually based in a conflict zone before the "Black UN" armies. "Black UN" also departs before the "Blue UN" upon completion of mandated tasks. "Blue UN" usually undermines "Black UN" and does not feel comfortable with the presence of "Black UN."[34] Cedric De Coning noted the problems that arose within the context of an integrated mission, observing that

> Whilst the UN Integrated Mission has been accepted as the mission structure of choice at the highest levels within Member States, the UN secretariat and within UN agencies, these problems at country level still bedevils its acceptance at the operational level. The degree of resistance to, and frustration with the integrated mission model at the country-level is in-itself, causing dysfunction and have resulted in the implementation of the concept having unintended consequences.[35]

Moreover, "Blue UN" considers that only they promote and work to sustain peace and development in a conflict-ridden country. In contrast, "Black UN" considers that their presence plays a key role in managing the conflict, and "Blue UN" hardly plays any role in overall peace efforts.[36] Assessing this complex dynamic, Haysom observes that "Militaries will rarely have a purely humanitarian role, even in natural disaster response. Humanitarian organizations should accept this, and focus on … areas of common ground, such as the protection of civilians."[37]

The UN agencies also remain vulnerable to institutional competition as well as poor coordination among key organizations. Although the UN High Commission for Refugees, UN Children's Fund and the UN Development Programme are technically under the legal authority of the UN, each has its own governing body, funding and mandate.[38] Arguably, they remain jealous of their reputations and autonomy. In contrast, UN peace operations components work under a unified chain of command. Within the UN secretariat, peacekeeping missions are the responsibility of the Department of Peacekeeping Operations (renamed as the Department of Peace Operations from January 1, 2019); humanitarian affairs are the domain of the Office for the Coordination of Humanitarian Affairs and Inter Agency Standing Committee; and peacemaking and peacebuilding (including electoral assistance and outreach to NGOs and civil society) are the mandate of the Department of Political Affairs.[39]

An overview of policies and concepts of CIMIC

The CIMIC concept emerged from the UN peace operations in the 1990s as the result of cumulative experience rather than an organized approach – there was no policy or doctrine. For instance, with respect to the humanitarian assistance mission in Somalia, according to Cedric De Coning, "TCCs units' coordinated requests for security escorts for food convoys by the NGOs through formal coordination meetings. However, these coordination meetings were not uniform in nature and varied from outfit to outfit."[40]

46   The Emergence of Modern Civil-Military Coordination

In the 2000s, military concepts and capabilities for CIMIC grew, as military forces from different parts of the world began to participate frequently in peace operations. However, the North Atlantic Treaty Organization (NATO) also developed its own concept for civil-military cooperation in the 1990s and used it to replace UN forces in the Former Yugoslavia.[41] There are differences between the functioning of CIMIC in NATO versus UN peace operations. These differences are related to the organization and tasks of CIMIC in an operating environment. For instance, in NATO, military units have dedicated CIMIC elements and doctrine. Civil-military cooperation in the Canadian army refers to "a military function that supports the commander's mission by establishing and maintaining coordination and cooperation between the military force and civil actors in area of operations."[42] In contrast, in UN peace operations, most of the TCCs' units from Asia and Africa do not have a dedicated CIMIC element.

Modern CIMIC evolved out of a Cold War separation of military and civilian functions. Moreover, as more and more Third World armies became involved in UN operations, experiences in building state infrastructure became problematic. Many Third World armies came from recently war-torn states, or from one-party or dictatorial regimes. They could not be counted on to develop and manage state-building efforts as well as their security tasks. Therefore, the UN Office for the Coordination of Humanitarian Affairs facilitated the development of a series of humanitarian CIMIC policies and guidelines. These included guidelines on the Use of Military or Armed Escorts for Humanitarian Convoys, developed in 2000, and the 2004 Guidelines on the Use of Military and Civil Defence Assets to Support UN Humanitarian Activities in Complex Emergencies (revised in 2006).[43] These policies are mostly applicable for UN agencies and other humanitarian stakeholders. However, CIMIC personnel need to acquire knowledge of these policies and guidelines to better equipped in order to function effectively in humanitarian crises.[44]

During the 1990s and 2000s, various militaries were deployed in increased numbers in multidimensional environments along with other components, which resulted in frequent interaction in different fields of peace operations. Additionally, military resources were used in emergency humanitarian relief, and were becoming involved in reconstruction and rehabilitation projects.[45] Thus, the UN developed the first CIMIC policy in 2002 in order "to create scope for enhancing interaction between military elements, and humanitarian and development organizations and the local civilian populations."[46] The salient aspects of this policy are discussed later in this chapter. After 2002, several other policies related to humanitarian assistance developed as shown in table 2.1.

The 2008 Capstone Doctrine was based on recommendations of the 2002 Brahimi Panel Report and was formulated covering the principles and guidelines of UN peace operations.[47] The doctrine acknowledged that, the UN Country Team (UNCT) are responsible for long-term development as well as capacity-building efforts, and UN peace operations are neither designed nor equipped to engage in such efforts. However, UN peace operations have a choice to initiate or prepare the ground for longer-term institution and capacity-building efforts, due to the inability of other actors to take the lead.[48] The doctrine also stipulated that the

The Emergence of Modern Civil-Military Coordination   **47**

TABLE 2.1 Development of policies/guidelines related to CIMIC.

Year	Policies/Guidelines
2003	Use of Military and Civil Defence Assets (MCDA) Guidelines.
2005	United Nations Humanitarian Civil-Military Coordination Concept.
2005	Report of the Office of Internal Oversight Services on the review of military involvement in civil assistance in peacekeeping operations.
2006	Secretary General's Note of Guidance on Integrated Mission.
2007	Revised Oslo Guidelines.
2008	The United Nations Peacekeeping Operations Policy Directive on Civil Affairs.
2008	The UN Peacekeeping Operations Principles and Guidelines – the Capstone Doctrine.

Source: Developed by the author.

responsibility for the provision of humanitarian assistance rests primarily with the relevant UN agencies, and the NGOs. But various actors engaged in peace operations, including TCCs, became involved in humanitarian activities to support UN objectives. Such involvement of TCCs are based on a community assistance role as the military is deployed all over the area in a UN mission. Additionally, lack of capacity by humanitarian communities to render assistance in huge area of operations resulted in the involvement of the military in humanitarian assistance programme.

The concept of an integrated UN mission was introduced by the 2008 Capstone Doctrine.[49] An integrated mission is a strategic partnership between a multi-dimensional UN peace operation, the UN Country Team, and the Humanitarian Country Team. The introduction of a Resident Coordinator as head of the UN Country Team and the Humanitarian Coordinator as the head of the Humanitarian Country Team made coordination relatively convenient from the 2000s onward. Since then, the Deputy Special Representative to the Secretary General (DSRSG)/ Resident Coordinator (RC)/Humanitarian Coordinator (HC) remains responsible for the coordination of both humanitarian operations and development activities, and for maintaining links with governments, donors, humanitarian and development communities.[50] Therefore, coordination remains on track between the peacekeeping components, development partners, and humanitarian communities. The Chief of Civil-Military Coordination represents the military component of a UN peace operation featuring such coordination. The details of the coordination structure in UN peace operations are discussed at a later stage of the chapter.

The UN also introduced the "Policy Directive and Guidelines on Quick Impact Projects (QIPs)" in 2007 (reviewed in 2009). QIPs, small-scale projects within a budget of US\$ 25,000 (later increased to US\$ 50,000 in 2013) were designed to promote peace and development for local populations in a rapid, concrete manner.[51] The projects are also designed to promote the presence of the UN through peace dividends. The correct identification, effective planning and implementation of QIPs also assist in state-building affairs in order to contribute to

48 The Emergence of Modern Civil-Military Coordination

sustained peace and development. According to the 2008 Capstone Doctrine, "these QIPs were not a substitute for humanitarian and/or development assistance and may take a number of forms, including infrastructure assistance or short-term employment generation activities." QIPs also support the mission's objectives by building confidence in its mandate. Coordination and consultation with humanitarian communities in regard to the identification of QIPs is essential too, as the humanitarian communities may have concerns about the QIPs or CIMIC projects, or "local confidence building activities," or pacification projects that are of a humanitarian nature.[52] Ashraf Ghani and Clare Lockhart argued that "these projects were in poor quality, and caused frustration and resentment in Afghanistan."[53] There local people would rather take more time to undertake QIPs-related initiatives, for instance, to build reliable water, power, and sanitation services.[54] However, not all QIPs followed the same approach and some QIPs were designed and coordinated with the Afghan National Development Strategy. Additionally, at the tactical level, sometimes QIPs were only used to attain local military objectives.

The UN-CIMIC Policy was reviewed in 2010 due to some adjustments of other relevant UN policies and doctrine related to the Integrated Mission Planning Process (IMPP), Protection of Civilians (POC), Joint Mission Analysis Centres (JMAC), and Joint Operations Centres (JOC). Based on these policies, the 2010 Civil-Military Coordination in UN Integrated Peacekeeping Missions (UN-CIMIC) was developed.[55] The Chief of CIMIC in Sudan was involved in the review process of existing guidelines and incorporated comments based on his experience on the ground. The 2010 UN-CIMIC Policy covered the role and responsibilities of the UN-CIMIC function, which are discussed later in this chapter.

Along with the UN-CIMIC Policy, in 2010, there was a requirement to re-examine the gamut of peace operations to address the new challenges. In 2000 when the Report of the Panel on UN peace operations was prepared by Brahimi, the UN was dealing with 25,000 peacekeepers. Ten years, it was 120,000 peacekeepers. Therefore, "New Horizon" was launched with the goal of forging a greater consensus on the future direction of UN peacekeeping between three essential partners: the Security Council, the Troop and Police Contributing Countries (TCCs and PCCs), and the UN Secretariat.[56] The Under Secretary-General of the Department of Peacekeeping Operations advocated UN peacekeeping as a partnership.[57] "New Horizon" focused on "a shared vision on growing a partnership between the UN Security Council, TCCs/PCCs and the UN field mission into an effective action on the ground, and on developing a system together to support future peacekeeping."[58]

Development of the UN concept of CIMIC

There are three phases of tasks in UN peace operations: immediate, mid-term, and long-term according to a study by the US Institute of Peace in 2006.[59] Immediate tasks of peace operations relate to initial setting-up, disarming warring factions, and establishing security apparatuses. Mid-term tasks relate to assistance with state-building, and long-term tasks include efforts for national reconciliation, empowering civil

The Emergence of Modern Civil-Military Coordination   **49**

society, and other actions to sustain peace. These tasks and issues were deliberated in the 2000 Brahimi Report. Cedric De Coning discussed all these tasks in different phases of peace operations: stabilization phase, transition phase, and consolidation phase.[60] The stabilization phase encompasses immediate and mid-term tasks, the transition phase involves mid-term and long-term tasks, and the consolidation phase relates to long-term tasks. CIMIC tasks to assist in national-level state-building mostly fit into mid-term tasks, which may overlap with immediate and long-term tasks.

CIMIC tasks demand the national/local authorities to become owner of a project. Becoming owner of a project or "local ownership" is only possible when some form of government institution is established in the area of the UN peace operation. So, if CIMIC functions start earlier than the mid-term tasks. Then the mission component will have to manage the QIPs and CIMIC projects or "local confidence building activities" for the subsequent handover to the local authorities when the situation improves. However, as discussed in Chapter III, the UN civilian operations in the Congo (ONUC, 1960–64) started state-building activities simultaneously with the mandate of technical assistance from the beginning of the operation. Therefore, it is also possible to plan ahead, with involvement in some of the sectors related to government functioning or socio-economic development areas. CIMIC projects result in assisting state-building endeavours. Therefore, such projects need to integrate with the national plans of the host government, the UN humanitarian action plan, UN Development Assistance Framework (UNDAF),[61] and the Sustainable Development Goals (SDGs 2030)[62] of the UN.

The Establishment of UN Peace Operation CIMIC (UN-CIMIC) and UN Humanitarian CIMIC (UN-CMCoord)

Civil-Military Coordination is used by different organizations and countries to suit their requirements. For instance, in NATO, the European Union (EU), and countries in Europe and Canada, it is known as "Civil-Military Cooperation."[63] In the United States (US), "the terms 'Civil Affairs' and 'Civil Military Operations (CMO)' address civil-military cooperation indirectly or implicitly."[64] In UN peace operations, it is known as "UN-Civil-Military Coordination (UN-CIMIC)[65]" and for the humanitarian community, it's termed "Humanitarian Civil-Military Coordination (CMCoord)." CIMIC in the UN context follows a different approach from NATO, the EU, the US, and Canada. According to Cedric De Coning, "NATO operations are coalition type operations and deployed in a more contested environment as peace enforcement operations."[66] In contrast, a UN peace operation is a consent-based operation, based on the core principle of consent of the parties and operations are under civilian led activities. Therefore, the application of CIMIC varies between NATO operations and UN peace operations.

UN-CIMIC refers to the coordination mechanisms and procedures used by civilian partners and the UN military within the UN System.[67] Whilst UN-CIMIC refers to a military staff function to support UN Mission objectives, UN Humanitarian CIMIC (UN-CMCoord) refers more to a "dialogue" and interaction for humanitarian purposes.[68] The humanitarian CIMIC provides an interface between humanitarian and military actors to protect and promote humanitarian principles and achieve humanitarian objectives in complex emergencies and natural disaster situations. UN-CMCoord and UN-CIMIC functions thus complement each other on the ground, as illustrated in Figure 2.1.[69]

Figure 2.1 shows the relationship between the UN-CIMIC and UN-CMCoord, where the UN-CIMIC provides "the interface between political and security objectives on the one hand, and humanitarian, development and peacebuilding objectives on the other. UN-CIMIC focuses on the preservation of appropriate relations with the civilian and humanitarian aspects."[70] As a whole, UN-CIMIC entities involve coordination between the military component of the peacekeeping mission and a wide range of civilian actors.

The advent of complex emergency guidelines introduced UN-CMCoord in the 1990s during the proliferation of humanitarian organizations in conflict-ridden areas.[71] From a humanitarian perspective, complex emergency guidelines refer the UN-CMCoord to promote civil-military coordination in humanitarian operations within the purview of humanitarian principles. The complex emergency guidelines also stress that coordination remains a shared responsibility facilitated by liaison and joint training. As a whole, the UN guidelines for humanitarian-military coordination (UN-CMCoord) is summarized in the following six operating principles:

1. Decision to accept military assets must be made by humanitarian organizations.
2. Military assets should be requested only where there is no comparable civilian alternative and only the use of military assets can meet a critical humanitarian need and its use should be as a last resort.
3. A humanitarian operation using military assets must remain under the overall authority and control of the humanitarian organization responsible for that operation.
4. Countries providing military personnel to support humanitarian operations should ensure that they respect the humanitarian principles.

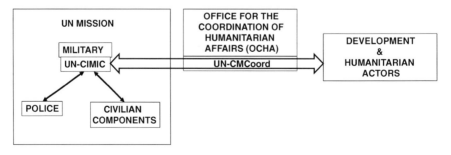

FIGURE 2.1 Relationship between UN Mission and Development, Humanitarian Actors through UN-CIMIC and UN-CMCoord.
UN Department of Peacekeeping Operations and Department of Field Support, 'Policy: Civil-Military Coordination in UN Integrated Peacekeeping Missions (UN-CIMIC)', 16. (Developed by the author)

5. The large-scale involvement of military personnel in the direct delivery of humanitarian assistance should be avoided.
6. Any use of military assets should ensure that the humanitarian operation retains its international and multilateral character.[72]

The 2002 UN-CIMIC policy (reviewed in 2010) stated the basic principles and core tasks for UN-CIMIC.[73] According to the basic principles, it is important for effective CIMIC to have a solid understanding of the civilian effort, as well as the ways in which the military can make a constructive contribution. On the other hand, "the civilian components need to similarly understand the role of the military and how UN-CIMIC serves as a mission coordination tool to leverage the capabilities of the military component in support of the overall mission effort."[74] Therefore, planning and implementation of UN-CIMIC activities addresses the comparative strengths of military, police and civilian contributors in order to minimize the duplication of efforts and enable the effective use of resources.

Core tasks of UN-CIMIC thus include "liaison and information-sharing/ management, and civil assistance."[75] Liaison and information-sharing are the main tasks to provide support in the management of CIMIC. Civil assistance is "a support function that includes two types of related activities undertaken by the military component of a UN integrated mission: mission support and community support."[76] Mission support refers to the support provided by the UN mission to requests for assistance from humanitarian and development organizations. When mission support operations are undertaken, UN-CIMIC remains responsible for planning, coordinating, and facilitating the actions of the military units responsible for executing the task. Community support facilitates the interaction between the mission and host government as well as local populations. Community support projects are related to different activities/projects such as water supply and training on livelihood related activities that could be requested by any of the mission components, or the host government or local populations. Through the community support activities, UN-CIMIC can reach out to local populations and thus contribute to national-level state-building.

In the context of UN-CIMIC, it is important to study the principles, concepts and functions of UN-CMCoord. Most of the local humanitarian actors engaged in humanitarian work are present in conflict-ridden areas long before the arrival of UN peacekeepers and will continue their functions after their departure. Therefore, UN-CIMIC personnel need to understand the network of humanitarian assistance, which includes all national and international organizations.[77] Similarly, for UN-CMCoord, it is important to be aware of why UN military forces may undertake actions that can trespass into humanitarian space. Thus, the functions of UN-CMCoord include liaison and information-sharing as well.

Necessity of CIMIC in UN Peace Operations

Three central qualities of CIMIC have been stipulated by the UN Department of Peacekeeping Operations: interdependence, duplication, and leverage.[78] The

52 The Emergence of Modern Civil-Military Coordination

various components of a peace operation are interdependent. However, a combined and sustained effort is significant for a successful peace operation. In this context, coordination is the process that ensures that the entities work together within the entire gamut of a peace operation. In the absence of meaningful coordination, overlap, duplication and above all an uneconomic or inefficient application of resources will be the result. In the context of assisting in national-level state-building, a better coordination with different pillars: mission components, host government, and local populations will result in an efficient outcome of an activity or project. Effective coordination also helps to allocate of funds appropriately to any Quick Impact Project (QIP).

Leverage is also achieved through the exchange of information, joint planning, mutual support, coordination, and feedback. For instance, by coordination of the various components, a QIP can be materialized in an education sector. Here, for example, to construct or renovate a school, UNICEF can provide reading and writing materials, the mission can provide funds for furniture as a QIP, the host government can provide teachers with salary, and the private sector can support the construction or renovation of the school. This project can be coordinated by the UN-CIMIC, where the UN military may also render assistance by providing its assets and manpower during the construction phase. One of the local NGOs may also become an implementing partner of the project.

The recommendation of the 2015 High-level Panel on Peace Operations – "More people-centric UN peace operations" – demand CIMIC activities as well as QIPs "should maintain the closest possible interaction with the communities and support national initiatives regarding rural and local development."[79] Cedric De Coning argues that, "at the strategic level, CIMIC is used to suggest a multidimensional, whole-of-government approach."[80] Therefore, CIMIC activities should be a part of national strategy connecting to UN's global efforts of Sustainable Development Goals (SDGs) 2030.

UN-CIMIC in certain state-building functions

Since the end of the Cold War state-building activities are usually directly or indirectly part and parcel of the mandate of UN peace operations. Peacebuilding activities take place in peace operations at any stage to assist in state-building. Both the military and civilian partners are engaged in activities related to assisting in state-building, to achieve a specific outcome towards sustained peace and development. Thus, a close cooperation between military and civilian partners in peacebuilding activities would assist appropriate CIMIC activities in benefiting local populations.

One of the major recommendations of the 2000 Report of the Brahimi Panel on UN Peace Operations was to introduce a more integrated approach to multi-dimensional peace operations. Another recommendation was to link the different dimensions of peacekeeping/peacebuilding components (political, development, humanitarian, human rights, rule of law, social and security) into a coherent support strategy. These components play a significant role in assisting in state-building activities

The Emergence of Modern Civil-Military Coordination 53

and as such, in order to coordinate amongst the components, UN-CIMIC's role is crucial for certain state-building functions such as project management and conflict management.[81] These functions greatly contribute to assisting national-level state-building efforts.

Project management is an important area where UN-CIMIC can be effective. QIPs were not unique to peace operations and were first introduced by the UN High Commission for Refugees in 1991 in Nicaragua to undertake small-scale low-cost projects for the refugees and returnees.[82] QIPs may take a number of forms in different sectors such as education, health, agriculture, or overall economic livelihood, and may include infrastructure assistance or short-term employment-generating activities. QIPs establish and build confidence in the mission, its mandate, and the peace process.[83] They are not a substitute for humanitarian/ development assistance but do assist with national-level state-building endeavours. QIPs need to be coordinated by UN-CIMIC with the humanitarian stakeholders in order to avoid concerns of stepping into humanitarian space.

Military contingents from a given Troop Contributing Country (TCC) may identify potential projects in their areas of operation, in close consultation with beneficiaries, community leaders and Civil Affairs/Humanitarian Affairs counterparts. Any other mission components may identify and propose QIPs. UN-CIMIC personnel may coordinate such efforts and thus be involved in project management activities – identification, monitoring and evaluation of the project.

UN-CIMIC may also address gender sensitive issues of the project through employing a gender mainstreaming approach.[84] This gender mainstreaming would integrate female peacekeepers as and when necessary, considering the sensitivity of any CIMIC activities or QIPs. Gender mainstreaming in CIMIC can be achieved by gender training for CIMIC personnel, inclusion of female(s) in CIMIC entities, and articulating clear guidelines on gender sensitive issues. For instance, female staff members can contribute significantly to deal with women-related issues within a community.

UN-CIMIC personnel irrespective of gender may be involved in negotiation and mediation to assist in conflict management. CIMIC personnel may manage conflict through communication and negotiation related to the identification, prevention, and resolution of conflicts.[85] For negotiations as well as mediation, UN-CIMIC personnel may also become the focal point for communication with local populations, host government representatives, and other appropriate stakeholders.

Coordination structure in UN peace operations

In the 2000s, the UN had begun to develop a complex system integrating a CIMIC component into peace missions. Thus, it is pertinent to study a typical coordination structure of a UN system before discussing activities of UN-CIMIC in UN peace operations. The coordination structure is shown in Figure 2.2.[86]

54 The Emergence of Modern Civil-Military Coordination

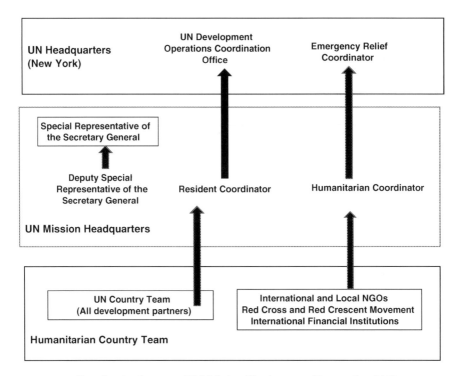

FIGURE 2.2 Coordination between UN Mission Headquarters (Deputy Special Representative of the Secretary General/Resident Coordinator/Humanitarian Coordinator), UN Country Team, and Humanitarian Country Team with entities at the UN Headquarters.

Department of Peacekeeping Operations & Department of Field Support, *United Nations Civil-Military Coordination (UN-CIMIC) Specialized Training Materials*, 69. (Developed by the author)

In the UN system coordination structure, a senior UN official who is the Resident Coordinator (RC), usually the UNDP Resident Representative connects all development partners. This RC can be designated through the UN Development Operations Coordination Office (DOCO) based in New York.[87] The RC's office or RC's Support Office (RCSO) serves as the secretariat in the UN RC system. The RC also serves as the Humanitarian Coordinator (HC) in the absence of a UN Mission. The Deputy Special Representative of the Secretary-General (DSRSG) acts as both RC and HC when the UN field mission or peace operation is in place in any country. Thus, the DSRSG usually wears three hats to promote synergy between a UN peace operation's component and its development partners (UN Country Team-UNCT) and any humanitarian stakeholders (Humanitarian Country Team-HCT).

As per the definition by the Office for the Coordination of Humanitarian Affairs (OCHA), the Humanitarian Country Team (HCT) is comprised of the heads of UN humanitarian agencies, international humanitarian organizations, international NGOs, donor representatives, and other related stakeholders.[88] That means that the HCT is the UNCT plus international and local NGOs, the Red Cross/Red Crescent Movement and international financial institutions. The HCT is the coordinating body to deal with humanitarian issues. The triple hatted DSRSG has different reporting lines depending on the function. The DSRSG reports directly to the SRSG on matters related to a UN peace operation; as the RC he/she reports directly to the UN Development Operations Coordination Office; and as the HC, he/she reports directly to the Emergency Relief Coordinator. However, these reporting channels only take care of issues at the headquarters level of the three bodies, and so it remains a challenge to bring synergy at the mission and local level. Therefore, coordination becomes a key consideration at the different tiers of the mission. Thus, the role of CIMIC becomes more crucial for coordination between the UN military and other stakeholders involved.

In an integrated UN peace operation, UN-CIMIC serves as a link between UNCT or HCT through UN-CMCoord, who is based in Office for the Coordination of Humanitarian Affairs.[89] Such an integrated structure of UN peace operation is shown in the Figure 2.3.[90]

UN-CIMIC works in the chain of command of the UN military force commander. It has coordination links with the CIMIC officers in the peace operation's components – sectors and other concerned components. However, UN-CIMIC maintains the coordination link with the UNCT and HCT through UN-CMCoord as discussed earlier.

In an integrated mission, the Special Representative of the Secretary-General (SRSG), is normally supported by customized components to facilitate integration between the mission's components: Joint Operations Centre (JOC) to coordinate

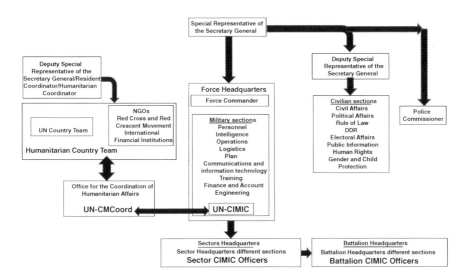

FIGURE 2.3 Coordination structure in an integrated UN peace operation.
Department of Peacekeeping Operations & Department of Field Support, *United Nations Civil-Military Coordination (UN-CIMIC) Specialized Training Materials*, 71. (Developed by the author)

56 The Emergence of Modern Civil-Military Coordination

daily mission activities of all components; Joint Mission Analysis Cell (JMAC) for the management and analysis of information and reports of the mission's civil and military information in support of the decision-making process; Joint Logistics Operations Centre (JLOC) to coordinate the logistical support; and Director Mission Support (DMS), which includes civilian and military logisticians.[91] Under these joint arrangements, UN-CIMIC may also be represented in the JOC to facilitate better coordination with different entities.[92]

Conclusions

The basic principles and core tasks of UN-CIMIC are related to promoting better understanding of the civilian effort and an appropriate contribution by the military to assist in national-level state-building. The planning and implementation of UN-CIMIC activities, therefore, demands utilization of the comparative strengths of military, police and civilian stakeholders. This, in turn, facilitates minimizing any duplication of efforts and ensures an effective use of resources.

Through the core tasks of UN-CIMIC – liaison and information sharing, and civil assistance – coordination is undertaken to support the management of civil-military interaction and to achieve the UN objectives. The establishment of liaison arrangements requires clear lines of communication between the military forces and the humanitarian communities, and a regular exchange of information. Information-sharing between humanitarian and military actors is also required for undertaking both the humanitarian as well as military operations in UN peace operations.

Civil assistance – mission support and community support – remains one of the important tools for the UN-CIMIC to assist in national-level state-building. Community support projects – fostering a people-centric approach – are undertaken through QIPs and CIMIC projects or "local confidence building projects." Through these projects UN peace missions assist in country- and community-level state-building. The military remains responsible to help secure the environment on the ground and at the same time through CIMIC assists in country- and community-level state-building. The UN military has the capacity and capability to implement a project within the shortest possible timeframe.

CIMIC related tasks in UN peace operations can assist in reaching out to local populations through different activities and projects, and thus assist in national-level state-building. However, what sounds good in theory, is often more challenging in practice. Thus, how these CIMIC activities and projects were in practice will be discussed in the following chapter as case studies.

Notes

1 UN Peacekeeping Best Practices Unit, "Handbook on United Nations Multidimensional Peacekeeping Operations", 37.
2 Cedric De Coning, "Civil-Military Coordination Practices and Approaches Within United Nations Peace Operations", *Journal of Military and Strategic Studies* 10, no. 1 (1 September 2007): 1–2, https://jmss.org/article/view/57636.

The Emergence of Modern Civil-Military Coordination 57

3 Gerard Lucius and Sebastiaan Rietjens, *Effective Civil-Military Interaction in Peace Operations: Theory and Practice* (Springer, 2016), 64.

4 Department of Peacekeeping Operations and Department of Field Support, *United Nations Peacekeeping Operations: Principles and Guidelines*, 21–22.

5 Christopher Ankersen, *Civil-Military Cooperation in Post-Conflict Operations: Emerging Theory and Practice* (Routledge, 2007), 22.

6 UN Department of Peacekeeping Operations and Department of Field Support, "Policy: Civil-Military Coordination in UN Integrated Peacekeeping Missions (UN-CIMIC)", 2.

7 Ankersen, *Civil-Military Cooperation in Post-Conflict Operations*, 70.

8 Department of Peacekeeping Operations and Department of Field Support, "Policy: Civil-Military Coordination in UN Integrated Peacekeeping Missions (UN-CIMIC)", 1.

9 "OCHA was established in 1991 to coordinate humanitarian activities.", "Humanitarian Civil-Military Coordination: Publications | OCHA", accessed 15 February 2018, https://www.unocha.org/legacy/what-we-do/coordination-tools/UN-CMCoord/publications; Office for the Coordination of Humanitarian Affairs (OCHA), *Civil-Military Coordination Handbook* (Geneva: OCHA, 2003); Department of Peacekeeping Operations and Department of Field Support, "Policy: Civil-Military Coordination in UN Integrated Peacekeeping Missions (UN-CIMIC)"; UN Department of Peacekeeping Operations & Department of Field Support, *United Nations Civil-Military Coordination (UN-CIMIC) Specialized Training Materials.*

10 Ankersen, *Civil-Military Cooperation in Post-Conflict Operations*, 26.

11 Michael W. Doyle and Nicholas Sambanis, "Peacekeeping Operations", in *The Oxford Handbook on The United Nations*, First (New York: Oxford University Press, 2007), 324.

12 UN Department of Public Information, "United Nations Peace Operations 2009: Year in the Review", January 2010, 42.

13 United Nations, "Report of the High-Level Independent Panel on Peace Operations", Review on Peace Operations (New York, 16 June 2015), 14, https://peaceoperations review.org/wp-content/uploads/2015/08/HIPPO_Report_1_June_2015.pdf. The HIPPO held its Regional Consultation for Asia Pacific in Bangladesh in January 2015. The author was the Director Overseas Operations at the Army Headquarters. He took personal initiative to organize the forum and presented a keynote paper, "Challenges and Way Ahead for UN peace operations: Experience of Bangladesh." A few issues were addressed in the final report of the HIPPO from the paper.

14 United Nations, 39.

15 Youssef Mahmoud, "People-Centric Approaches to Peace: At Cross Roads Between Geopolitics, Norms, & Practices", in *United Nations Peace Operations in a Changing Global World* (Springer, 2018), 94–95.

16 African Centre for the Constructive Resolution of Disputes (ACCORD), "The African Civil-Military Coordination Programme 2006", 2006, 250–51.

17 Joshua S. Goldstein, *Winning the War on War: The Decline of Armed Conflict Worldwide* (New York: Plume, 2012), 104.

18 James V. Arbuckle, *Military Forces in 21st Century Peace Operations: No Job for a Soldier?* (Routledge, 2006), 44.

19 Arbuckle, 44.

20 African Centre for the Constructive Resolution of Disputes (ACCORD), "The African Civil-Military Coordination Programme 2006", 251–55.

21 Ashraf Ghani and Clare. Lockhart, *Fixing Failed States: A Framework for Rebuilding a Fractured World* (Oxford; Oxford University Press, 2008), 176, http://public.eblib.com/choice/publicfullrecord.aspx?p=415309.

22 Simone Haysom, "Civil-Military Coordination: The State of the Debate", ODI HPN, 1 January 2013, https://odihpn.org/magazine/civil%c2%96military-coordination-the-sta te-of-the-debate/. Simon Haysom is a Research Officer in the Humanitarian Policy Group.

23 Rietjens, *Civil-Military Cooperation in Response to a Complex Emergency: Just Another Drill?* (BRILL, 2008), 22.

24 African Centre for the Constructive Resolution of Disputes (ACCORD), "The African Civil-Military Coordination Programme 2006", 254.

25 African Centre for the Constructive Resolution of Disputes (ACCORD), 254.

26 Lucius and Rietjens, *Effective Civil-Military Interaction in Peace Operations*, 64.

27 "The Chief of CIMIC section in UNMIS (2009–10) was the author".

28 OCHA, "Agenda for the 95th UN-CMCoord Course, Nairobi, Kenya, November 8–13, 2009", 28 October 2009.

29 Lucius and Rietjens, *Effective Civil-Military Interaction in Peace Operations*, 65–66.

30 David Curran, *More than Fighting for Peace?: Conflict Resolution, UN Peacekeeping, and the Role of Training Military Personnel* (Springer, 2016), 95.

31 Michelle Berg is an independent consultant from Canada expressed her views during an interview on NGOs: The way it functions and requirement of training, Washington DC, 3 April 2019.

32 Lorraine Elliott, "The United Nations and Social Reconstruction in Disrupted States", in *From Civil Strife to Civil Society: Civil and Military Responsibilities in Disrupted States* (New York: United Nations University Press, 2003), 262.

33 "The Chief of CIMIC in UN Mission in Sudan (UNMIS) was the author (2009–10)". He experienced the organizational culture related to "Blue UN" and "Black UN."

34 Michelle Berg, "UN Mandate to Protect-Meaning and Mission Considerations Regarding Civilian Population, UN Agencies, and Affected Personnel" (Lecture, Inter American Defense College, Washington DC, USA, 3 April 2019). She also expressed the same opinion on "Blue UN" and "Black UN."

35 Coning, "Civil-Military Coordination Practices and Approaches Within United Nations Peace Operations", 28; Victoria Metcalfe, Simone Haysom, and Stuart Gordon, "Trends and Challenges in Humanitarian Civil–Military Coordination: A Review of the Literature", *Humanitarian Policy Group and Overseas Development Institute*, 1 May 2012, 8–9.

36 "The Chief of CIMIC in UNMIS was the author (2009–10)."

37 Haysom, "Civil-Military Coordination",14.

38 "UN Funds, Programmes, Specialized Agencies and Others", 18 November 2014, http://www.un.org/en/sections/about-un/funds-programmes-specialized-agencies-and-others/index.html.

39 Elliott, "The United Nations and Social Reconstruction in Disrupted States", 268.

40 Cedric De Coning, "Civil-Military Coordination in United Nations and African Peace Operations", *The African Centre for the Constructive Resolution of Disputes (ACCORD)*, UN Complex Peace Operations, n.d., 50.

41 African Centre for the Constructive Resolution of Disputes (ACCORD), "The African Civil-Military Coordination Programme 2006".

42 National Defence Government of Canada, "Civilian-Military Cooperation| Influence Activities | 5th Canadian Division | Canadian Army", 25 February 2013, http://www.army-armee.forces.gc.ca/en/5-cdn-div-ia/cimic.page.

43 "Guidelines on the Use of Military and Civil Defence Assets to Support United Nations Humanitarian Activities in Complex Emergencies", OCHA, 22 May 2017, https://www.unocha.org/publication/guidelines-use-military-and-civil-defence-assets-support-united-nations-humanitarian.

44 Cedric De Coning, "Civil-Military Relations and U.N. Peacekeeping Operations", *World Politics Review*, 19 May 2010, 8. Coning explained "Humanitarian space is about protecting humanitarian action from political influence and interference. Humanitarian space protects the right of the victims to receive humanitarian assistance by protecting the right of humanitarian actors to have free access to the beneficiaries. If one does not emphasize and clarify this distinction, then it becomes impossible to accurately delineate the role that UN peacekeeping operations can play in support of humanitarian action."

45 Department of Peacekeeping Operations, "The United Nations Civil-Military Coordination Policy 2002" (United Nations, 9 September 2002), 1.

46 Department of Peacekeeping Operations, "The United Nations Civil-Military Coordination Policy 2002".

47 Department of Peacekeeping Operations and Department of Field Support, *United Nations Peacekeeping Operations: Principles and Guidelines*.

The Emergence of Modern Civil-Military Coordination 59

48 Department of Peacekeeping Operations and Department of Field Support, 28–29.
49 Department of Peacekeeping Operations and Department of Field Support, 53.
50 UN Department of Peacekeeping Operations and Department of Field Support, 69. "Reform of UN in 2019 kept the same provision in UN peace operations", Economic and Social Council General Assembly, "Repositioning the United Nations Development System to Deliver on the 2030 Agenda: Our Promise for Dignity, Prosperity and Peace on a Healthy Planet" (New York: United Nations, 21 December 2017), 19, https://digitallibrary.un.org/record/1473546?ln=en.
51 United Nations, "United Nations Department of Peacekeeping Operations/ Department of Field Support Policy on Quick Impact Projects" (United Nations, 21 January 2013), 5.
52 Department of Peacekeeping Operations and Department of Field Support, *United Nations Peacekeeping Operations: Principles and Guidelines*, 30.
53 Ashraf Ghani and Clare. Lockhart, *Fixing Failed States: A Framework for Rebuilding a Fractured World* (Oxford; Oxford University Press, 2008), 5, http://public.eblib.com/choice/publicfullrecord.aspx?p=415309.
54 Ashraf Ghani and Clare. Lockhart, *Fixing Failed States: A Framework for Rebuilding a Fractured World* (Oxford; Oxford University Press, 2008), 178, http://public.eblib.com/choice/publicfullrecord.aspx?p=415309.
55 UN Department of Peacekeeping Operations and Department of Field Support, "Policy: Civil-Military Coordination in UN Integrated Peacekeeping Missions (UN-CIMIC)".
56 UN Department of Public Information, "United Nations Peace Operations 2009: Year in the Review", 6.
57 Under Secretary-General Department of Peacekeeping Operation Jean-Pierre Lacroix, CIMIC in State-Building, Oral, Dhaka, 25 May 2018.
58 Department of Public Information, "United Nations Peace Operations 2009: Year in the Review", 12.
59 William J. Durch and Tobias C. Berkman, "Restoring and Maintaining Peace: What We Know So Far", in *Twenty-First-Century Peace Operations*, First (Washington, D.C.: US Institute of Peace, 2006), 21.
60 Cedric De Coning, "Civil-Military Coordination and UN Peacebuilding Operations", *The Yearbook of International Peace Operations*, International Peacekeeping, 11 (2007): 4.
61 UN Sustainable Development Group, "UN Development Assistance Framework Guidance", 2017, https://undg.org/document/2017-undaf-guidance/.
62 United Nations, "SDGs: Sustainable Development Knowledge Platform".
63 Coning, "Civil-Military Coordination and UN Peacebuilding Operations", 97–98.
64 Stijn van Weezel, "CIMIC Concepts & Capabilities: Research into the CIMIC Operationalization of Nations", *Civil-Military Co-Operation Centre of Excellence, The Hague, The Netherlands*, no. August, 2011 (2011): 14.
65 Coning, "Civil-Military Coordination Practices and Approaches Within United Nations Peace Operations", 12.
66 Coning, "Civil-Military Coordination and UN Peacebuilding Operations", 99; Coning, "Civil-Military Coordination Practices and Approaches Within United Nations Peace Operations", 5.
67 Department of Peacekeeping Operations and Department of Field Support, "Policy: Civil-Military Coordination in UN Integrated Peacekeeping Missions (UN-CIMIC)".
68 Department of Peacekeeping Operations and Department of Field Support.
69 UN Department of Peacekeeping Operations & Department of Field Support, *United Nations Civil-Military Coordination (UN-CIMIC) Specialized Training Materials*, 16.
70 Victoria Metcalfe, Simone Haysom, and Stuart Gordon, "Trends and Challenges in Humanitarian Civil–Military Coordination: A Review of the Literature", *Humanitarian Policy Group and Overseas Development Institute*, 1 May 2012, 2.
71 Coning, "Civil-Military Relations and U.N. Peacekeeping Operations", 7.
72 Office for the Coordination of Humanitarian Affairs (OCHA), *Civil-Military Coordination Handbook*.

73 UN Department of Peacekeeping Operations and Department of Field Support, "Policy: Civil-Military Coordination in UN Integrated Peacekeeping Missions (UN-CIMIC)".

74 UN Department of Peacekeeping Operations and Department of Field Support.

75 Coning, "Civil-Military Coordination and UN Peacebuilding Operations", 109.

76 Cedric De Coning and Stephen E. Henthorne, "Civil-Military Coordination (CIMIC)", ed. Harvey J. Langholtz (Peace Operations Training Institute, VA, USA, 2008), 13.

77 Office for the Coordination of Humanitarian Affairs (OCHA), *Civil-Military Coordination Handbook*.

78 UN Department of Peacekeeping Operations and Department of Field Support, *United Nations Peacekeeping Operations: Principles and Guidelines*.

79 Mahmoud, "People-Centric Approaches to Peace: At Cross Roads Between Geopolitics, Norms, & Practices", 98.

80 Coning, "Civil-Military Coordination Practices and Approaches Within United Nations Peace Operations", 1.

81 African Centre for the Constructive Resolution of Disputes (ACCORD), "The African Civil-Military Coordination Programme 2006".

82 Brent C Bankus, "Military-Enabled Quick Impact Projects Improve Quality of Life of Local Populations", n.d., 26.

83 United Nations, "United Nations Department of Peacekeeping Operations/ Department of Field Support Policy on Quick Impact Projects", 4.

84 UN Women, "How We Work: UN System Coordination: Gender Mainstreaming", UN Women, accessed 28 January 2019, http://www.unwomen.org/en/how-we-work/un-system-coordination/gender-mainstreaming. Gender mainstreaming is defined as "The process of assessing the implications for women and men of any planned action, including legislation, policies or programmes, in all areas and at all levels. It is a strategy for making women's as well as men's concerns and experiences an integral dimension of the design, implementation, monitoring and evaluation of policies and programmes in all political, economic and societal spheres so that women and men benefit equally, and inequality is not perpetrated. The ultimate goal is to achieve gender equality."

85 African Centre for the Constructive Resolution of Disputes (ACCORD), "CIMIC and Peacebuilding Operations", *African Journal of Conflict Resolution* 5, no. 2 (2005): 89.

86 Department of Peacekeeping Operations & Department of Field Support, *United Nations Civil-Military Coordination (UN-CIMIC) Specialized Training Materials*, 69.

87 UN Department of Peacekeeping Operations & Department of Field Support, *United Nations Civil-Military Coordination (UN-CIMIC) Specialized Training Materials*.

88 Office for the Coordination of Humanitarian Affairs (OCHA), *Civil-Military Coordination Handbook*.

89 Department of Peacekeeping Operations & Department of Field Support, *United Nations Civil-Military Coordination (UN-CIMIC) Specialized Training Materials*.

90 Department of Peacekeeping Operations & Department of Field Support, 71.

91 UN Department of Peacekeeping Operations & Department of Field Support, 71–75.

92 UN Department of Peacekeeping Operations & Department of Field Support, 71–75.

3

UNITED NATIONS PEACE OPERATIONS IN THE DEMOCRATIC REPUBLIC OF CONGO

State-Building vis-à-vis Civil-Military Coordination

Introduction

Maintaining international peace and security was the first purpose listed in the first chapter of the United Nations (UN) Charter. Through the Charter, the primary and the most difficult responsibility assigned to the UN was keeping the peace. Peacekeeping, in a broader sense, "refers to the various means that the UN employs on the spot to prevent disputes from arising, or to stabilize the situation where trouble has arisen."[1] As early as 1945, Chapter VI and VII of the UN Charter articulated the measures for the settlement of disputes as well as actions related to threats to international peace and security. These prescribed military interventions have become identified as the UN's primary peacekeeping or peace making role. Article 55 of Chapter IX, however, related to "International Economic and Social Cooperation," which entailed assistance in state-building affairs, required for sustained peace and development, a requisite for a successful UN peace operation.

Historian Evan Luard identified the initial period of UN history 1945–1955 as "the years of Western domination of the UN, and the emergence of the Cold War."[2] This political reality dominated and shaped the UN and brought peacekeeping into operation. During the early postwar era the UN also had to deal with conflicts in Africa resulting from the process of decolonization and the Cold War. From 1956–64 the UN experienced two different dimensions of peacekeeping, in Suez in 1956 through the UN Emergency Force (UNEF)[3] and in the Congo from 1960–1964 through the UN Operations in the Congo (Opération des Nations Unies au Congo, or ONUC). As the proverb states, "no two crises are the same," thus the experience of UNEF was not straightforwardly applicable to ONUC. Moreover, the peacekeeping operation in the Congo was initiated by the UN Security Council, whereas the Suez intervention was initiated by the General Assembly.[4]

DOI: 10.4324/9781003275404-4

62 United Nations peace operations in the Democratic Republic of Congo

Both peace operations occurred in a context of Cold War tensions due to ideological differences between the West and the Soviet Union. UNEF's involvement resulted from the disruption of a vital trade route, the Suez Canal. ONUC was the outcome of economic interest as well as failure to develop state-building during the long colonial era. Where UNEF dealt with the Israeli and Egyptian state military forces, ONUC dealt with a "toxic brew of great-power rivalry, local tribal conflicts, and the fresh trauma of seventy years of colonialism."[5]

Historian Christopher D O'Sullivan observes that "postcolonial Africa desperately needed investment, development assistance, relief from poverty and famine, educational reform, health care, and support for emerging institutions of self-government. The outside world was more interested in geopolitical gains and securing and extracting Africa's resources."[6] The Congo was the first case of such ventures for geopolitical gains and as well as pursuit of economic interest by the world powers in post-colonial Africa. ONUC was also the first operation where UN had to use force to fulfill its mandated tasks. In the Congo, apart from maintaining peace and security, the UN undertook massive state-building activities through its civilian operations involving a very considerable body of experts from the UN and its specialized agencies to help build a stable society. The UN's 1960–64 intervention in the Congo became a major test of "first generation" peacekeeping.[7] ONUC's civilian operation adopted a "top-down" approach to state-building efforts that were drawn from concepts of the UN Relief and Rehabilitation Administration (UNRRA), discussed in Chapter I. The civilian operations became an integral aspect of an integrated approach to maintaining security and assisting with state-building – a new dimension of the peacekeeping mission.

The United Nations (UN) withdrew from the Congo in 1964 and new UN peace operations did not occur in Africa until the end of Cold War in 1989. Perhaps this long pause was because of the UN's experience in the Congo including the controversy surrounding the death of the Prime Minister Patrice Lumumba, the loss of the UN Secretary-General Dag Hammarskjold, and the costs associated with operations.[8] The civilian operation in the Congo was discontinued in 1967 due to the unwillingness of member states to continue funding the operation as well as lack of support from the Congolese government. From 1965 to 1989, the Cold War rivalry was at its peak. The United States (US) intervention in Vietnam (1965–73), the Arab-Israel War (1967 and 1973), the Soviets' invasion of Afghanistan (1979–89), and the Iran-Iraq War (1980–88) kept the focus of the international community away from Africa. In his 2012 book, *Winning the War on War: The Decline of Armed Conflict Worldwide*, Joshua S. Goldstein argued that the "Security Council had long been immobilized by the Cold War standoff, since each superpower had a veto."[9] Although Africa experienced widespread internal conflicts, the international community largely stayed away.

Civil wars and internal unrest plagued Africa during the 1970s-1980s: Somalia, Chad, Sudan, Ethiopia, Eritrea, Uganda, Guinea Bissau, Southern Rhodesia, and the Democratic Republic of the Congo (DRC).[10] Namibia, Mozambique, and Angola all fought wars of independence, followed by subsequent civil wars in

Mozambique and Angola. These issues affected international peace and security. The superpowers supported a proxy civil war involving Angola. This is clear through an examination of the UN Security Council Resolution proceedings in the 1970s and 1980s. From 1970–86, twelve resolutions were tabled at the UN Security Council concerning situations in Southern Rhodesia, Namibia, and Angola. These were vetoed mostly by the United States (US) and the United Kingdom (UK).[11] In his 2014 book, *United Nations Peacekeeping in Africa Since 1960*, Norrie Macqueen argued that the "discussions took place in the Security Council concerning destructive conflicts within independent Africa in the 1960s and 1970s."[12] Nor did these discussions bring any peacekeeping intervention by the UN. In June 1975, the US, the UK, and France vetoed a Security Council Resolution declaring South Africa's presence in Namibia a threat to international peace and security under the terms of Charter VII of the UN Charter.[13] Consequently, no new peacekeeping was undertaken in select African conflicts until the involvement of the UN in the independence process in Namibia and the Cuban military withdrawal from Angola in 1989.

The end of the Cold War changed international relations and opened avenues for the UN to take the lead in resolving long-standing conflicts in nations that had largely been the victims of the superpowers' influence. The UN's agenda for peace and security rapidly expanded with the end of the Cold War. Goldstein argued that "the UN Security Council suddenly got a fresh wind, started to operate as intended, and a rapid expansion of peacekeeping followed."[14] The UN also established a separate entity, the Department of Peacekeeping Operations, in 1992, in order to manage new peacekeeping scenarios.[15] The dynamics of peacekeeping varied during the Cold War, whereas after the Cold War, peacebuilding or stabilization operations became part and parcel of peacekeeping. After the Cold War, the UN entered a new era of comprehensive peace and stability building in Africa marked by more participation from non-western countries.

During the 1990s and 2000s, Africa experienced thirteen major armed conflicts – the highest total for any region of the world.[16] The UN then engaged in Angola, Namibia, Western Sahara, Mozambique, Somalia, Rwanda, Liberia, Sierra Leone, Ethiopia, Eritrea, the Central African Republic, the DRC, Burundi, Ivory Coast (Côte d' Ivoire), Sudan, and Chad. In his 2016 book, *War & Conflict in Africa*, Paul D. Williams argued that "Of the UN peace operations deployed since 1989, almost ninety percent were sent to trouble areas with at least some, if not primary, internal conflict components."[17] Therefore, UN engagements also involved managing internal conflicts. The UN had a variety of mandates in these countries, ranging from the verification of ceasefires to the protection of civilians, and to assistance in state-building, including peace enforcement. The UN faced some of its toughest challenges and also suffered several failures while operating in African countries still struggling with the harsh realities of colonial era under development and exploitation while attempting state-building endeavours.[18] However, state-building efforts turned to partnership with host governments in these missions as a contrast to "top-down" approach of the UN civilian operation in the Congo.

64 United Nations peace operations in the Democratic Republic of Congo

In trying to meet many of the peacekeeping challenges in the mid-1990s, the UN experienced some dramatic failures. Somalia and Rwanda represent a turning point in the history of the UN and international community's involvement in Africa. The killing of twenty-three Pakistani and eighteen US peacekeepers in Somalia, arguably, discouraged further troops commitments by countries. The outcome was also noticed while managing the UN mission in Rwanda, where 800,000 Tutsis (and moderate Hutus) were massacred.[19] The genocide resulted in two million Rwandans, mostly Hutus, becoming refugees in neighbouring countries, mostly in the DRC. Amy Sayward argued "the Rwandan genocide caused shock waves that forced the international community to review its ability to intervene."[20] After the experiences of Rwanda (also Srebrenica[21]), the first mission to be equipped with an explicit protection of civilians-mandate was the UN Mission in Sierra Leone in 1999.[22] Therefore, the approach of peacekeeping operations gradually changed from traditional peacekeeping to protection-related responsibilities.

The UN reviewed its role in peacekeeping by evaluating its successes (for instance, in Namibia and Mozambique) versus its failures (Angola in 1991 and 1997, Somalia in 1993, Rwanda in 1994, and Bosnia in 1995),[23] the nature of the conflicts, and the lessons of the peace operations of the 1990s. The UN Secretary-General Kofi Annan asked a high-level group of experts to assess the UN system's shortcomings, so as not to repeat that experience, as demand for peace operations surged again at the end of the decade.[24] The 2000 Report of the Panel (known as the "Brahimi Report" after the Panel chair, UN Under Secretary-General Lakhdar Brahimi) offered an in-depth critique of the conduct of UN operations and made specific recommendations for change.

The Brahimi report recommended the integration of all entities in the UN system,[25] and a major paradigm shift from "traditional peacekeeping" to "multi-dimensional peacekeeping" covering "robust doctrines," "realistic mandates" and rapid deployment.[26] The UN later developed the "Capstone doctrine"[27] and therefore, a coherence was established between the UN Country Team (development partners), the Humanitarian Country Team (humanitarian stakeholders) and the UN peace operation (responsible for peace and security) in an integrated mission.[28]

Paul Williams argued that "the UN used Africa to professionalize peace operations."[29] In fact, by trying out different approaches to peacekeeping in multi-dimensional scenarios, the approach of the UN to peacekeeping grew in capability via lessons learned. In the 1990s, the mindset of peacekeepers was oriented towards "traditional peacekeeping." But the review of peacekeeping through the 2000 Brahimi Panel changed the approach of multidimensional and integrated peacekeeping. Thus, the UN achieved greater success in its missions in the 2000s. Additionally, the UN's ability and capacity, including logistics arrangement from the UN headquarters, developed in the 2000s. The establishment of a separate department (Department of Field Support) at the UN headquarters in 2007 began a new chapter to support UN peace operations in an integrated fashion.[30] The capacity of the Troop Contributing Countries was also enhanced at the same time.

The UN developed knowledge and expertise in African state-building by its peace operations in the 2000s. As far as assistance in state-building endeavours is concerned, the UN did its part through its involvement by conducting elections in Sierra Leone, Liberia, Ivory Coast, Namibia, and Mozambique. Disarmament, Demobilization and Reintegration (DDR) and Security Sector Reform (SSR) are two important state-building tasks where military involvement was useful. The success of DDRs in Namibia, Mozambique, Sierra Leone, Liberia, and Ivory Coast demonstrates their capacity for state-building. The civil-military coordination related tasks in Sierra Leone, Liberia, and Ivory Coast assisted the missions in reaching out to populations through community development projects, thus contributed to national-level state-building. Goldstein observes that "economic development and peacekeeping need better integration".[31]

The involvement of the UN in Africa in the 1990s and 2000s seems to have resulted in the reduction in the upward trend of conflict in the region. The UN contributed to peacebuilding as well as state-building endeavours through an integrated approach in several African countries. In his 2004 book, *The UN's Role in Nation-Building: From the Congo to Iraq*, James Dobbins argued that, "During the 1990s, deaths from armed conflict were averaging over 200,000 per year."[32] Lakhdar Brahimi pointed out that, "Over the last decade [1990s], the United Nations has repeatedly failed to meet the challenge, and it can do no better today."[33] However, by 2006, more than half of the conflicts in Africa came to an end, and deaths from armed conflicts there substantially decreased, though according to the UN High Commissioner for Refugees, "The refugee crisis in great lakes region of Africa is without precedent in history of UNHCR in 1997."[34] Despite the downward trend in African armed conflict as well as refugee issues, the challenge of maintaining peace and stability nonetheless continued in countries like the Democratic Republic of Congo (DRC) and Sudan. The mandate of both these UN missions was related to peace enforcements under Chapter VII of the UN Charter.

The DRC has undergone an unsettled and violent history both during the colonial era and after independence in 1960. The Belgians and the Congolese did not focus on developing a robust state. The UN Operation in the Congo (Opération des Nations Unies au Congo, ONUC) from 1960–64 focused on state-building through its civilian operations. At the end of ONUC's mandate, the UN military withdrew from the Congo with some measurable accomplishment. However, the dictatorship of military leader Joseph Mobutu followed, and so too did by the systematic failure of state-building and major post-independence conflicts. By the late 1990s civil war had claimed the lives of some three million Congolese.[35] Thereafter, the second round of UN involvement took place in the DRC, beginning in 1999 with the UN Organization Mission (Mission de l'Organisation de Nations Unies en République Démocratique du Congo, MONUC). MONUC was a result of the 1999 Lusaka Peace Agreement, established to combat ethnic rebel groups in the northeastern region, to support the central government and prevent Congolese turmoil from endangering regional stability.[36] In 2004, through UN Security Council Resolution 1565/2004, the mission was mandated to assist in state-building endeavours

66 United Nations peace operations in the Democratic Republic of Congo

through the provision of support for the adoption of legislation, the electoral process, and security sector reform. However, unlike the civilian operation component of ONUC, MONUC did not have a dedicated component for state-building.

During an eleven-year period (1999–2010) in the DRC, fifty-six UN Security Council resolutions were adopted to maintain the security and stability of the vast country, in addition to other associated mandated tasks.[37] The mission endeavoured to address the roots of the conflict related to the economic exploitation of natural resources and the involvement of neighbouring countries in the affairs of the DRC and assist with development for state-building. Due to the comparatively improved security situation, the mission turned to stabilization operations in mid-2010.

This chapter analyzes the UN peace operations – with the mandates of peace enforcements as well as assistance with state-building – in the Congo during the 1960s and 2000s. While doing so it introduces peacekeeping through the UN Charter on peace and security as well as economic development aspects related to assisting in state-building. The chapter makes a bridge between the UN mission in the Congo (1960–64) and the launching of the second mission in 1999. While analyzing ONUC (the Congo), the study focuses on both the military as well as civilian operations. Thereafter, the efforts of the UN are discussed, covering its role to improve security situations and to assist with state-building. Therefore, the study of the UN peace operations in the Congo will help develop understanding of how the UN sought to bring peace and stability as well as address state-building during this period.

The objective of this chapter is also to discuss Civil-Military Coordination (CIMIC) practices in the DRC to comprehend their contribution to national-level state-building efforts and how CIMIC efforts offered a "bottom-up" approach to delivering state-building programmes. It considers CIMIC activities with the UN mission in the DRC from 2005–10. The section on UN-CIMIC activities in the DRC is brief due to the limited availability of declassified sources material. The author endeavoured to obtain data from the UN Archives in New York in July–August 2018, but sources were only accessible before 1998 as a policy of the archives. Additionally, the UN headquarters and mission headquarters were contacted in 2018 and 2019 to obtain primary sources, but these were also unavailable. Nevertheless, a brief comparison of CIMIC activities in the DRC helps to illuminate the great difference in policy and practice between the DRC and Sudan. Perhaps the most important observation from this practical CIMIC examination in both peace operations in Africa is that UN security building and CIMIC worked best when delivered side by side in order to effectively rebuild viable and stable post-conflict states. This study will provide an understanding of the origin of the complex peace enforcement operations and concurrent assistance with state-building and civil-military coordination of the UN.

UN Charter on peace and security, and economic development related to state-building

The UN Charter addressed matters related to the promotion and maintenance of global peace and security.[38] The concept of maintaining international peace and security was institutionalized in Chapter VI and VII of the UN Charter, which articulated measures for the settlement of disputes as well as actions related to threats to international peace and security. Chapter VI dealt with "Pacific Settlement of Disputes." In particular, Chapter VI's Articles 33 to 38 indicated peaceful means of settlement such as "…negotiation, enquiry, mediation, conciliation, arbitration, judicial settlement, resort to regional agencies or arrangements, or other peaceful means of own choice."[39] Chapter VII was – and remains – more robust. It covered "action with respect to threats to the peace, breaches of the peace, and acts of aggression," with Articles 39 to 51 examining actions such as "… any measure to maintain or restore international peace and security, [including] economic [development], [and] use of force allowing the inherent right of individual or collective self-defen[c]e, if an armed attack occurs against a Member of the [UN]."[40] Norrie Macqueen observes that "Article 39 of Chapter VII …made the Security Council responsible for deciding when a situation required collective security action and what form that action should take."[41] Thus, Chapter VI action is the traditional "Blue helmet" peacekeeping: intervention between warring parties who are looking for a way to stop. Chapter VII empowers the UN to take all necessary means to establish peace.

Significant attention was also devoted to economic and social cooperation while articulating the UN Charter. Thus, a UN Economic and Social Council (ECOSOC) was created as a principal organ in 1945.[42] While Chapters VI and VII are related to maintenance of peace and security, Chapter IX Article 55 relates to "International Economic and Social Cooperation," setting out the following objectives:

> With a view to the creation of conditions of stability and well-being which are necessary for peaceful and friendly relations among nations based on respect for the principle of equal rights and self-determination of peoples, the [UN] shall promote: [(1)] higher standard of living, full employment, and conditions of economic and social progress and development; [(2)] solutions of international economic, social, health, and related problems; and international cultural and educational cooperation.[43]

Thus, by means of inclusion of these provisions of Chapter IX opened the way for the UN to become a future pillar of global economic governance.[44] In other words, it lets the UN assist in state-building affairs, which is required for sustained peace and development.

Peacekeeping, in a broader sense, refers to the various means to stabilize the situation in trouble prone areas.[45] In Africa, the UN stepped into its first peace operation during the Suez crisis in 1956. The UNEF was designed as a response to a specific situation and placed military forces between regular national armed forces, whose governments had agreed to a ceasefire. The mandate was clear and there was no involvement in internal conflicts or politics of parties. The main party, Egypt, cooperated with the UN and did not interfere with the deployment

68   United Nations peace operations in the Democratic Republic of Congo

of UNEF. The Suez Crisis was one of the high scale international conflicts which tested the capability of the UN to contain such confrontations. It was also the first test case for deploying UN troops under Chapter VI in Africa to defuse tension and stabilize a war zone. While the operation of UNEF was ongoing, the world's attention turned towards the Congo as it was securing independence in June 1960.

UN Operation in the Congo, ONUC (1960–64): the political and security dynamics

The Congo plunged into violent conflict upon its independence, and its new government soon called for UN assistance. According to Norrie Macqueen, "The Congo crisis was in many ways a model subject for UN peacekeeping in the early 1960s."[46] The UN Operation in the Congo (Operation des Nations Unies au Congo, or ONUC) from July 1960 until June 1964, marked a milestone in the history of UN peacekeeping in terms of the responsibilities it had to assume, the size of its area of operation and the manpower involved. In addition to a peace-keeping force which comprised nearly 20,000 personnel, it included a civilian operation component.[47] In ONUC, Peter argued that, "peacekeepers became caught up in an armed conflict between two groups of warring factions supported by the USSR and the US."[48]

The Congo, a former Belgian colony, became independent on June 30, 1960. In the late 1950s, Congolese began to demand independence led by Patrice Lumumba and Joseph Kasavubu. Lumumba, a vibrant advocate of decolonization, attended the All-Africa People's Conference in December 1958, where he met leaders like Nkrumah and authors like Frantz Fanon amongst other figures. He was inspired by these leaders and dreamt for unity to defeat colonialism. Upon return to the Congo Lumumba and Kasavubu separately declared independence and sent a copy of their Declaration to the Soviet Union, including a request for military aid. This move surprised the Belgians.

In the meantime, due to internal conflict within the Force Publique, the para-military colonial police force (later renamed as Congolese National Army, ANC), Congolese soldiers mutinied, with unrest rapidly spreading to garrisons across the country. The anarchy and chaos continued for months, prompting the Belgians to respond on January 13, 1959 by promising independence. Later riots erupted in October-December 1959 in Kasai, Stanleyville, and Leopoldville involving black and white civilians. This rioting led to political crisis in Belgium and a consequent compromise with the Congolese. Thus, a round table conference in early 1960 was called by the Belgian government to discuss the road to independence. During the conference a treaty of friendship was signed between the two countries, indicating a conference to settle economic issues in April 1960 and the holding of national elections that May 1960, with the date of independence set for June 30.[49]

The period after independence was marked by more violence and serious Cold War rivalry, which led to a very high-profile involvement by the international community. The ideological differences between the Soviets and the US became a

United Nations peace operations in the Democratic Republic of Congo **69**

bone of contention, however, both the superpowers opted for the deployment of UN forces to maintain stability of the Congo.[50] On July 4, just a few days after independence, General Emile Janssens, a Belgian, reminded the Congolese soldiers of their subordinate position by writing on a blackboard for all of the officers and soldiers to read, "After Independence = Before Independence."[51] This further angered the Congolese soldiers, who were receiving extremely low pay, and on July 5, Congolese soldiers mutinied and drove out their Belgian officers.[52] The mutiny spread all over the country, including the police; Belgian officers were overwhelmed by soldiers in different areas, and tens of thousands of Europeans were held by the mutineers. Later the mutineers were joined by workers, who began to strike. On July 9, Belgium sent reinforcements comprising 10,000 para-troopers to maintain security, as well as to protect its citizens there, without the consent of the Congolese government.[53] President Kasavubu and Prime Minister Lumumba demanded the withdrawal of Belgian forces and consequently asked for UN assistance on July 10. Meanwhile, on July 11, provincial leader Moise Tshombe declared the independence of Katanga from the Congo and requested Belgium to continue its technical, financial, and military support. This resulted in a pull back of Belgian forces from all over the Congo to Katanga. Katanga was of vital economic importance to the new state as its exports constituted about eighty percent of the Congo's trade revenues.[54] It was also the key focus of foreign investors and mineral companies.

The Belgian decision to support the secession of mineral-rich Katanga complicated US long-term policy. It was clear that "Belgium backed the de facto independence of Katanga to protect its substantial investments there, especially the mining giant of Brussels, Union Minière du Haut Katanga (UMHK)."[55] These unilateral actions by the Belgians brought the international community into crisis. Both the US and USSR believed that an internationalization of the crisis would work in their favour and thus agreed to the deployment of a UN peacekeeping force in 1960 to stabilize the situation.[56] The US wanted to prevent the Soviet Union from directly inter-vening in the Congo and show the world that the Cold War would not spread to Africa. The Soviet Union's goal was to expand its influence in the Congo. For their part, the Congolese requested UN intervention to prevent Katanga's secession, as the principal resources of the Congo were in Katanga and thus the vast country would require the resources of Katanga for its development. Finding the UN uncoopera-tive, Lumumba sought Soviet assistance to end Katanga's secession. Arguably, Lumumba's decision to seek such assistance escalated Cold War rivalry.

Upon request for UN assistance, the UN Security Council decided to launch peace operations. The UN Secretary-General Dag Hammarskjold invoked Article 99 of the UN Charter to convene the Security Council,[57] and within forty-eight hours, contingents from different countries including Asian and African States began to arrive in the Congo by US and Soviet planes. The Belgians commenced withdrawal on July 16, 1960 but subsequently delayed it. At the same time, UN civilian experts started arriving in the Congo to provide technical assistance, according to the mandate of the Security Council.

70 United Nations peace operations in the Democratic Republic of Congo

ONUC was established by Security Council resolution 143/1960 of July 14, 1960, which empowered "the Secretary-General to take the necessary steps, in consultation with the Government of the Republic of the Congo, to provide the Government with such military assistance as might be necessary until, through that Government's efforts with [UN] technical assistance, the national security forces might be able, in the opinion of the Government, to meet fully their tasks."[58] Later, according to the UN Security Council Resolution 8/5002 dated November 24, 1961, the mandate was reviewed:

> To maintain the territorial integrity and political independence of the Congo, to assist the central government in the restoration and maintenance of law and order, to prevent the occurrence of civil war in the Congo, to secure the immediate withdrawal and evacuation from the Congo of all foreign military, para-military and advisory personnel not under the [UN] command, and all mercenaries; and to render technical assistance.[59]

To fulfill the obligations of the mandate, UN contingents entered the Congo to prevent total collapse and to keep out the power blocs. Meanwhile, the Belgians were giving Tshombe advice and financial support for Katanga's secession. Therefore, the UN's efforts to achieve its mandated task of retaining unification of the Congo became challenging and difficult.

It was evident that in order to unify the Congo, the UN would have to use force to subdue Katanga.[60] Thus, in February 1961, the UN force was given unprecedented latitude to use force if necessary to prevent civil war in the Congo, as well as to retain its territorial integrity, and so a new resolution was passed with the Belgians' immediate withdrawal from Katanga and entry of the UN force. Within two weeks, most of the Belgian troops left Katanga. However, Tshombe formed gendarmerie forces with remaining Belgian officers and consolidated his position, while the UN did nothing to resist him.[61] Due to the delay by the UN, Lumumba planned to bring an end to Katangan independence with the assistance of the Soviet Union.

Lumumba's planning was based on assistance from the Soviet Union, which provided about one-hundred trucks and eleven transport planes in late July 1960.[62] The US Central Intelligence Agency (CIA) was then given permission to assassinate Lumumba, who was labeled a Soviet pawn.[63] Soviet planes flew the Congolese army to first stage of operations in South Kasai, resulting in outbreak of tribal war. The Secretary- General then authorized ONUC to use force, if necessary, to halt the Congolese army. Lumumba's invitation to the Soviet Union to deploy troops to South Kasai, led the Congolese President Kasavubu to dismiss him on September 3, 1960 and broadcast that Joseph Ileo was the new prime minister. Lumumba, in turn, dismissed President Kasavubu, which led to a constitutional crisis. Later both were reinstated by the parliament and the senate. The UN then closed all airports and radio station by order of the Special Representative to the Secretary-General of ONUC, Andrew Cordier (successor of Ralph J. Bunche), who did not consult the Secretary-General. This UN action led Guinea and Ghana

United Nations peace operations in the Democratic Republic of Congo **71**

to threaten to pull out their forces from the Congo, and the impartiality of UN became a question.[64]

Under pressure, mainly from the Soviets and Afro-Asian countries, the UN Secretary-General replaced Cordier with an Indian UN official Rageshwar Dayal, who met with the president and prime minister and assured them of the neutrality of UN. By this stage, the crisis was spiralling out of control. On September 14, 1960, Colonel Mobutu, the Chief of Staff of the Congolese army, seized power and announced the expulsion of all communist forces from the Congo. Consequently, a new UN Security Council resolution was adopted which barred the member states from providing military assistance to the Congo without UN approval.[65] Such moves by the Security Council changed the dynamics of international politics as well as the security situation in the Congo.

The new Security Council resolution, the subsequent killing of Lumumba, fighting between the Congolese army and UN forces as well as the death of the Secretary-General radically changed the situation in the Congo. On November 27, 1960, Lumumba left his residence, abandoning UN protection, and was arrested by the Congolese army after three days in Kasai province. Thereafter, Indonesia, Ceylon, Morocco, Guinea, United Arab Republic and Yugoslavia, all decided to withdraw their forces after the UN failed to protect Lumumba. According to Kevin Spooner, "ONUC assisted Mobutu in finding Lumumba and tacitly assisted in his arrest."[66]

Lumumba was later transferred to Katanga by Mobutu on order from Kasavubu, who received instructions from the Harold d' Aspremont Lynden, the Belgian minister of African affairs.[67] It is certain that, in addition to the CIA, the elimination of Lumumba was also being planned by the Belgian secret service. UN leaders also persisted with their project to eliminate Lumumba politically. According to a telegram of August 26 from the US permanent mission to the UN, Hammarskjold was convinced that "Lumumba must be broken."[68] Lumumba was killed by a group of Belgian and Congolese soldiers on January 17, 1961 upon orders from Captain Julien Gat, a Belgian officer – later an investigation by the Belgian parliament suggested that Brussels was directly implicated in the affair[69] – and the announcement was made public by radio after three weeks on February 13, 1961.[70] This led the UN to adopt a strong resolution covering the withdrawal of all Belgians, including those in administration, reconvening of the parliament, reorganization of the Congolese army, prevention of foreign interference, and a UN decision to resolve the situation by the use of force as a last resort, if necessary.[71] President Lumumba was a victim of Cold War rivalry and his assassination later resulted in the establishment of US influence in the Congo. Lumumba was a clear victim of both nineteenth century-style imperialism and the realities of the post-1945 Cold War.[72]

The strong UN resolution adopted in the wake of Lumumba's death was not accepted by Kasavubu and thus fighting broke out between the Congolese army and UN forces. Katanga authorities also boycotted all UN personnel, viewing the UN as but one faction in a civil war. ONUC forces then took over radio stations, Ministry of Interior and post offices to expel the Belgians by force from Katanga and succeeded. Tshombe then escaped and moved to the Rhodesian border.

72 United Nations peace operations in the Democratic Republic of Congo

Meanwhile, UN Secretary-General Dag Hammarskjold lost his life on September 17, 1961 in the plane crash on the way to Rhodesia where talks were to be held for the cessation of hostilities.[73]

Hammarskjold will be remembered for his leadership as well as steering the UN in the Congo during the Cold War rivalry. His role took the UN to a new height and changed the dimension of the peacekeeping. He was criticized for not consulting with Lumumba from time to time as he did with President Nasser in 1956 during the operation of UNEF. He dealt directly with Tshombe about the withdrawal of Belgian forces without consulting the central government. The Soviets accused him of being a tool of US, France and Belgium when he ordered UN forces to close down the central radio station and the national airport.[74] A few countries decided to withdraw their forces from the Congo due to alleged UN failure, too. U Thant became the new Secretary-General and ONUC continued its efforts to unify the Congo.

ONUC undertook the most important mandated tasks of retaining territorial integrity of the Congo by resorting to military action and asserting its control in Katanga. On December 20, 1961, the UN apparently sought military solution through use of air and military power. A general ceasefire was declared on December 21, 1961 when Tshombe signed the eight-point Declaration. However, hostilities continued and by January 1963, UN established full control over Katanga and Tshombe announced his readiness to end the secession. In the meantime, in August 1962, the UN proposed a plan of National Reconciliation covering a united Congo under a federal constitution.[75]

The National Reconciliation Plan, also known as the "U Thant Plan," was proposed by the Secretary-General to settle the differences between the Central Government and Katanga. This was accepted by both parties. The plan proposed the adoption of a constitution for a federal system of government; the division of revenues and foreign exchange earnings; the unification of the currency; the integration and unification of all military, paramilitary, and gendarmerie units into a national army.[76] With the implementation the National Reconciliation Plan, the military phase of ONUC operations drew to a close.

ONUC withdrew from Katanga in mid-1963, and UN forces were completely withdrawn from the Congo by June 30, 1964, yet instability continued. Although the military phase of the ONUC had ended, the civilian operation, which started almost simultaneously with military operations, for undertaking national-level state-building continued. This state-building phase was the largest single programme of assistance undertaken until that time by the UN and its agencies in 1964 and beyond.

UN civilian operations in the Congo 1960–64: An approach to state-building

The UN Civilian Operation in the Congo, a component of ONUC, focused on state-building, which was the first of its kind undertaken by the UN. The civilian operation preserved the economy of the Congo and its administrative structure.[77] King Gordon in his 1962 book *UN in the Congo: A quest for peace* argued, "In one area the UN was already playing a positive role. Its civilian operations had prevented a general breakdown of the economy and public services and, in spite of enormous difficulties, were mapping out a long-range [programme] of training and assistance."[78] The civilian operation was initiated through the specific mandate of the UN Security Council, "to render technical assistance," as requested by the Congolese government. Thus, the UN involved all its machineries to make the operation successful and through its resolution emphasized and added "specialized agencies to render assistance to the UN as requested."[79] The civilian operation employed an integrated approach to maintaining security alongside state-building programmes – a new dimension in UN peace operations. However, these efforts resulted in "top-down" strategies which bore similarities to foreign imposed colonial methods of state-building.[80]

The civilian operations were conducted by groups from the UN's specialized agencies as well as technicians and experts from different countries. These groups advised Congolese officials and trained Congolese personnel. Starting from the government machineries at the different tiers, financial institutions, and socio-economic development, the civilian operations attempted classic state-building endeavours. Hammarskjold once said that, "while the military operations were in the Congo pending reorganization of the Congolese security capacity, the Civilian operations were to make the essential and long-term contribution of the UN to the Congo."[81] The long-term contribution needed the financial capacity of the UN and as such until the end of 1963 the civilian operations were financed entirely by the Congo Fund, supported by voluntary contributions, established by the General Assembly in 1960. A vast range of operations were undertaken from the directive of the UN headquarters, focusing on a long-term plan of state-building.

At the UN headquarters, the civilian operations were the responsibility of the Secretary-General and no part of the civilian operations had executive authority on behalf of the Congolese government. In his 1978 book *The U.N. in the Congo: The Political and Civilian Efforts,* Arthur House argued that "The executive capacity for civilian operations under the Secretary-General had no legal status for its organization, staffing, operating procedure, or establishment of priorities."[82] The scope and purpose of civilian operations were:

(1) to provide the country with expert assistance in the interim period between independence and the complete Africanization of the administration and economy, (2) to assist the Congolese authorities to adapt the economic and administrative institutions to the needs of an independent nation, (3) to enable the Congolese to acquire the necessary professional skills within the shortest possible time.[83]

The civilian operations were thus structured for both establishing and strengthening the real independence of the Congo. To undertake these tasks, the operation focused on two approaches. First, the prevention of large-scale disasters such as famine, epidemics, tribal warfare, and refugee dislocation, and second, a long-term approach of preserving the structure of services for the social well-being of the people.[84] In order to fulfill these tasks, operations were structured keeping both the civilian and military stature as equal, with each commanded by an official of equivalent rank while incorporating other experts. The organization chart of the civilian operation within the framework of ONUC is shown in Figure 3.1.[85]

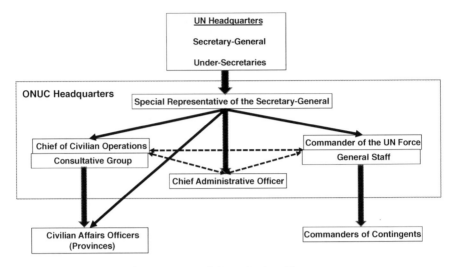

FIGURE 3.1 ONUC Civilian Operations' Organization Chart
J. King. Gordon, The United Nations in the Congo; A Quest for Peace. ([Place of publication not identified]: Carnegie Endowment for International Peace, 1962), 62. (Modified by the author)

In the ONUC organization, high level experts were appointed as "consultants," who were in charge of each functional group. These consultants were attached to the Chief of the Civilian Operations and together formed the Consultative Group.[86] Advisers from the UN specialist agencies were integrated with the Consultative Group and were responsible to advise the corresponding Congolese ministries. The specialist agencies' representatives reported to the Secretary-General resulting in a unique coordination through one chain of command.

The coordination of the civil organization needed the military for security, while the military often needed the civilian staff for provision of basic services. Thus, the civilian and military staffs were in close contact with each other, demonstrating a beginning of civil-military coordination in a UN peace operation. Every category of civilian operations had to coordinate with military for their security. Similarly, certain military affairs, which necessitated political considerations, were also coordinated with the civilian leadership. For instance, when thirteen Italian airmen were killed in Kindu in November, 1961, the military requested bombing operations, which were denied upon request from ONUC civilian leadership.[87] Apart from civil-military coordination, the functioning of civil affairs at the provincial level was placed under the Under Secretary-General in charge of the Civilian Affairs at ONUC Civilian Operations Headquarters and the Officer in charge of the province used to be known as Civilian Affairs Officer. Later, upon the withdrawal of the military this officer was called the "Administrative Officer."[88]

Civil-military coordination was a necessity in ONUC, but (arguably), the UN military forces, who were drawn mostly from the developing countries, were not much accustomed to such coordination mechanisms. Arguably, the UN was not also ready to initiate the civil-military coordination due to volatile security situation in the Congo, the dynamics of Cold War and, therefore, ran the two pillars "military" and "civilian" in parallel with limited coordination and did not involve military units to assist in the state-building affairs.

The UN delivered programs for the Congolese to run their country by involving them in different fields of state-building. From the beginning of the civilian operations, the UN got involved in different state-building fields – security, public administration, finance, economics, foreign trade, justice, natural resources, public works, health, education, agriculture and food supply, communications, labour, and social affairs. The civilian operations' task was to render advice and to work with parts of the government in these fields, the planning for and implementation of which were obtained from the ONUC's monthly and annual reports. For instance, the report of the UN Civilian Operation in the Congo, May 1, 1963, prepared by ONUC Staff in New York, assessed two and half years of the ONUC activities and the programme of assistance for 1963. The report indicated that by January 1962, the Congo Fund received $40,000,000 volunteer contributions and ONUC civilian operations spent $19,000,000 for technical assistance in different fields, 693 Congolese were trained in the Congo, 242 abroad; 985 Congolese were attending in-service training in the Congo, 400 attended various short-term seminars, 858 persons were recruited to ensure maintenance of essential public services, and 1135 experts and 554 secondary school teachers were in the Congo.[89]

Similarly, the UN Press Release dated March 1962 mentioned the involvement of about 1000 experts in a wide variety of services as well as a plan to provide 2329 Congolese training at home and abroad in different fields in 1962 with a cost of about $16,000,000.[90] The ONUC also coordinated bilateral arrangements in these fields provided by different countries. For instance, 1,861 Belgian experts were hired through bilateral arrangements and ONUC civilian operations, while a Belgian technical assistance programme ran simultaneously.[91] A close examination of ONUC's involvement in these fields of assistance makes it clear that the UN efforts in the state-building in the Congo, can be considered as a model. The facts and figures of the fields of assistance are based on the reports, documents, journal articles, and letters obtained through archival research at the UN Archives, New York, and Library and Archives Canada, Ottawa, Government of Canada. This dimension of ONUC activities remain little known compared to the more infamous military portion.

Security sector

Assistance to the security sector involved the training of the Congolese army and police forces. It was mandated by the UN Security Council, which never gave any direction to ONUC to reform or retrain the Congolese army. The task of such training was given to the Civilian Operations, who were not capable of the job. Major-General H.T. Alexander, the acting force commander from Ghana, who arrived with the first military troops, attempted to disarm the army for a possible

76 United Nations peace operations in the Democratic Republic of Congo

retraining arrangement. This procedure was not accepted by the UN due to serious resistance from the Congolese government. Later ONUC began a retraining programme in August 1960 under the Deputy Force Commander Hammou Kettani of Morocco. Approximately fifty percent of soldiers attended the training, but some recruits fled with equipment. The training was discontinued from September 1960 due to lack of interest from the Congolese government, which preferred a bilateral arrangement of training with Belgium. The Congolese government also arranged military training under US stewardship in 1962 involving six countries: Canada for communication; Italy for air force; Norway for navy; Israel for paratroopers; Belgium for Headquarters staff, base management and military instructions; the US provided equipment. This arrangement was opposed by the Soviets, but it remained in place until the UN officially took away ONUC's retraining responsibilities in June 1963.

Similarly, ONUC civilian operations undertook police advisory services and training.[92] ONUC experts helped to organize the central identification bureau of the Criminal Investigation Department, imparted training and conducted refresher courses. A comprehensive long-term programme of training for 400 recruits for the territorial police was set up at the Police School in Leopoldville since November 1961. Additionally, over 600 police were trained in the provinces, while 380 police personnel were trained for urban security operations in Leopoldville (300) and Stanleyville (80).[93] ONUC also coordinated a bilateral arrangement of police training. Thus, a UN project titled "Police Training" was planned in March 1963 in coordination with the US, Belgium, and Nigeria.[94] Like the security sector, in every field of operations, the main problem was lack of trained civil servants to direct public administration.

Public administration

The assistance to administration covered basic government functions including financial and monetary matters, foreign assistance programmes, commerce, foreign exchange, judicial system, training of civil servants, and management of development programmes. ONUC experts, in collaboration with the Congolese authorities, began to reform the administration in 1960 through establishing comprehensive organizational plans to set up the central government services. The Ministry of Public Administration and ONUC experts were thus integrated and made progress, but ministerial departments were mostly not willing to accept their roles contained in the organizational plan. To enhance their efforts, in 1961, ONUC experts prepared draft legislation which would involve seconding one official each from the departments and trade unions. The number of experts involved in the ONUC Public Administrative Section was one in 1960, three in 1961, four in 1962, and ten in 1963.[95] These experts were involved in the training of the civil servants as well as students.

In 1962, ONUC identified a number of tasks related to Public Administration: to study the administrative structure of ministries through a joint survey by the Congolese and the ONUC, to assist provincial governments – including arrangement to work in the new provinces – and to provide operational staff from the UN to the provinces.[96] ONUC depended on Belgian technical assistance for these tasks due to a shortage of ONUC experts as well as lack of funds. Organizing administration proved challenging due to presence of the Congolese, ONUC experts and Belgians all in the same office. ONUC first planned to establish a National School of Law and Administration to train both magistrates and civil servants. ONUC undertook two kinds of training in public administration: immediate, accelerated training for the senior officials, and a long-term, more thorough preparation of university level graduates. In the first short course 300 participated from sixteen principal government agencies.

The training for senior civil servants started with 176 officials from all sixteen government departments. Such training was also organized for the postal adminis- trators. The 1962 Plan of Administration covered training of lower and mid-levels by fourteen experts as well as 100 accelerated training programmes for the administrative officials.[97] ONUC also provided study grants to the students of administration and judicial services. The number of students receiving study grants for the National School of Law and Administration was 160 in 1960–61, 150 in 1961–62 and 200 in 1962–63.[98] Through this school, the training of the judiciary system was integrated.

Like public administration, the judiciary system did not get much attention before the independence of the Congo. At the time of independence 400 Belgian lawyers were in the Congo and within a month upon independence only fifteen to twenty remained. There were no Congolese lawyers and UN recruited lawyers just to keep the city courts functioning. ONUC arranged entry into judicial service through the graduate programme of the National School of Law and Administration. Thereafter, the 1962 Plan of Civilian Operations included a program to recruit sixty judges.[99] At the same time ONUC planned for sixty scholarships in judicial service, each amounting to 36,000 Congolese francs a year.[100] ONUC experts were attached to the ministry and gave advice on draft legislation and archive management as well as in the elaboration of the constitution in 1964. The training and management of all these experts and students were however constrained by the economic situation, which was very challenging.

Economic, transportation, and communication services

ONUC was also involved in economic development, transportation, and com- munication services in the Congo. The International Monetary Fund (IMF) worked on the economic and financial aspects of the plan and reported that the unification of currency of Katanga and rest of the Congo remained the main issue in the economic field. By the end of 1961, in Katanga 1 US$ was worth 50 Katanga francs, whereas, in rest of the Congo 1 US$ was 64 Congo francs. This difference resulted in a trade imbalance, a deficit in the national budget as well as differences in foreign exchange earnings. Thus, the IMF's phased plan included the reintegration of foreign exchange earnings and customs revenues of Katanga with those of the rest of the Congo, resumption of trade and payments between the two

78 United Nations peace operations in the Democratic Republic of Congo

parts of the Congo, and establishment of one currency in the two parts of the Congo.[101] In the economic field, the implementation of the National Reconciliation Plan was a major challenge. Apart from the implementation of the National Reconciliation Plan, ONUC experts carried out surveys of natural resources and addressed the development of the mining sector too.

Mining was the largest business in the Congo and the principal source of national revenue and foreign exchange earnings. The industry was mainly the domain of the Belgians. ONUC planned to train the Congolese in technical fields in order to restore the mining economy. But political factors discouraged the ONUC contribution in this field and, as such, the Belgian and French advisers exercised greater influence in this field than their ONUC advisers. The 1962 ONUC Plan for the development of the mining sector planned to establish a National Mining School, for which ONUC provided twenty-one experts and sustained fifty trainees on a yearly basis.[102] Although the involvement in the mining economy proved problematic, the involvement in public works was well coordinated.

Economic development was pursued through public works, one of the most important areas of the civilian operations. In 1957, 27,000 kilometres of roads, 13,700 kilometres of navigable river and 5,120 kilometres of rail network were available in the Congo.[103] In 1960, US$ 630,000 was allocated by ONUC for a single month to undertake public works and by 1960 close working relations was established between the ONUC advisers and the Ministry of Public Works of the Central Government as well as at the Provinces.[104] The 1962 Plan for the Public Works helped establish a National School for Building and Public Works and provided fellowships to 100 Congolese.[105] Meanwhile, emergency public works started with US$ 1,130,000 through a number of projects in different parts of the Congo. These works were jointly coordinated by the ONUC advisers and the concerned ministry officials.[106] Public works included maintenance of 22,000 kilometres of road, maintenance of infrastructure for waterways and the railroads, repair services for electric power facilities, repair of runways, and flood control measures. All these public works were planned and undertaken by the ONUC experts employing Congolese after appropriate training.

ONUC employed forty-four experts in public works and trained about forty Congolese as specialists in public works until 1967. As of October 1964 public works undertaken by ONUC included but were not limited to office construction and repair, road repair, barrage repair, housing construction and repair, school repair and construction, anti-erosion projects, and garbage and waste management.[107] Similarly, a letter written by Deputy Chief Civilian Operations ONUC to Assistant Director USAID Leopoldville, dated June 7, 1963 demonstrated evidence of the public works related to repair of Avenue Baudoin in Eastern part of the Congo, construction of a dormitory at the National Pedagogical Institute, repair of the Bukavu-Usumbura road, construction of the Port of Coquilhatville, and levelling of the waters of Lake Tanganyika.[108] Additionally, a few public works were undertaken in the communication fields.

Assistance to the communication field included civil aviation, transport, meteorology, and telecommunications and postal services. The UN civil aviation team had thirty-three advisers and experts assigned to key airports. They repaired radio navigational equipment, provided training to airport staff, engineers, and worked to develop Air Traffic Control School in Leopoldville. However, the team experienced difficulties with the Congolese Ministry of Transport and Communications.[109] The 1962 Plan in the communication field called for 135 experts as well as the training of 139 students.[110] In telecommunications and postal services, as of 1960, thirty-four experts were involved in the major cities, two Congolese were sent for fellowships programme on telecommunications, three postal experts were assigned in the main post office, and sixty-three senior officials had participated in post office related training. Similarly, in meteorology, six experts worked to ensure consistent service, and in the transport sector ONUC experts ensured that river pilots kept the waterways functional and initiated a training scheme for Congolese river pilots with ONUC assistance.[111]

Social welfare services

ONUC civilian operations were also deeply involved in social welfare activities in the Congo. In 1960, social welfare services included assistance to refugees, community development to promote economic recovery and advanced standards of living, training facilities for social and community development workers, and the reduction of unemployment. The first relief activity was organized by the ONUC for supplying emergency aid to refugees; it integrated experts from UN agencies and the Red Cross. Social Affairs advisers were involved with the Ministry of Social Affairs in different provinces to address unemployment issues and other social problems.[112] In the absence of an authentic survey (last sample survey was conducted for the period between 1953 to 1955), ONUC Bureau of Social Affairs undertook research and proposed to conduct a census by the 600 university students from social sciences.[113] The bureau also got involved in the rural development of the Congo. ONUC established a Social Service Training Institute and trained thirty individuals in 1963–64.[114]

ONUC civilian operations were also involved in the field of labour management through the International Labour Organization (ILO), which as a lead agency undertook several initiatives. For instance, in 1960, three candidates were selected for ILO fellowships in Europe. Additionally, training programs for labour inspection and industrial hygiene were planned and thirty-four trainees underwent the course to assume senior posts.[115] The 1962 Plan of Labour Management called for the hiring of twenty-four experts and awarding fellowships to twenty-nine students for advanced study.[116]

Health sector

In the health sector, ONUC focused on primary health care as well as development of a public health system. The World Health Organization provided advisory assistance at the central and provincial level. Over 100 specialists were deployed by

80 United Nations peace operations in the Democratic Republic of Congo

1960. The WHO also planned for the training of local personnel to replace foreign doctors and technical advisers. The Congo had no doctors and as such the medical assistants were sent abroad in phases for advance training to complete that long course and become a full doctor. Additionally, 130 operational health personnel were seconded by the WHO to the ministry and three were sent to Europe for training as doctors to make the total number of doctors to sixty-eight by 1961. A significant number of students were also sent abroad for medical education on ONUC grants.[117] The 1962 Plan on Health envisioned medical training for eighty-six students as well as manning the nation's health services with 200 public health doctors out of 244 medical experts.[118] As a whole, ONUC arranged medical degree course for the students: three in 1961, nine in 1962, fourteen in 1963, seventy-seven in 1964, 134 in 1965 and 192 in 1968.[119]

Education sector

ONUC civilian operations undertook education programmes with the assistance from the UN Educational, Scientific and Cultural Organization (UNESCO). It was involved at the primary, secondary, and advanced levels: advising the central and provincial ministries of education, assisting in the effort to reform education, and providing for the formation of qualified Congolese to carry in the country's educational system. In 1960, sixty-four teachers were brought in, and sixteen experts were working as advisers. As of June 22, 1964, 800 UNESCO and twenty-six expert teachers were in the Congo. An additional requirement to recruit 250 secondary school teachers was sent to the Secretary-General at the request of the Government of the Congo.[120] UNESCO upgraded the level of teachers through training and courses. There were only 152 secondary graduates available in 1960. The secondary enrolment increased to 54,000 in 1961–62 from 28,900 in 1959–60. A National Pedagogical Institute was founded in 1961, which was designed to provide training to primary and secondary level teachers.

The 1962 Plan of Education involved over 1500 fellowship holders to receive educational training and thereafter absorption of 110 fellows as primary school inspectors and administrators. In addition, the involvement of over 100 ONUC experts and professors were planned to strengthen the Congo's educational system.[121] The National Mining School was established in 1962 with the aim to train Congolese mining inspectors and engineers. The National Institute for Building and Public Works was founded in 1962 to train civil engineers. A Vocational Training Institute was established in 1964 to train and develop the skills of the Congolese in different fields. Training was also organized in journalism and radio broadcasting. UNESCO initiated fellowships to the students and in 1962, 1000 grants were provided where eighteen students went abroad and in 1963, 3000 such fellowship grants were provided with fifteen for the overseas programme. In 1966, UNESCO helped and prepared the ministry officials to handle hiring and thereafter the education programme gradually phased out. Apart from UNESCO, ONUC worked with UNDP and UNICEF for collective development in the education sector. Belgian and French technical assistance personnel were not also cooperating much with UN's reforms in education resulting in frictions from time to time.

Agriculture sector

The economy of the Congo depended on mines in Katanga and South Kasai, but for the majority of the population agriculture remained the most important livelihood. The Food and Agricultural Organization undertook activities related to administrative reorganization, advisory support to the ministry, education and training, improvement of nutrition, adoption of commercial agreements, and employment of unemployed workers. In 1960, a total budget of US$ 741,000 supported advisory services, farm mechanics training centres, accelerated courses for agricultural assistants, a poultry training centre and veterinary courses.[122]

ONUC handled food security through emergency provisions in different provinces in 1960. ONUC supplied 7,288,160 pounds of food received through donation and shipped 6,360,860 pounds in November 1960 to alleviate the emergency in Kasai, Kivu, and Katanga provinces. It also covered the worsening situation involving 250,000 refugees in the South Kasai province in order to prevent a famine. To tackle the emergency UNICEF allocated US$ 250,000 for the purchase of vehicles for the mobile health team of World Health Organization and 74,000 children received milk through a distribution programme during 1960.[123]

Apart from emergency provisions, ONUC was involved in extensive training and advisory services in the agricultural sector. For instance, in 1960, in the field of agriculture and food supply, the advisory capacity targeted forty experts nationally and locally. ONUC arranged general, civic education and agricultural training for batches of 2,000 youths from May 1960 by establishing youth camps in Leopoldville. The Food and Agricultural Organization established an Advanced School for Tropical Agronomy at Lovanium University in Leopoldville to offer a three-year course of study. There, twenty-five candidates were selected for the 1960–61 academic year with four professors provided by the Food and Agricultural Organization. It also established a Farm Mechanization Centre and trained 307 students from 1961 to 1966. The Butembo Veterinary School began operations in 1961 with instructors provided by the Food and Agricultural Organization and the school produced twenty-two veterinary assistants. The 1962 Plan of Agriculture arranged for twenty-one experts to provide consultative services while 130 trainees were equipped with modern agricultural know-how.[124] By the end of 1962, over fifty fellowships were awarded to the Congolese in the agriculture field. Efforts to train and hire foreign experts continued in 1963–64.

According to a letter from the Food and Agricultural Organization to the Under-secretary General for Civil Affairs ONUC dated May 27, 1963, some 542 foreign experts on agriculture were available before independence. A total of 118 foreign experts were working in 1963 and Congolese government demanded 233 more; however, the Food and Agricultural Organization could only provide twenty-three.[125] The principal agricultural commodities of the Congo were palm

82 United Nations peace operations in the Democratic Republic of Congo

products, cotton fibres, Robusta coffee, Arabica coffee, rubber, cocoa beans, tea, and bananas. The production of most of the products went down from 1960 to 1966 due to crises and continued thereafter. For instance, before independence, Congo palm oil and palm nuts represented about a quarter of the world's palm products (185, 549 tons in 1959). In 1962, it fell to 150,000 tons and it was on the downward curve from 1967 (109,038 tons).

These approaches to state-building continued until 1964 under the flagship of ONUC. When ONUC military forces were withdrawn on June 30, 1964, 2,000 men and women remained from the UN and its specialized agencies to continue assisting in the work of state-building. Then authority over civilian operations passed to the Resident Representatives of the Technical Assistance Board and the Director of the Special Fund Programme.[126] Upon withdrawal of military, the technical assistance tasks became secondary to the Congolese due to rebellions. Civilian operations had to work within their own budgets, which were provided by voluntary contribution. As a whole, civilian operations struggled without the support of military. As the rebellions grew from 1965, twelve members of the UN programme were killed and in August 1964, all the dependents of personnel of civilian operations withdrew from the Congo. In 1966, few ministries could not yet stand alone and needed UN technicians to continue assistance.

Assessment of ONUC

To undertake an assessment of ONUC, first the sources of conflict in the Congo (as briefly discussed in chapter I) need to be assessed. The sources of conflict related to Cold War rivalry, failure of state-building, and local and political dynamics was addressed in the mandate either directly or indirectly. Support for state-building was provided as "technical assistance" which was handled through ONUC's civilian operations. The civilian operations attempted to train the Congolese in mining operations in order to ensure "local ownership" of Congo's extensive resources. The National Reconciliation Plan, which assisted unification of Congo, also dealt with economic issues. Moreover, bilateral arrangements as well as high profile business involvement by the US and Belgium in the field of natural resources kept ONUC away from the economic scene.

From 1960 to 1964, more than ninety-three thousand troops served in ONUC and 20,000 were present at any one time. The total cost of military operations was US $ 402 million.[127] John Allphin Moore and Jerry Pubantz in their 2006 book *The New United Nations: International Organization in the Twenty-First Century* argued that, "In Congo, the UN attempted to expand the meaning of peacekeeping by going beyond simply separating two independent states and monitoring an armistice or a [ceasefire]."[128] The mission entangled the UN in Cold War rivalry and UN's action forced Katanga to remain part of the Congo. Joshua Goldstein argued "ONUC succeeded in holding the Congo together."[129]

ONUC turned into an early experiment in state-building, a "top-down" approach directed from UN headquarters. Its civilian operations were affected by a

United Nations peace operations in the Democratic Republic of Congo   83

number of factors: the state of the available civilian infrastructure; low living standards and hardships; a weakened administration and a disrupted economy; non-cooperation from government officials; limited availability of resources and finance for UN operations; regular criticism by the Europeans and Congolese; a perception by many Congolese that the UN was simply a replacement for the Belgians; and the accusation by the Belgians that UN was trying to recolonize the Congo. Civilian operations were also affected by the lack of a smooth transition before independence by the Belgians. Also, when ONUC experts became involved in the administration bilateral cooperation between Belgium and the Congo continued, and Belgian officials sometimes worked to undermine UN experts, leading to hostile relationships. According to Arthur House, "There was also a lack of harmony in civil service between the Congolese, Belgians and ONUC personnel."[130] However, the maximum funding was provided by the US as well as through Belgians' bilateral assistance, which were vital to steering the civilian operations. Finally, Africans were united at the UN in trying to solve the Congo crisis. As a whole, Gibbons and Morican conclude, the "UN rescued and helped [the Congo] back on the road to prosperity. A threat to world peace was dealt with through UN though Mobutu established an exploitative dictatorship in 1965."[131] Above all, the concept of civilian operations can be considered a model of state-building by the UN.

UN Organization Mission in the DRC (MONUC)

Background

The UN's withdrawal from the Congo in 1964, began an era of dictatorship and state collapse. Joseph Mobutu mounted a coup in the Congo following a political stalemate, which occurred after the elections in March 1965 and was due to differences between Prime Minister Moise Tshombe and President Joseph Kasavubu. In his 2009 book, *Africa's World War: Congo, the Rwandan Genocide, and the Making of a Continental Catastrophe*, Gerard Prunier argued that "the coup in 1965 was sponsored by the Central Intelligence Agency of the United States."[132] Regardless of the truth of Prunier's claim, the post-independence period in the DRC was shaped by the international context of Cold War rivalry. Patience Kabamba claimed that, "To secure access to the Congo minerals, the United States and European powers financed the Mobutu regime."[133] The period of Mobutu rule was marked by the exploitation of economic resources and gradual decay of state institutions.

The Congo experienced a systematic state failure as well as systematic looting of the nation's wealth. During Mobutu's thirty-two-year rule as president (1965–97), within the first ten years of Mobutu's takeover, the Congo started its journey towards state collapse. Young and Turner suggested that an important part of the pathology of state decay is expressed by three processes: shrinkage in the competency, credibility, and probity of the state.[134] There was no central point of command in the DRC. Kabamba argued that "Instead multiple, fragile, interconnected and contested centres of military might, welfare provision, ethnoreligious and local

84 United Nations peace operations in the Democratic Republic of Congo

loyalties claimed sovereignty over people."[135] Alex Thomson stated that "Mobutu's political decisions caused both a crisis of accumulation and a crisis of governance."[136]

The Congo's crisis of accumulation was created by a combination of poor policy and widespread corruption.[137] The failing economy and a failure of governance led to systematic state collapse. According to Joshua Goldstein, by the 1990s, "the country's economy was near complete collapse due to economic mismanagement, corruption, and political instability."[138] The DRC experienced a higher magnitude of political instability after the end of the Cold War. According to Norrie Macqueen, "The decline of the superpowers' military aid and their patronage in general was crucial in explaining the collapse of the DRC."[139] The local Congolese resorted to the smuggling of natural resources and took up arms to establish a reign of terror, which resulted in the massive displacement of populations. These displaced villagers formed their own militias, and within a short time a complete militarization of society took place.[140] Thereafter, the internal conflict in the DRC fuelled cycles of regional and international confrontation. Neighbouring countries exploited the internal conflict of the DRC due to the instability. Rwanda and Uganda used the Congo as a base of operations and became involved in the internal affairs of the Congo from the 1990s.

The Congo crisis, also known as the Great Lakes crisis of 1997–2001, was the first large-scale African regional war of the postcolonial era.[141] The war attracted the forces of nine African countries and a number of rebel factions operating in the conflict zone. While neighbouring countries got involved with the affairs of the Congo, the anti-government forces, led by Laurent Kabila, obtained assistance from Rwanda, as Mobutu had previously supported Rwandese rebels in the eastern Congo.[142] Kabila's forces also received logistical support from the US. After the Rwandan genocide, according to Prunier, the US began to train the Rwandan army and at the same time provided direct logistical support to Kabila's forces in area of operation by C-130 flights.[143] Consequently, Kabila with the assistance from the Rwandan and Angolan armies overran the already decaying Congolese army. Mobutu finally succumbed to an alliance of Congolese and regional forces led by Kabila.[144] In May 1997, Kabila overthrew Mobutu and became the president.

Like Mobutu, Kabila did not focus on state-building affairs.[145] He remained occupied with the affairs of different rebel groups, and expelled Rwandan forces from the eastern Congo in 1998 (the latter consisting of Hutu refugees, who came to the Congo from Rwanda when the Tutsi led Rwandan Patriotic Front won the election in July, 1994), resulting in formation of a new rebel group, the Congolese Rally for Democracy (RCD), which was supported by Rwanda and Uganda.[146]

It was above all Rwanda, with its provision of well-equipped and battle-hardened troops, that ultimately decided the conflict.[147] The RCD captured a few major cities and threatened Kinshasa. Angola, Zimbabwe, Namibia, Sudan, Chad, and Burundi backed the Kabila government against the rebel movement. Thus, nine African countries got involved in the conflict, and by 2004 an estimated 3.8 million people lost their lives.[148] Kabila relied on military support from his allies to compensate for the weakness of the Congolese army. In return, Kabila offered these governments

United Nations peace operations in the Democratic Republic of Congo **85**

lucrative mining contracts, including trade in diamonds, the mineral *columbo tantalite (coltan),*[149] and timber.[150] The abundant supplies of coltan in the eastern Congo, according to Goldstein, "mined without much equipment or technology, empowered armed groups that fought to control the deposits and illegally export the coltan."[151] Due to the UN Security Council's continued pressure on the Southern African Development Community (SADC), neighbouring countries ultimately came together to establish a peace agreement in Lusaka.[152]

African leaders came to a consensus through the Lusaka agreement in July 1999, which was signed by the Congolese government, the warring regional states and the Congolese rebel groups. The Lusaka agreement reformed the Congo's political system so that it would be more democratic, inclusive, and secure a sustained peace. The agreement called for an inter-Congolese dialogue on the country's future, the normalization of the DRC's border, the disarmament of the militias, and the establishment of a Joint Military Commission.[153] The UN Security Council endorsed the agreement by its Resolution 1258/1999 on August 6, 1999 and deployed a UN liaison group with ninety personnel to the capitals of the signatory states and to the Joint Military Commission provisional headquarters. The UN Security Council did not follow completely the obligations of the agreement and thus, the resolution ended up being an under-resourced UN mission (MONUC).[154] Arguably, such under-resourced arrangements were the result of a lack of commitment by the international community.

Mandate vis-à-vis implementation of tasks by MONUC

MONUC was initiated in July 1999 through the UN Security Council Resolution 1275/1999 to provide assistance in the implementation of the 1999 Lusaka Ceasefire Agreement. It was mainly tasked with liaising with the Joint Monitoring Commission to provide technical assistance in the implementation of the Ceasefire Agreement and the disengagement of forces.[155] MONUC was mandated to protect civilians in 2000. Fighting had recommenced between Rwandan and Ugandan forces in Kisangani, which resulted in the deaths of hundreds of Congolese. Therefore, UN Security Council Resolution 1291/2000 authorized up to 5,537 personnel to operate under Chapter VII as peace enforcement operations.[156] MONUC was then tasked with the demobilization, disintegration and reintegration (DDR) of foreign as well as Congolese armed groups, and the support of confidence-building measures between the DRC, Rwanda, and Uganda.

The UN Security Council began to address one of the most serious roots of the conflict in 2000 – the economic exploitation of resources. UN Security Council Resolution 1291/2000, dated February 24, 2000, formed a panel to report on the matter related to the illegal exploitation of resources, their use to fuel conflict and the illicit flow of arms.[157] The panel submitted its final report on October 23, 2003.[158] The report was endorsed by the UN Security Council through its resolution 1533 dated March 12, 2004. The panel recommended consequent actions by the countries and a few steps for peace dividend (as mentioned in Box 3.1) in conflict areas.[159] Actions for the countries included conducting investigations of companies and individuals, strengthening monitoring capacity of civil societies, enactment of the Codes related to natural resources, reforms in different sectors of natural resources, and the establishment of a government body or commission to review and revise all natural resource concessions and contracts.[160]

BOX 3.1. PEACE DIVIDEND MEASURES RECOMMENDED BY THE UN PANEL OF EXPERTS ON THE ILLEGAL EXPLOITATION OF NATURAL RESOURCES AND OTHER FORMS OF WEALTH FROM THE DRC.

United Nations Security Council, 'UN Panel of Experts on the Illegal Exploitation of Natural Resources and Other Forms of Wealth from the DRC', UN Documents, 23 October 2003, https://www.undocs.org/S/2003/1027., 20. (Developed by the author)

- Local confidence building activities in conflict areas to quickly convince the people that peace is better than conflict. (Details of these activities are discussed in Chapter III and IV).
- Undertaking Quick Impact Projects (QIPs) to break the dependency link between armed groups carrying out natural resource exploitation and the local communities. (Details of QIPs are discussed in Chapter III and IV).
- Functioning of hospitals, clinics and schools are needed to be ensured and assistances provided in this regard.
- Undertaking massive development works for job creation involving the repair of roads, sanitation systems, and public buildings.

MONUC undertook peace dividend measures from time to time throughout its deployment areas. Additionally, the government of the DRC took steps recommended by the panel in due course, assisted by MONUC. Thus, the UN and MONUC endeavoured to address one of the roots of conflict: illegal exploitation of natural resources from the DRC, even though Joshua Goldstein concludes that "the UN could do little to stop it."[161] Nonetheless, these measures were interconnected with the issue of maintaining peace and stability, and assistance for state-building, especially effective governance.

The UN mission's initiative resulted in the signing of the Global and All-Inclusive Agreement on the transition in the DRC in 2002 and thereafter, the government and the rebel groups reached an agreement on a transitional regime. Under this agreement, President Joseph Kabila (son of Laurent Kabila, who was assassinated in 2001) accepted terms for a transitional government that would share power with rebel parties, and he agreed to elections by 2005. The UN then placed its full resources behind the agreements. It also used its military forces to combat ethnic rebel groups in the north-eastern region.

The UN mission faced a difficult security situation from 2003. The security situation deteriorated in the eastern DRC in 2003 due to ethnic violence.[162] Thus, the UN authorized quick deployment of a French-led Interim Emergency Multinational Force for three months (June-August 2003).[163] This attempt was to stabilize the situation and give time to the UN for subsequent deployment. The force operated in coordination with the UN mission, stabilized the situation and was replaced by UN force with a robust mandate including assistance for Disarmament, Demobilization, and Reintegration (DDR). As part of planning process, the UN approached member states including Bangladesh to contribute forces in the DRC within a shortest possible time in April 2003.[164] Being a desk officer of the peacekeeping affairs at the army headquarters of the Bangladesh army, the author had a unique experience to undertake an operational reconnaissance to the DRC to study the security situation in order to ensure effective performance by the Bangladesh' peacekeepers upon deployment.

The author's experience from April 21 to May 1, 2003, related to the affairs of the mission, its mandates, and issues of state-building as well as the volatile security situation in the eastern DRC. He was a member of the thirty-five-member reconnaissance team, which was composed of representatives from troop contributing countries India, Pakistan, Nepal, Indonesia, and officials of the UN and MONUC headquarters. The author experienced a snapshot of conflict-ridden Congo with an extremely unpredictable and unstable situation upon arriving in the eastern city of Bunia. It was a barren city with hardly any infrastructure or road network. There was insignificant presence of state apparatus; overall it was a textbook example of the results of a failed state. Only an ad hoc UN office with a few hundred peacekeepers and European forces was present. Armed groups of militias, including children, equipped with modern weapons fully loaded with ammunition – awaiting to press the trigger at their whims – patrolled the streets. The UN team was briefed about the ferocious militias, who recently killed two UN peacekeepers and eaten their delicate organs. During the reconnaissance the team faced a combat situation, when it got stranded as the militias opened fire on to the local briefing site. A couple of reconnaissance team members had to be taken for medical emergency by an armoured personnel carrier ambulance in the hours of darkness. The following day, the team had to run on the runway to board a moving C-130 UN special cargo flight in order to leave Bunia. They had witnessed a snapshot of conflict-ridden Congo. Thus, a new UN Security Council Resolution 1493/2003 resulted from the escalation of crisis in the Ituri region and authorized up to 10,800 personnel to take over from the European forces.

Like the Ituri region of the DRC, other eastern areas experienced an eruption of conflict in 2004.[165] The eastern Congo again became the site of terrible violence, as power struggles took place between ex-rebel and government commanders within the new, integrated Congolese army. Thus, UN Security Council approved a robust mandate through its resolution 1565/2004 which increased strength of peacekeepers to 23,900, who would deploy in key regions of instability, deterring violence in the Kivus and elsewhere.[166] The mission therefore adopted aggressive means to weaken the militias and at the same time became a target too. In

88 United Nations peace operations in the Democratic Republic of Congo

February 2005, nine Bangladeshi peacekeepers were killed during an ambush in Ituri. Thereafter, the approach of the mission became more robust, and the pressure rose on all armed groups.

The UN mission in the DRC was also mandated to assist in state-building through providing support for the constitution, adoption of legislation, electoral reform, and security sector reform (SSR). From the outset of the new mandate, the mission was engaged in state-building affairs in different forms. These included building institutions of the government at different levels, including the parliament, the electoral commission, the Congolese armed force (Forces Armées de la République Démocratique du Congo, FARDC), the police, the civil and military judicial system. Consequently, the UN then supported a referendum for a new constitution in 2005, assisted in the elections in 2006, and completed the transition process by 2007. The country's first free and fair election in forty-six years took place on July 30, 2006, with voters electing a 500-seat National Assembly.[167] Following the elections, the mission continued to implement multiple political and military reforms, ensure the rule of law and promote capacity-building tasks as mandated.

The UN enforced peace and protection of civilians in coordination with the Congolese armed forces. It operated alongside Congolese troops in offensive operations to protect civilians and forcefully disarmed militia groups.[168] It also conducted joint operations against foreign armed groups, such as the Forces démocratiques de Libération du Rwanda (FDLR), from Rwanda, and the Lord's Resistance Army (LRA), from Uganda.[169] These operations were related to the mandate to assist internal security forces to evict foreign armed groups from the DRC.

MONUC supported Congolese armed force operations by providing ground and tactical mobility, fuel, medical supplies, evacuation of casualties, and rations. MONUC personnel also prepared a standing operating procedure in coordination with the Congolese armed forces for rendering support. According to a UN report, Belgium and South Africa trained the Congolese armed forces under bilateral agreements. Thus, Congolese armed forces were able to deploy troops to neutralize the conflict in different places. The mission further assisted the preparation of the Congolese army by preparing a draft memorandum of understanding between the Mission and the Government to screen personnel for training by the UN. For instance, the UN police trained 8,625 national police officers and 210 judiciary police officers in 2009 and the mission and UNDP jointly trained 709 police officers in the same year.[170]

The security situation again deteriorated after the election between 2007 and 2008 in the eastern DRC (Kivus), resulting in a new UN Security Council Resolution 1856/2008 with a maximum strength of 22,016 personnel, tasked with concentrating efforts to develop a lasting solution to the conflict in the eastern DRC. The resolution also mandated the UN to provide training to the Congolese armed forces with basic training, human rights, international humanitarian law, and prepare them to handle security in respective area of responsibility as part of security sector reform. The mission was also tasked with preventing the provision

United Nations peace operations in the Democratic Republic of Congo **89**

of support to illegal armed groups, including support derived from illegal economic activities. These tasks were difficult for the UN mission due to its dispersed deployment as well as lack of capacity. However, the mission expanded its monitoring capacity by engaging local communities to assist in undertaking these tasks.

Assessment of MONUC

Philip Roessler and John Prendergast concluded that, "MONUC had put up its best effort with peace implementation, but there were serious deficiency in local leaders' willingness to support the peace, marginal international political will to take risks for peace, and equally little willingness to expend the necessary resources to create it."[171] The revolutionary leader, Che Guevara, had expressed the same feeling about the leaderships of different tiers of the Congo (including Laurent Kabila) when he assisted the training of the rebels on guerilla warfare in the mid-1960s.[172] Bearing these problems in mind, it is worth noting that the UN ensured the end of the civil war, helped to attain a comparatively better security situation, and organized successful elections in 2006. Additionally, it assisted with improved relations between the neighbouring countries.

The 2010 UN Secretary-General's closing report (31st report) on the mission highlighted the achievements, challenges and suggested ways forward.[173] The Congolese armed forces had developed the capacity, with the assistance of the UN, to launch small-scale offensives against the rebels, with some significant successes.[174] MONUC also scaled down inter communal clashes as well as attacks on the humanitarian actors through supporting the operations conducted by Congolese armed forces and police. The Congolese armed forces and police also attained the capability to conduct operations on a limited scale, either independently or jointly.

MONUC attempted to address the conflict through eliminating the main foreign armed groups from Rwanda and Uganda, including a couple of local armed groups. The UN assisted DDR programmes for the ex-militias of these armed groups including a sensitization programme and reintegration support by coordinating with UN agencies, donors, the Government of Sudan, and the Government of Uganda in 2009.[175]

MONUC stabilized the conflict in affected areas, consolidated peace across the country and initiated development projects. However, state institutions were still weak, and the progress made with respect to the training and professional development of the Congolese armed forces had its limits. Amalgamation of soldiers from former armed groups resulted in poor loyalty, indiscipline, and disruption of chains of command. The situation was further aggravated by inadequate budget, lack of equipment, poor logistics, a non-functional pay system, and human rights violations.[176] A similar situation occurred with the police, which also absorbed former armed group members.

Yet overall, MONUC contributed to the recovery of the DRC from conflict and to the improvement of peace and security from 1999 to June 2010. Thereafter, it turned into a stabilization operation (the UN Organization Stabilization Mission in the

90 United Nations peace operations in the Democratic Republic of Congo

DRC, MONUSCO) from July 1, 2010 through the UN Security Council Resolution 1925/2010. Ongoing tasks thus remained for the stabilization mission were protection of civilians, humanitarian assistance, DDR, security sector reform, support to national institutions building, and civil-military coordination tasks for community outreach programmes. Part of MONUC in general and MONUSCO in particular reflected the latest emerging trends in UN stability building practice in Africa.

Civil-Military Coordination (CIMIC) in the UN Organization Mission in the DRC (MONUC)

The MONUC is being considered here as a comparative example to the more detailed case of Sudan. Unlike Sudan, the mission in the DRC was mandated to assist in state-building endeavours four years after it launched. The MONUC operated from November 30, 1999 to June 30, 2010 with 26,413 personnel comprising military, police and civilians.[177] In MONUC, the area of operations was divided amongst brigades comprising mixed military forces mainly from Bangladesh, India, Morocco, Pakistan, South Africa, Tanzania, Tunisia, and Uruguay.

In MONUC, the UN-CIMIC unit and the Office for the Coordination of Humanitarian Affairs jointly developed "Guidelines for Interaction between MONUC Military and Humanitarian Organizations."[178] These guidelines established the principle of cooperation between Troop Contributing Countries (TCCs) military forces and humanitarian actors. Therefore, they maintained a clear distinction between their roles and responsibilities. Generally, the guidelines were followed by all concerned stakeholders – military, UN agencies, civilian sections, and NGOs.[179] According to the guidelines, the role of the UN-CIMIC unit was to enhance and support military operations by achieving humanitarian relief through coordination, liaising, facilitation, information-sharing and mutual support between the TCCs' military forces, the Office for the Coordination of Humanitarian Affairs, and the local authorities. In particular, CIMIC activities in the mission supported the program of Disarmament, Demobilization, Repatriation, Resettlement, and Reintegration (DDRRR) and the electoral process.[180]

The mission established joint protection working groups from 2006, known as Provincial Protection Clusters, comprising concerned UN agencies, NGOs, and TCC military forces.[181] In practice, different humanitarian activities were coordinated through these clusters at the community-level. Additionally, regular CIMIC meetings were held at the mission headquarters at Kinshasa, division headquarters at Kisangani, and other brigade headquarters. As a unique arrangement, these meetings were co-chaired by the head of the CIMIC sections concerned and the head of the humanitarian assistance sections.[182]

The guidelines also spelt out which CIMIC activities were to be funded from TCCs' own means to create a positive relationship with the host community. By this guideline, MONUC attempted to formalize CIMIC activities rendered by TCC military forces. These activities included the development of infrastructure, the provision of public and social services, and activities related to training of personnel, socio-economic development, cultural activities, and sports. These efforts required prior coordination with the concerned humanitarian organization in the deployment area.[183] However, the following paragraphs demonstrate that, like the UN mission in Sudan (discussed in the following chapter), these CIMIC activities were applied unevenly.

The objectives of CIMIC in the DRC were "to create a favourable atmosphere and to build confidence in local authorities, interest groups and populations."[184] In order to achieve these objectives, good coordination with the civil and humanitarian agencies within all respective area of operations was needed. Therefore, the role of CIMIC was mainly related to assisting in the protection of civilians, projects for local populations, and assessment of the civilian environment.[185]

In MONUC, CIMIC unit's key tasks were liaising with authorities, the Congolese armed forces (Forces Armées de la République Démocratique du Congo, FARDC), NGOs, civil society organizations, local populations, and UN agencies. To fulfill the requirement of the 2003 "MONUC: Force Commander's Directive on CIMIC," CIMIC units' tasks targeted confidence-building measures to support the FARDC, NGOs and local populations.[186] Thus, at the community-level, the relevant CIMIC unit was involved in the identification and implementation of potential CIMIC projects in close coordination with the respective Head of the Office of MONUC at the brigade level, local authorities, and NGOs. This approach contributed to creating a positive relationship between the different deployed military units and local populations.

In this section the discussion of CIMIC activities in the DRC is brief due to the limited availability of declassified source material. A summary of broad CIMIC activities in the DRC from 2000 to June 2010 covered the regular provision of medical support to local populations through the establishment of medical camps/clinics in remote locations. The repair of roads, bridges, culverts, and runways were undertaken along with the establishment of water points, the construction of roads, the renovation of offices, schools, and community centres. The necessary provision was made for humanitarian assistance through convoy escorts, as well as transport support to UN agencies. Additionally, the training of local populations on computers was undertaken, football matches were organized between UN military forces and local populations, and provision was made for stationery and reading materials to schools and of medicines to hospitals.

QIPs in the DRC

In the DRC, QIPs were executed, to the maximum extent possible, by TCC personnel with the support and the practical collaboration of the FARDC. Liaising was undertaken on a weekly basis with the UN Civil Affairs Section as well as with concerned UN agencies and NGOs.

The UN mission in the DRC received a budget of US$ 1 million each year for small community-based projects and has undertaken a good number of QIPs since 2001. As of May 2010, the mission completed 724 projects, and seventy-six projects were underway.[187] In general, the QIPs were neither broad-based nor part of a well-orchestrated plan. TCCs military contingents undertook QIPs in their respective

92 United Nations peace operations in the Democratic Republic of Congo

TABLE 3.1 QIPs undertaken by TCCs in the DRC (2004–10).

Year	QIPs
2004	• The renovation of a centre for the deaf, and of a residence in Kisangani University.
2008	• The rehabilitation of a training college for mothers with badly nourished children as part of a poverty reduction programme, which was supported by the World Food Programme and UN Children's Fund. A total of approximately 5,639 families were the beneficiaries from this initiative.
2010	• The rehabilitation of a territory's administrative office and a market shed – these projects were a dire necessity for the population in and around the city of conflict-ridden Dungu, Orientale province. Upon renovating the building, the capacity of the office increased, and local populations were getting better and more hygienic service than before.
	• The construction of a pavilion as overhead protection for a local farmers' market in the Baokandia district of Dungu. This project not only protected the vendors but provided better sanitary conditions for the sale of local produce.

Source: Brent C Bankus, 'Military-Enabled Quick Impact Projects Improve Quality of Life of Local Populations', 26; https://monuc.unmissions.org/en/monuc-rehabilitating-two-important-buildings-dungu; https://reliefweb.int/report/democratic-republic-congo/dr-congombandaka-monuc-finances-new-quick-impact-project-iyonda;https://reliefweb.int/report/democratic-republic-congo/drc-monuc-funds-two-quick-impact-projects-kisangani. (Developed by the author)

areas of operation. According to the report of the ReliefWeb on "MONUC's Quick Impact Projects-Democratic Republic of the Congo," about seventy-five percent of QIPs were implemented by local NGOs, and the remaining twenty-five percent were implemented by TCCs contingents and other entities.[188] QIPs undertaken by TCC military forces resulted in the UN-CIMIC playing a role. A summary of QIPs undertaken by TCCs from 2004–10[189] is shown in table 3.1 (major locations are shown in map at Appendix 2).

Conclusions

Since its inception in 1945, the UN has played a significant role in maintaining peace and security when the world powers were in conflict. By and large the UN prevented a confrontation of Great Powers through its involvement in Suez and the Congo. In both the cases, the World Powers were interested in geopolitical gains as well as securing their economic interests. UNEF represented a straightforward effort to maintain peace and security in the wake of a clash between states. On the other hand, ONUC had to handle an internal conflict to maintain peace and security.

In ONUC the mandated tasks were also short-term. Although ONUC attempted to instil "local ownerships" amongst the Congolese through the various efforts of its civilian operations, the mandate was most successful in addressing short-term conflict and ensuring the unity of the Congo. ONUC was not a failure but a contentious endeavour. The UN delivered different programs for the Congolese to run the country. It ran courses for different professionals through thousands of UN experts. Congolese were sent abroad on UN fellowships to study and prepare themselves to administer the country. The UN also prevented a possible famine and tacked refugee situations.

ONUC was a model of the "top-down" approach to state-building. The leadership of Dag Hammarskjold, who channelled the UN agencies through the Secretary-General, remained as an example of unity of command for steering military and civilian operations. ONUC achieved a substantial proportion of its mandate but non-cooperation on the part of Belgium and elements of the Congolese population posed major obstacles. A vacuum was created in governance upon independence and the withdrawal of Belgians, which affected the start of the civilian operations. Nevertheless, UN civilian operations prevented economic collapse and the complete breakdown of public services. The education and health sectors benefitted enormously from UN assistance in state-building, though the mining sector avoided key reforms due to the economic interests of the stakeholders. Capacity building of the military and police is an important tool of state-building, which ONUC got engaged in, but ultimately bilateral arrangements became the dominant solution. When ONUC forces were withdrawn on June 30, 1964, groups of experts remained from the UN and its specialized agencies and continued the job of state-building. After the UN's departure Mobutu seized power with US backing and continued the greedy exploitation of Congo's wealth for his own personal fortune. Goldstein stated, "The country stayed desperately poor during his thirty years rule."[190]

The DRC first experienced UN involvement from 1960–64 and thereafter succumbed to gradual state failure from 1965 to 1997, which featured increased communal violence and the involvement of foreign armed groups of neighbouring countries into the conflict. Thereafter, the UN Organization Mission in the DRC (MONUC) intervened in support of the Lusaka Ceasefire Agreement of 1999. From 1999 until 2010, MONUC gradually implemented its mandated tasks and as such converted to a stabilization operation after 2010. This study related to the first UN peace operations in the Congo had set the scene for subsequent study of state-building as part of case study. Additionally, the model of state-building demonstrated through civilian operations in the Congo provides a point of reference for the study of subsequent civil-military coordination in UN peace operations to assist in national-level state-building.

The civil-military coordination related tasks were not much visible in the DRC due to the nature of conflict as well as the priority of maintaining security. However, state-building endeavours geared up in the DRC at a later stage of the mission especially in the political development and security sectors reform. The following chapter investigates the UN peace operations in Sudan.

Notes

1 Clarke M. Eichelberger, *UN: The First Twenty Years* (New York: Harper & Row, 1955), 28.

2 Evan Luard, *A History of the United Nations, Volume 1: The Years of Western Domination, 1945–1955* (London: Macmillan, 1982), 93–105.

94 United Nations peace operations in the Democratic Republic of Congo

3 "UNEF was later renamed as 'UNEF I' upon launching of the UN peace operation UNEF II after the 1973 Arab-Israel War.", n.d.
4 Eichelberger, *UN: The First Twenty Years*, 31.
5 Joshua S. Goldstein, *Winning the War on War: The Decline of Armed Conflict Worldwide* (New York: Plume, 2012), 69.
6 Christopher D O'Sullivan, *The United Nations: A Concise History* (Malabar, Fla.: Krieger Pub. Co., 2005), 67.
7 O'Sullivan, 68.
8 James Dobbins, *The UN"s Role in Nation-Building: From the Congo to Iraq* (Santa Monica, CA: RAND Corp., 2004), 31, http://catdir.loc.gov/catdir/toc/ecip054/2004027669.html.
9 Goldstein, *Winning the War on War*, 5.
10 "The Congo was renamed as Zaire in 1971 and the Democratic Republic of the Congo in 1997".
11 Joëlle Sciboz, "Research Guides: Security Council – Quick Links: Vetoes", research starter, accessed 11 February 2019, //research.un.org/en/docs/sc/quick/veto.
12 "A few examples in Africa were the war between Ethiopia and Somalia over the Ogaden, the Nigerian civil war, and the Tanzanian intervention in Uganda".
13 Norrie Macqueen, *United Nations Peacekeeping in Africa Since 1960* (London, United Kingdom: Routledge, 2014), 14–16, 111; John MacKinlay, "The Commonwealth Monitoring Force in Zimbabwe/Rhodesia, 1979–80", in *Humanitarian Emergencies and Military Help in Africa*, ed. Thomas G. Weiss, Issues in Peacekeeping and Peacemaking (London: Palgrave Macmillan UK, 1990), 38–39, https://doi.org/10.1007/978-1-349-11582-2_3; "Commonwealth Monitoring Force, Rhodesia", accessed 15 February 2019, http://www.pcacekeepers.asn.au/operations/OpAGILA.htm. However, the international community got involved in a crisis associated with Rhodesia (a former colony of the UK) in 1979 – not by the UN, but by the Commonwealth led by the UK. In December 1979, the Commonwealth Monitoring Force (CMF) was established to supervise the implementation of the Lancaster House Agreement between the government of Southern Rhodesia and the guerilla forces of the Patriotic Front. The CMF was tasked with monitoring the agreement and resembled a UN observer mission. It assisted to conduct general election in 1980 and independence was achieved by the new Republic of Zimbabwe. Arguably, the UK"s national interest played a role for such involvement during the Cold War.
14 Goldstein, *Winning the War on War*, 74.
15 Goldstein, 115.; Department of Peacekeeping Operations, "United Nations Peacekeeping", United Nations Peacekeeping, accessed 13 February 2019, https://peacekeeping.un.org/en/node.
16 Paul D. Williams, *War & Conflict in Africa*, 2nd ed. (Cambridge UK and Maiden, USA: Polity Press, 2016), 5.
17 Williams, 31–32.
18 United Nations Security Council, "Special Report of the Secretary-General on the United Nations Mission in Liberia", Final Report (New York, 15 November 2016), 7, https://unmil.unmissions.org/sites/default/files/special_unmil_sg_report_15_november_2016.pdf.; United Nations Security Council, "Final Report of the Secretary-General on the UN Operation in Mozambique", Final Report (New York, 23 December 1994), 4, https://documents-dds-ny.un.org/doc/UNDOC/GEN/N94/515/76/PDF/N9451576.pdf?OpenElement. For instance, in Sierra Leone, a former British colony, the British were steering the affairs in the UN Security Council and were involved in the training of Sierra Leone Armed Forces through bilateral arrangements. Similarly, the French were extensively involved in the political and security affairs of Ivory Coast. The US was engaged with Liberian affairs, including screening and the training Liberian Armed Forces. South Africa was also engaged frequently in Namibian affairs. Portugal assisted with the training of Mozambique

military. However, former colonial powers assisted in bringing the parties of the conflicts to the negotiation table in order to sign peace agreements.

19 Roméo A. Dallaire, *Shake Hands with the Devil: The Failure of Humanity in Rwanda* (Toronto: Vintage Canada, 2004), 5.

20 Amy L Sayward and Jeanna Kinnebrew, "Making and Keeping the Peace: U.N. Peacekeeping and Refugee Assistance Operations", in *The United Nations in International History* (London, Oxford, New York, New Delhi, Sydney: Bloomsbury, 2017), 139.

21 "The fall of the town of Srebrenica and its environs to Bosnian Serb forces in early July 1995 made a mockery of the international community's professed commitment to safeguard regions it declared to be 'safe areas' and placed under United Nations protection in 1993. United Nations peacekeeping officials were unwilling to heed requests for support from their own forces stationed within the enclave, thus allowing Bosnian Serb forces to easily overrun it and – without interference from UN soldiers – to carry out systematic, mass executions of hundreds, possibly thousands, of civilian men and boys and to terrorize, rape, beat, execute, rob and otherwise abuse civilians being deported from the area.", Human Rights Watch 350 Fifth Avenue, 34th Floor | New York, and NY 10118–3299 USA | t 1.212.290.4700, "The Fall of Srebrenica and the Failure of UN Peacekeeping | Bosnia and Herzegovina", Human Rights Watch, 15 October 1995, https://www.hrw.org/report/1995/10/15/fall-srebrenica -and-failure-un-peacekeeping/bosnia-and-herzegovina.

22 Hilde Frafjord Johnson, "Protection of Civilians in the United Nations: A Peacekeeping Illusion?", in *United Nations Peace Operations in a Changing Global World* (Springer, 2018), 133.

23 Goldstein, *Winning the War on War*, 75.

24 William J. Durch et al., *The Brahimi Report and the Future of UN Peace Operations* (Washington, D.C.: The Henry L. Stimson Center, 2003), https://www.stimson.org/ sites/default/files/file-attachments/BR-CompleteVersion-Dec03_1.pdf.

25 Goldstein, *Winning the War on War*, 115.

26 Michael W. Doyle and Nicholas Sambanis, "Peacekeeping Operations", in *The Oxford Handbook on The United Nations*, First (New York: Oxford University Press, 2007), 334.

27 UN Department of Peacekeeping Operations, "United Nations Peacekeeping Operations: Principles and Guidelines" (United Nations, 2008), https://peacekeeping. un.org/sites/default/files/capstone_eng_0.pdf.

28 Cedric De Coning, "Civil-Military Coordination in United Nations and African Peace Operations", *The African Centre for the Constructive Resolution of Disputes (ACCORD)*, UN Complex Peace Operations, n.d., 53.

29 Williams, *War & Conflict in Africa*, 232.

30 Goldstein, *Winning the War on War*, 119.

31 Goldstein, 106.

32 Dobbins, *The UN"s Role in Nation-Building*, 272.

33 Lakhdar Brahimi, "Letter Dated 17 August 2000 from the Chairman of the Panel on United Nations Peace Operations to the Secretary-General", Report of the Panel on United Nations Peace Operations (New York, 17 August 2000), 8.

34 "High Commissioner says refugee crisis in Great Lakes Region of Africa without precedent in history of UNHCR | Meetings Coverage and Press Releases", accessed 16 September 2019, https://www.un.org/press/en/1997/19971103.GASH3433.html.

35 Kevin A. Spooner, *Canada, the Congo Crisis, and UN Peacekeeping, 1960–64* (Vancouver, Canada: UBC Press, 2009), 3.

36 United Nations Security Council, "UN Security Council Resolution 1279 (1999) – MONUC" (United Nations, November 30, 1999), http://www.un.org/en/ga/search/ view_doc.asp?symbol=S/RES/1279(1999).

37 MONUC, "Resolutions of the Security Council on MONUC – United Nations Organization Mission in the Democratic Republic of the Congo," MONUC: United Nations Organization Mission in the Democratic Republic of the Congo, 2010 1999, https://peacekeeping.un.org/sites/default/files/past/monuc/resolutions.shtml.

38 Stephen Buzdugan and Anthony Payne, *The Long Battle for Global Governance* (Routledge, 2016), 40.
39 UN Department of Public Information, "UN Yearbook: 1946–47", The Yearbook of the United Nations: The authoritative reference work on the UN System, 47 1946, 835, https://www.unmultimedia.org/searchers/yearbook/page.jsp?bookpage=180&volume=1946-47.
40 UN Department of Public Information, 835–36.
41 Macqueen, *United Nations Peacekeeping in Africa Since 1960*, 4.
42 Buzdugan and Payne, *The Long Battle for Global Governance*, 40.
43 UN Department of Public Information, "UN Yearbook: 1946–47", 837.
44 Buzdugan and Payne, *The Long Battle for Global Governance*, 41.
45 Eichelberger, *UN: The First Twenty Years*, 28.
46 Macqueen, *United Nations Peacekeeping in Africa Since 1960*, 35.
47 Spooner, *Canada, the Congo Crisis, and UN Peacekeeping, 1960–64*, 5.
48 Mateja Peter, "Peacekeeping: Resilience of an Idea", in *United Nations Peace Operations in a Changing Global World*, ed. Cedric De Coning (Springer, 2018), 30.
49 Jeanne M. Haskin, *The Tragic State of the Congo: From Decolonization to Dictatorship* (New York: Algora Publishing, 2005), 20–21.
50 Spooner, *Canada, the Congo Crisis, and UN Peacekeeping, 1960–64*, 6–7.
51 Nicole Hobbs, "The UN and the Congo Crisis of 1960", *Yale University EliScholar – A Digital Platform for Scholarly Publishing at Yale*, 2014, 14; Spooner, *Canada, the Congo Crisis, and UN Peacekeeping, 1960–64*, 26–27.
52 Spooner, *Canada, the Congo Crisis, and UN Peacekeeping, 1960–64*, 3.
53 O'Sullivan, *The United Nations*, 69.
54 Macqueen, *United Nations Peacekeeping in Africa Since 1960*, 38–39.
55 Macqueen, 39.
56 "ONUC", accessed 30 January 2018, https://peacekeeping.un.org/sites/default/files/past/onucB.htm.
57 Terry M. Mays, *Historical Dictionary of Multinational Peacekeeping* (Scarecrow Press, 2010), 321.
58 United Nations, "ONUC Mandate", UN peacekeeping, Republic of the Congo – ONUC, 14 July 1960, https://peacekeeping.un.org/sites/default/files/past/onucM.htm.
59 ONUC Staff New York, "Report of the United Nations Operation in the Congo as on May 1, 1963", Yearly (New York: United Nations, 1 May 1963), MG 30, C241, Volume 32, Personal stuffs of John King Gordon, Senior Information Officer, United Nations, Library and Archives Canada, Government of Canada.
60 Philip Deane, "A UN Failure in Congo May Depose Hammarskjold", *Toronto Global and Mail*, 2 February 1961, RG 25, Volume 5221, Library and Archives Canada, Government of Canada.
61 Evan Luard, *A History of the United Nations, Volume 2: The Age of Decolonization, 1955–1965* (London: Macmillan, 1989), 217–39.
62 Luard, 240.
63 Haskin, *The Tragic State of the Congo: From Decolonization to Dictatorship*, 26–27.
64 Macqueen, *United Nations Peacekeeping in Africa Since 1960*, 47–51; Spooner, *Canada, the Congo Crisis, and UN Peacekeeping, 1960–64*, 5.
65 Luard, *A History of the United Nations, Volume 2: The Age of Decolonization, 1955–1965*, 243–56.
66 Spooner, *Canada, the Congo Crisis, and UN Peacekeeping, 1960–64*, 115–16.
67 Lise A. Namikas, *Battleground Africa: Cold War in the Congo, 1960–1965*, Cold War International History Project Series (Washington, D.C.: Woodrow Wilson Center Press, 2013), 125.
68 Ludo de Witte, *The Assassination of Lumumba* (Verso, 2002), 17.
69 Macqueen, *United Nations Peacekeeping in Africa Since 1960*, 52.
70 Haskin, *The Tragic State of the Congo: From Decolonization to Dictatorship*, 29; Namikas, *Battleground Africa*, 125–26.

71 Luard, *A History of the United Nations, Volume 2: The Age of Decolonization, 1955–1965*, 267.
72 Namikas, *Battleground Africa*, 3.
73 Luard, *A History of the United Nations, Volume 2: The Age of Decolonization, 1955–1965*, 283.
74 Luard, 198–216.
75 Luard, 293.
76 United Nations, *The United Nations and the Congo: Some Salient Facts* (New York: United Nations, 1963), 10.
77 Arthur H. House, *The U.N. in the Congo: The Political and Civilian Efforts* (Washington: University Press of America, 1978), 60.
78 J. King. Gordon, *The United Nations in the Congo; a Quest for Peace*. ([Place of publication not identified]: Carnegie Endowment for International Peace, 1962), 61.
79 House, *The U.N. in the Congo*, 79.
80 Lacroix, Interview with the UN Under-Secretary-General of the Department of Peace Operations on "The United Nations Peace Operations in Africa", Dhaka, 24 May 2018. During the interview, the Under-Secretary-General mentioned that, the Congo example was a "top-down approach" of state-building. Not all host governments would accept this colonial method of state-building. Therefore, the approach of UN towards state-building demands the consent of the host government.
81 House, *The U.N. in the Congo*, 2.
82 House, 67.
83 United Nations, Library and Archives Canada, Government of Canada, United Nations Press Services Office of Public Information, "UN Civilian Operations in the Congo: The Largest Technical Assistance Operation Ever Undertaken", Press Release (New York, 1 March 1962), 3, MG 30, C241, Volume 32, Personal stuffs of John King Gordon, Senior Information Officer.
84 House, *The U.N. in the Congo*, 77.
85 Gordon, *The United Nations in the Congo; a Quest for Peace.*, 62; House, *The U.N. in the Congo*, 90–91.
86 House, *The U.N. in the Congo*, 80.
87 House, 86.
88 House, 178.
89 UN Archives, ONUC Staff New York, "Report of the United Nations Operation in the Congo as on May 1, 1963".
90 UN Archives, United Nations Press Services Office of Public Information, "UN Civilian Operations in the Congo: The Largest Technical Assistance Operation Ever Undertaken", 2.
91 House, *The U.N. in the Congo*, 193.
92 H. Kaufman, "Police Advisory Services and Training", 2.
93 UN Archives, ONUC Public Administration Section, "Public Administration and Police Training", Report of 1963 (Leopoldville, 1963), 3–4, S-0728, Box 31, File 2, United Nations Archives Records Management Section.
94 UN Archives, ONUC HQ, "An Interim Report – Congolese Civil Police Problems and Possible Solutions" (Leopoldville, 19 June 1963), S-0728, Box 30, File 2, United Nations Archives Records Management Section.
95 UN Archives, ONUC Public Administration Section, "Public Administration and Police Training", 1–3.
96 UN Archives, Chief Civilian Operations ONUC, "Public Administration", Letter to Under Secretary in charge of civilian affairs, ONUC, 12 December 1962, 1–4, S-0728, Box 31, File 2, United Nations Archives Records Management Section.
97 UN Archives, United Nations Press Services Office of Public Information, "UN Civilian Operations in the Congo: The Largest Technical Assistance Operation Ever Undertaken", 4–5.
98 UN Archives, ONUC Public Administration Section, "Public Administration and Police Training", 1–3.

98 United Nations peace operations in the Democratic Republic of Congo

99   UN Archives, United Nations Press Services Office of Public Information, "UN Civilian Operations in the Congo: The Largest Technical Assistance Operation Ever Undertaken", 4–5.
100 Library and Archives Canada, United Nations Civilian Operations in the Congo, "Progress Report on United Nations Civilian Operations in the Congo (1–30 November, 1960)", Monthly Report (Leopoldville, 12 May 1960), 16, RG 25, Volume 5221, Library and Archives Canada, Government of Canada.
101 UN Archives, International Monetary Fund, "Currency Unification in the Congo", 1 July 1963, 1–8, S-0728, Box 11, File 5, United Nations Archives Records Management Section.
102 UN Archives, United Nations Press Services Office of Public Information, "UN Civilian Operations in the Congo: The Largest Technical Assistance Operation Ever Undertaken", 4–5.
103 UN Archives, Military Information, "Report on Communication Network: 1963", Short Report, HQ ONUC (Leopoldville, 5 March 1963), 1, S-0728, Box 6, File 4, United Nations Archives Records Management Section.
104 UN Archives, United Nations Civilian Operations in the Congo, "Progress Report on United Nations Civilian Operations in the Congo (1–30 November, 1960)", 20.
105 UN Archives, United Nations Press Services Office of Public Information, "UN Civilian Operations in the Congo: The Largest Technical Assistance Operation Ever Undertaken", 4–5.
106 UN Archives, United Nations Civilian Operations in the Congo, "Progress Report on United Nations Civilian Operations in the Congo (1–30 November, 1960)", 19.
107 UN Archives, Bureau of Technical Assistance, ONUC, "Public Works Related Photos", Photos on public works activities by ONUC Civilian Operations (Bukavu, October 1964), S-0728–0038, Box 38, File 1, United Nations Archives Records Management Section.
108 UN Archives, Deputy Chief Civilian Operations ONUC, "Agenda for Meeting on Public Works by ONUC Civilian Operations", Letter to Assistant Director, USAID, 6 July 1963, S-0729, Box 1, File 16, United Nations Archives Records Management Section.
109 UN Archives, United Nations Civilian Operations in the Congo, "Progress Report on United Nations Civilian Operations in the Congo (1–30 November, 1960)", 10.
110 UN Archives, United Nations Press Services Office of Public Information, "UN Civilian Operations in the Congo: The Largest Technical Assistance Operation Ever Undertaken", 4–5.
111 UN Archives, United Nations Civilian Operations in the Congo, "Progress Report on United Nations Civilian Operations in the Congo (1–30 November, 1960)", 10.
112 United Nations Civilian Operations in the Congo, 22.
113 UN Archives, Senior Consultant, Bureau of Social Affairs, ONUC, "Social Research", Letter to Senior Consultant Finance, ONUC Leopoldville, 14 December 1962, S-0728, Box 36, File 4, United Nations Archives Records Management Section.
114 UN Archives, Chief Civilian Operations ONUC, "Rural Development", Letter to Senior Adviser, Social Affairs, ONUC Leopoldville, 1 December 1963, S-0728, Box 36, File 4, United Nations Archives Records Management Section.
115 UN Archives, United Nations Civilian Operations in the Congo, "Progress Report on United Nations Civilian Operations in the Congo (1–30 November, 1960)", 18.
116 UN Archives, United Nations Press Services Office of Public Information, "UN Civilian Operations in the Congo: The Largest Technical Assistance Operation Ever Undertaken", 4–5.
117 UN Archives, United Nations Civilian Operations in the Congo, "Progress Report on United Nations Civilian Operations in the Congo (1–30 November, 1960)", 15.
118 UN Archives, United Nations Press Services Office of Public Information, "UN Civilian Operations in the Congo: The Largest Technical Assistance Operation Ever Undertaken", 4–5.
119 UN Archives, Executive Chairman Technical Assistance Board UN New York, "1964 Contingency Authorization – Public Health Advisory Services and Training –

Congo", 6 January 1964, S-0728, Box 21, File 7, United Nations Archives Records Management Section.

120 UN Archives, Chief Civilian Operations ONUC, "UNESCO Programme for School Year 1964/65", Formal Message No. ONUC 2391, 22 June 1964, S-0728, Box 11, File 1, United Nations Archives Records Management Section; Chief Civilian Operations ONUC, "Financial Guarantee of UNESCO Programme for Secondary Education by the Government of the Congo", Letter to Under Secretary Special Political Affairs, UN HQ, New York, 22 June 1964, S-0728, Box 11, File 1, United Nations Archives Records Management Section.

121 UN Archives, United Nations Press Services Office of Public Information, "UN Civilian Operations in the Congo: The Largest Technical Assistance Operation Ever Undertaken", 4–5.

122 UN Archives, United Nations Civilian Operations in the Congo, "Progress Report on United Nations Civilian Operations in the Congo (1–30 November, 1960)", 7–8; Spooner, *Canada, the Congo Crisis, and UN Peacekeeping, 1960–64*, 129–30.

123 UN Archives, United Nations Civilian Operations in the Congo, "Progress Report on United Nations Civilian Operations in the Congo (1–30 November, 1960)", 7–8; Spooner, *Canada, the Congo Crisis, and UN Peacekeeping, 1960–64*, 129–30.

124 UN Archives, United Nations Press Services Office of Public Information, "UN Civilian Operations in the Congo: The Largest Technical Assistance Operation Ever Undertaken", 4–5.

125 UN Archives, FAO, "Progress Report December 1962: Agriculture", Monthly Report, ONUC Civilian Operations (Leopoldville: FAO, January 1963), Series S-0844, Box 1, File 8 and S-0728, Box 1, File 1, United Nations Archives Records Management Section; FAO ONUC, "Need for FAO Experts in the Congo", 27 May 1963, S-0728, Box 1, File 1, United Nations Archives Records Management Section.

126 House, *The U.N. in the Congo*, 174–75.

127 Spooner, *Canada, the Congo Crisis, and UN Peacekeeping, 1960–64*.

128 John Allphin Moore and Jerry Pubantz, *The New United Nations: International Organization in the Twenty-First Century* (Upper Saddle River, N.J.: Pearson Prentice Hall, 2006), 199.

129 Goldstein, *Winning the War on War*, 72.

130 House, *The U.N. in the Congo*, 186.

131 S.R. Gibbons and P. Morican, *The League of Nations and UNO* (London: Longman Group Limited, 1970), 140–47.

132 Gérard Prunier, *Africa's World War: Congo, the Rwandan Genocide, and the Making of a Continental Catastrophe* (Oxford; Oxford University Press, 2009), 76, http://catdir.loc.gov/catdir/toc/fy0903/2008020806.html.

133 Patience Kabamba, *Business of Civil War: New Forms of Life in the Debris of the Democratic Republic of Congo* (Dakar, Senegal: Codesria (Conseil pour le Developpement de la Recherche Economique et Sociale en Afrique), 2013), 30, http://ebookcentral.proquest.com/lib/unb/detail.action?docID=1190896.

134 Crawford Young and Thomas Turner, *The Rise and Decline of the Zairian State* (Madison, UNITED STATES: University of Wisconsin Press, 1985), 399, http://ebookcentral.proquest.com/lib/unb/detail.action?docID=3445288.

135 Kabamba, *Business of Civil War*, 7.

136 Alex Thomson, *An Introduction to African Politics*, 4th ed. (London and New York: Routledge, 2016), 155.

137 Thomson, *An Introduction to African Politics*, 155–56.

138 Goldstein, *Winning the War on War*, 158.

139 Macqueen, *United Nations Peacekeeping in Africa Since 1960*, 58.

140 *King Leopold's Ghost*, Video file, 2016, https://digital-films-com.proxy.hil.unb.ca/PortalPlaylists.aspx?wID=106437&xtid=118372.

141 The US secretary of state, Madeleine Albright, described this conflict in the UN Security Council as Africa's "first world war", Macqueen, *United Nations Peacekeeping in Africa Since 1960*, 88.

142 Goldstein, *Winning the War on War*, 159.
143 Prunier, *Africa's World War*, 126–27.
144 Macqueen, *United Nations Peacekeeping in Africa Since 1960*, 59.
145 Goldstein, *Winning the War on War*, 159.
146 Goldstein, *Winning the War on War*, 159–60.
147 Macqueen, *United Nations Peacekeeping in Africa Since 1960*, 87.
148 Philip Roessler and Prendergast, "Democratic Republic of Congo", in *Twenty-First-Century Peace Operations* (Washington, D.C.: US Institute of Peace, 2006), 236.
149 United Nations Security Council, "UN Panel of Experts on the Illegal Exploitation of Natural Resources and Other Forms of Wealth from the DRC", UN Documents, 23 October 2003, https://www.undocs.org/S/2003/1027. Metal tantalum is extracted from the mineral columbo tantalite (coltan), Tantalum is used in the production of electronics components, e.g., mobile phones, laptops.
150 Roessler and Prendergast, "Democratic Republic of Congo," 237.
151 Goldstein, *Winning the War on War*, 160.
152 Macqueen, *United Nations Peacekeeping in Africa Since 1960*, 88–89.
153 Goldstein, *Winning the War on War*, 162.
154 Goldstein, 163; United Nations Security Council, "UN Security Council Resolution 1279 (1999) – MONUC".
155 United Nations Security Council, "UN Security Council Resolution 1279 (1999) – MONUC."
156 Macqueen, *United Nations Peacekeeping in Africa Since 1960*, 93.
157 United Nations Security Council, "UN Security Council Resolution 1457: UN Panel of Experts on the Illegal Exploitation of Natural Resources and Other Forms of Wealth from the DRC- Based on Actions on the Report Dated 15–10–2002" (United Nations, 24 January 2003), http://www.un.org/en/ga/search/view_doc.asp?symbol=S/RES/ 1457%282003%29. The panel submitted its first report on October 15, 2002, indicating list of countries and companies associated with such illegal extraction of resources. Consequently, the UN Security Council, through Resolution 1457 of January 24, 2003, took steps which included, but were not limited to: obtaining the reactions of the governments and companies involved; verifying and assessing the lists of companies involved; recommending measures to the DRC for establishing legal frameworks, and developing policies and administrative capacities to stop such illegal exploitation.
158 United Nations Security Council, "UN Panel of Experts on the Illegal Exploitation of Natural Resources and Other Forms of Wealth from the DRC".
159 United Nations Security Council, 20.
160 United Nations Security Council, 21.
161 Goldstein, *Winning the War on War*, 161.
162 Goldstein, 165.
163 United Nations Security Council, "United Nations Security Council Resolution 1484 (2003): Authorization of Deployment of Interim Emergency Multi National Force in the Eastern DRC" (United Nations, 30 May 2003), www.un.org/en/ga/search/view_doc.asp?symbol=S/RES/1484%282003%29.
164 United Nations Security Council, "UN Security Council Resolution 1493 (2003): Expansion of MONUC in the Eastern DRC" (United Nations, 28 July 2003), http:// www.un.org/en/ga/search/view_doc.asp?symbol=S/RES/1493%282003%29.
165 Goldstein, *Winning the War on War*, 167.
166 "UN Security Council Resolution 1565 (2004) /", 1 October 2004, http://digitallibra ry.un.org/record/531854.
167 United Nations, "United Nations Organization Mission in the Democratic Republic of the Congo (MONUC)", MONUC, accessed 15 November 2018, https://peacekeeping.un.org/sites/default/files/past/monuc/index.shtml. The entire electoral process on July 30, 2006 represented one of the most complex votes the UN had ever helped organize.

168 Cedric De Coning, "Civil-Military Coordination in United Nations and African Peace Operations," *The African Centre for the Constructive Resolution of Disputes (ACCORD)*, UN Complex Peace Operations, n.d., 56.
169 Goldstein, *Winning the War on War*, 169–70.
170 United Nations Security Council, 11–12.
171 Philip Roessler and John Prendergast, "Democratic Republic of the Congo", in *Twenty-First-Century-Peace Operations*, ed. William J. Durch (Washington, D.C.: United States Institute of Peace and The Henry L. Stimson Center, 2006), 311–18.
172 Goldstein, *Winning the War on War*, 158.
173 United Nations Security Council, "Thirty-First Report of the Secretary-General on the United Nations Organization Mission in the Democratic Republic of the Congo, 2010".
174 United Nations Security Council, 2.
175 United Nations Security Council, 3.
176 United Nations Security Council, 10–11.
177 "MONUC Facts and Figures – United Nations Organization Mission in the Democratic Republic of the Congo", accessed 28 February 2019, https://peacekeeping.un.org/sites/default/files/past/monuc/facts.shtml.
178 MONUC CIMIC Unit and OCHA, "Guidelines for Interaction between MONUC Military and Humanitarian Organizations" (MONUC, Kinshasa, 8 June 2006), 7.
179 Ross Mountain, "Letter on Guidelines for Interaction between MONUC Military and Humanitarian Organizations from Humanitarian Coordinator, the DRC to UN Heads of Agencies, MONUC Heads of Offices, Heads of Sections, and NGOs", Formal letter, 4 December 2006.
180 MONUC CIMIC Unit and OCHA, "Guidelines for Interaction between MONUC Military and Humanitarian Organizations", 10.
181 MONUC CIMIC Unit and OCHA, 18.
182 MONUC CIMIC Unit and OCHA, 19.
183 MONUC CIMIC Unit, 16–17.
184 MONUC Force Headquarters, "MONUC: Force Commander's Directive on CIMIC" (MONUC, 1 June 2003).
185 MONUC Force Headquarters.
186 MONUC Force Headquarters, 20.
187 "Thousands of Congolese Benefitting from MONUC"s Quick Impact Projects – Democratic Republic of the Congo", ReliefWeb, accessed 18 January 2019, https://reliefweb.int/report/democratic-republic-congo/thousands-congolese-benefitting-monucs-quick-impact-projects.
188 "Thousands of Congolese Benefitting from MONUC"s Quick Impact Projects – Democratic Republic of the Congo".
189 Brent C Bankus, "Military-Enabled Quick Impact Projects Improve Quality of Life of Local Populations", n.d., 26; "MONUC Rehabilitating Two Important Buildings in Dungu | MONUC", accessed 24 January 2019, https://monuc.unmissions.org/en/monuc-rehabilitating-two-important-buildings-dungu; "DR Congo/Mbandaka: MONUC Finances a New Quick Impact Project in Iyonda – Democratic Republic of the Congo", ReliefWeb, accessed 18 January 2019, https://reliefweb.int/report/democratic-republic-congo/dr-congombandaka-monuc-finances-new-quick-impact-project-iyonda; "DRC: MONUC Funds Two Quick Impact Projects in Kisangani – Democratic Republic of the Congo", ReliefWeb, accessed 18 January 2019, https://reliefweb.int/report/democratic-republic-congo/drc-monuc-funds-two-quick-impact-projects-kisangani.
190 Goldstein, *Winning the War on War*, 72.

4

THE UNITED NATIONS PEACE OPERATIONS IN SUDAN

State-Building vis-à-vis Civil-Military Coordination

Introduction

Like the Democratic Republic of Congo, Sudan bore the weight of its colonial legacy over the years. In particular, the colonizers did not pay much attention to Sudan's southern territories. A similar attitude was shown by the North towards the South after independence in 1956. The geographical, climatic, and ethnic differences between the South and the rest of the country are pronounced, resulting in differences and conflicts between the North and the South. According to a UN report, Arabs (from Northern Sudan) constituted thirty-nine percent and Africans (from Southern Sudan) sixty-one percent of the population. In the 1950s, seventy percent of the population followed Islam while the remainder, predominantly in Southern Sudan, followed local faiths (twenty-five percent) or Christianity (five percent).[1] Thus, socio-ethnic differences, disparity, and economic exploitation remained as sources of North-Sudan conflict. The Southerners resorted to guerilla warfare in 1963, and armed struggle was institutionalized through the establishment of a political and military wing in 1983. The conflict involved regional and international interventions through the 1972 Addis Ababa Agreement and the 2005 Comprehensive Peace Agreement (CPA), resulting in UN's involvement from 2005–11. The UN Mission in Sudan (UNMIS) was mandated to assist in implementing that CPA.[2] After the six years' period of the mission, South Sudan emerged as a new country on the world map.

The CPA delineated a systematic approach to state-building affairs related to structures of government. It outlined the timelines of different national events such as conducting a population and general elections at all levels of government. Giving almost six years' time in the CPA to implement mandated obligations was a waste of time and money. Nearly every CPA stipulation was delayed or only partially implemented, except one event, the referendum.[3]

DOI: 10.4324/9781003275404-5

The UN mission commenced civil-military coordination (CIMIC) related activities, including projects, from 2006 for the local populations in coordination with the UN High Commissioner for Refugees and NGOs.[4] CIMIC in the UNMIS followed principles, core tasks and also integrated humanitarian aspects of the CIMIC policy of the Office for the Coordination of Humanitarian Affairs. The responsibility for coordination with national, state, and local authorities was with the respective Office for the Coordination of the Humanitarian Affairs or Resident Coordinator's Support Office involving the relevant UN-CIMIC section. Such arrangements facilitated the implementation process of the Comprehensive Peace Agreement (CPA).

CIMIC activities mainly emerged from the initiatives of TCCs military forces, though applied unevenly. The UN-CIMIC entities at the sector or local levels engaged in the coordination process and the UN-CIMIC section at the headquarters oversaw activities of the sectors. This resulted in CIMIC activities to display the presence of the UN and arguably assisted in country- and community-level state-building. Quick Impact Projects (QIPs) undertaken in Sudan by TCCs as part of CIMIC activities also contributed towards the implementation of the CPA.

UN military forces (TCCs) were aware of serious lack of education and health facilities in Southern Sudan after thirty years of civil war. Consequently, TCCs military forces focused attention towards undertaking QIPs in the education and health sectors, apart from other sectors, to assist with national-level state-building. The UN-CIMIC in Sudan also undertook a number of QIPs, which remained a model of assistance in national-level state-building during 2009–10. QIPs targeted the key areas – education, agriculture, health, sports, and energy according to the needs of local populations, mostly in Southern Sudan. The projects were broad in nature, followed a "bottom up" approach for undertaking local or community-level state-building.

This chapter focuses on the UN operations in Sudan – with the mandates of peace enforcements as well as assistance with state-building. The chapter analyzes the civil war in Sudan as a background study, and efforts undertaken by the international community to reach at the peace agreement. The chapter excludes the issues and conflicts in Darfur due to a different dimension of that conflict, which requires a separate study.[5] At the end, the UN's role in implementing the Comprehensive Peace Agreement and aiding in state-building is discussed. This study will provide an understanding of the origin of the complex peace enforcement operations and concurrent assistance with state-building of the UN. A substantial portion of the chapter is based on observations, experience, and data gathered by the author while serving in the UN Mission in Sudan as the Chief of CIMIC section.

UN Mission in Sudan (UNMIS)

When UN peace operation was underway in the DRC, the thirty year-long bloody civil war was coming to an end in Sudan. Perhaps due to the US missile

104 The United Nations Peace Operations in Sudan

attack on Khartoum in 1998, 9/11 attacks on the US, and consequent pressure by the US on Sudan, the parties in the conflict from the North and South Sudan were brought to the negotiation table by the international community at the beginning of 2001. They reached a Comprehensive Peace Agreement by the end of 2004 involving different contentious issues. The UN Security Council also adopted a resolution to support the agreement at the beginning of 2005. Thus, UN Mission in Sudan was launched with a peace enforcement mandate in mid-2005.[6]

Background

The period of modern colonization in Sudan from the nineteenth century introduced conflict arising from socio-ethnic differences, economic exploitation, failure of state-building for the Southerners, not least because widespread enslavement resulted in an identity crisis tied closely to the massive displacement of people. The geographical, climatic, and ethnic differences between the South and the rest of the country are significant, resulting in differences and conflicts between the North and the South. The episodes of violence with the highest magnitude took place within three distinct armed conflicts: the North-South civil war between 1955 and 1972, the North-South civil war between 1983 and 2005, and the Darfur civil war from 2003 to 2006.[7]

Sudan is home to nineteen major ethnic groups and almost six hundred sub-groups, amounting to more than hundred languages and dialects spoken.[8] According to the census on ethnicity in 1956, Arabs (from Northern Sudan) constituted thirty-nine percent and Africans (from Southern Sudan) sixty-one percent of the population. At twelve percent of the national population, the Dinka were at that time the largest single group from Southern Sudan.[9] Seventy percent of the population reportedly followed Islam while the remainder, predominantly in Southern Sudan, followed local faiths (twenty-five percent) or Christianity (five percent).[10] These diverse populations hindered the development of a sense of unity in Sudan. Like the Congo, Sudan has enormous natural resources both explored and unexplored, including petroleum, natural gas, gold, silver, uranium, copper, cobalt, and granite.[11]

Sudan has borne the weight of its colonial legacy over the years. Turco-Egyptian rule brought civilization and culture to Sudan but introduced slavery and atrocities, and a struggle for ivory. During Anglo-Egyptian rule, Britain alone ruled in Southern Sudan and followed its divide and rule technique by introducing Christianity and the English language to counter the strong presence of Islamic culture in the North. The British introduced a separate policy for the South in the 1920s. However, they shifted to a policy of promoting unity in Sudan after the Second World War and during the process of decolonization. None of Sudan's colonizers paid much attention to its southern territories. A similar attitude was shown by the North towards the South after independence. Southern Sudan was dependent on the north for economic, educational, and health support, but the socio-ethnic differences, disparity, and economic exploitation remained as sources of North-South conflict.

Sudan experienced many transitions of civilian and military governments after independence in 1956, with varying approaches adopted towards the South. Self-government of the South introduced by the British in 1947 gradually turned to federal status in 1954 and upon independence in 1956. The movement for self-determination emerged in 1965. The Southerners resorted to guerilla warfare starting in 1963 and an armed struggle was institutionalized by establishing a political as well as military wing (Sudan People's Liberation Movement, SPLM and Sudan People's Liberation Army, SPLA) in 1983.[12] However, the SPLM did not develop its political organization and civil services, which were essential to institutionalize their demand.

The Addis Ababa agreement in 1972 brought an end to this warfare and resulted in some autonomy for southern Sudan.[13] According to Hilde Johnson, "this agreement was too weak, granting self-government but not self-determination."[14] However, Nahuel Arenas-Garcia argued that "the Agreement gave the southern regional government a high level of autonomy under the umbrella of a central government."[15] Although Islam was adopted as state religion in 1972, Christianity and other indigenous beliefs, mainly practised in the South, were permitted. From 1972–82, Sudan was mostly peaceful, the quietest era of its troubled post-independence history. However, the central government failed to implement fully the provisions of the agreement, which led to renewed political violence. Additionally, the discovery of oil in 1978 in the bordering areas also fueled the second civil war.[16] The second protracted period of civil war that prevailed from 1983 to 2005, resulted in more than two million deaths and four million persons displaced.[17] The conflict involved continued regional as well as international intervention and the 2005 Comprehensive Peace Agreement resulting in UN involvement from 2005–11.

The 2005 Comprehensive Peace Agreement (CPA)

The Sudanese CPA was signed between Government of the Republic of the Sudan and Sudan People's Liberation Movement (SPLM)/Sudan People's Liberation Army (SPLA) on January 9, 2005. The CPA was the outcome of negotiation under the stewardship of the Inter-Governmental Authority on Development (IGAD) peace initiatives. The main theme of the CPA recognized "the right of the people of Southern Sudan to self-determination but sought to make the unity of Sudan attractive during the interim period of six years."[18] In her 2016 book, *South Sudan: The Untold Story from Independence to the Civil War*, Hilde Johnson stated that "The CPA did not grant the Southerners independence; it guaranteed self-determination."[19] The CPA provided a political framework for a ceasefire and it also recognized that "the unequal development of the peripheral areas and the distribution of wealth were issues at the root of Sudan's civil war."[20] It contained a series of agreements enacted between May 2002 and December 2004 addressing the root causes of the conflict, establishing a framework for governance for power

106 The United Nations Peace Operations in Sudan

and wealth sharing, and implementing modalities covering permanent ceasefire and security arrangements, and resolution of the conflict in Southern Kordofan, the Blue Nile States, and the Abyei Area (map at Appendix 3). The CPA stipulated that at the end of the interim period a referendum would take place for the people of South Sudan to confirm the unity of the Sudan or to vote for secession.[21]

The CPA delineated a systematic approach to state-building affairs related to structures of government. It covered establishing the National Constitutional Review Commission and forming the National Government, the Southern Sudan level of Government to exercise authority in the South, governments at the state level, and local government throughout the Sudan. The CPA also outlined the timelines of different national events such as conducting a population census by June 2007, and general elections at all levels of government by June 2008. Until elections, the current incumbent President (or his successor) was the President and the current Sudan People's Liberation Movement's Chairman (or his successor) was the First Vice President (and the President of the Government of South Sudan).[22] At the national level, seat allocations of the National Assembly were: National Congress Party (fifty-two percent), Sudan People's Liberation Movement (twenty-eight percent), other Northern political forces (fourteen percent), and other Southern political forces (six percent).[23] The Government of Southern Sudan was to function in accordance with a Southern Sudan Constitution, with seventy percent of the deputies in the legislature coming from the Sudan People's Liberation Movement, fifteen percent from the National Congress Party, and fifteen percent from other Southern political forces.[24]

The CPA addressed the most important issue of the root of the conflict: the principles of an equitable sharing of the nation's wealth. While sharing the wealth, the priority was given to post-conflict construction/reconstruction, especially in Southern Sudan and other war affected and underdeveloped areas.[25] At least two percent of oil revenue was allocated to the oil producing states/regions in proportion to output produced in such states/regions. After payments to the oil producing states/regions, fifty percent of oil revenue derived from oil producing wells in Southern Sudan was allocated to the Government of South Sudan and the remaining fifty percent to the National Government and States in Northern Sudan.[26]

The Abyei region, a bridge between the North and the South, was a contested area (maps at Appendix 3 and 4). The Misseriya and other nomadic peoples retained their traditional rights to graze cattle and move across Abyei. There are three major oilfields in the area, whose 2005 to 2007 revenues were estimated in the region of US$ 1.8 billion.[27] During the interim period of CPA, Abyei was administered by a local Executive Council (appointed by the president). The oil revenues from Abyei were also proportionately allocated. Simultaneously with the referendum for southern Sudan, the residents of Abyei would cast a separate ballot to be part of the North or South.[28] Regarding the fate of Southern Kordofan and the Blue Nile States, the CPA agreed to undertake popular consultation as a democratic right and mechanism to ascertain the views of the people of these two states.[29]

The security arrangements of the CPA covered the status of the two-armed forces in the context of a united Sudan, provided the result of the referendum on self-determination confirmed unity. It covered the formation of the future army of Sudan that would be composed from the Sudan Armed Forces and Sudan People's Liberation Army. The two forces would remain separate during the six-year interim period and as such, would be redeployed within their respective North-South boundary in a different timeline with the exception of the Joint/Integrated Units (JIU).[30]

There would be formed JIUs consisting of equal numbers from both the armies during the interim period. The JIUs would constitute a nucleus of a post referendum army of Sudan, should the result of the referendum confirm unity. Otherwise, they would be dissolved, and the component parts integrated into their respective forces.[31] JIUs were to have five divisions and one independent brigade with a total of 39,000 personnel and would protect the oilfields and oil installations.[32]

The Mandate and its implementation

The UN Security Council resolution 1590/2005 established UN Mission in Sudan (UNMIS) under Chapter VII of the UN Charter.[33] The main task of UNMIS was to support implementation of the CPA.[34] The implementation of the mandate is discussed in this chapter mainly through an examination of reports which have been prepared by the mission and UN Secretary-General. These reports covered issues related to political development, wealth-sharing, security developments, protection of civilians, and the humanitarian situation. An examination of the reports gives a picture of the process as well as the progress of the implementation of the CPA during the six-year interim period from 2005–2011.

After launching the mission in mid-2005, the implementation of the CPA gained some momentum despite the delays following the death of First Vice-President John Garang on July 30, 2005.[35] With the death of Garang, the revolutionary character of the Sudan People's Liberation Movement changed overnight and a new understanding and approach to the CPA was applied. Garang was the last major southern leader to truly believe that unity might be both possible and desirable for both countries.[36] The North also saw him as a strong leader and his absence became an obstacle to implementing the CPA.[37] Rather than working towards the revolutionary transformation of the Sudanese state as the CPA provided, after the death of Garang the focus turned to Southern Sudan and the goal of independence.[38] Nevertheless, the Government of National Unity was formed in the North on September 20, 2005 without the Sudan People's Liberation Movement, and the Government of South Sudan was also formed on October 22, 2005.[39] There was one ceasefire violation by SPLA towards the end of 2005 due to SPLA's redeployment of troops from the east.[40] During 2005, there was some progress in addressing the situation in Abyei as per the CPA, as the Abyei Boundary Commission submitted its report on July 7, 2005.[41] The UN improved the

108 The United Nations Peace Operations in Sudan

security situation and implemented confidence-building measures in Abyei by increasing its military presence. At the same time, the UN agencies started planning humanitarian and developmental programmes in Abyei to help promote peaceful coexistence of the populations.[42]

The first year of the mission also marked coordination with the neighbouring UN missions in Africa. Collaboration with neighbouring UN missions in the DRC, Chad, and Darfur helped tackle conflicts, which had connections with neighbouring countries. There were also threats of renewed conflict between Eritrea and Ethiopia which had implications for stability and security in the Sudan and the whole region. Additionally, against a background of increased violence by the Lord's Resistance Army (LRA) in southern Sudan and neighbouring countries, Ugandan and Sudanese authorities, including the Sudan People's Liberation Movement, signed a protocol to allow the Ugandan People's Defence Forces (UPDF) to pursue LRA rebels within southern Sudan.[43]

During 2006 the implementation of the CPA did not go as planned. While the basic constitutional framework envisaged in the Agreement was in place and some of the political and security institutions were functioning, both the National Congress Party (NCP) and Sudan People's Liberation Movement were reluctant to take the difficult steps required to move towards sustainable peace that was "making unity attractive." Additionally, restriction on freedom of movement for UN personnel and logistics by the Sudanese became a routine difficulty.[44]

The year 2006 was notable both for the improvement of the security situation and the removal of the Special Representative of the Secretary-General from Sudan. The security situation improved due to deployment of ninety-seven percent UN personnel by April 2006 and the general situation in Sudan remained calm with only scattered tribal clashes in some parts of southern Sudan.[45] Towards the end of 2006, attacks by the Lord's Resistance Army in Southern Sudan also declined. The relations between the UN and Sudan (the North) became tense when the Special Representative of the Secretary- General (SRSG), Jon Pronk, was declared *persona non grata* in October 2006 for issues related to Darfur.[46] This act was a unique event in the UN history, where a head of the mission was expelled by a host government and the UN accepted it. Thereafter, the mission was run by the acting SRSG for about a year and the progress of the implementation of the CPA was very slow.

Though redeployment of both the armed forces continued in 2006, the formation of Joint/Integrated Units (JIU) was delayed due to lack of logistical support related to accommodations, transportation, and budget. In several areas, poorly disciplined JIU elements were responsible for a deteriorating security situation. The border demarcation between north and south made only slow progress. On the wealth-sharing agenda, both the parties reached agreement on rules of procedure for the National Petroleum Commission and a new national currency was launched on January 9, 2006 as part of a program of financial reform.[47]

The UN mission commenced civil-military coordination (CIMIC) related activities, including projects, from 2006 for the local populations in coordination with the

The CPA provision related to the demarcation of the boundary of Abyei progressed from 2007. The report of Abyei Boundaries Commission (ABC) sought to define and demarcate the Abyei Area, but the report was rejected by both the parties who claimed that the ABC crossed the limit of their mandate in the report. As a result, both the parties referred the matter to the Permanent Court of Arbitration (PCA) in the Hague through an Agreement on July 7, 2008.[50] PCA gave its ruling on July 9, 2009 and defined the boundary of Abyei Area.[51] Both the parties accepted the ruling and a committee was then appointed for demarcation of the boundary.[52] A history of the Abyei border agreements is illustrated in map at Appendix 4.[53]

UN High Commissioner for Refugees and NGOs.[48] The UN Secretary-General's report of 2006 covered CIMIC tasks by the military component in support of local communities, including the building and equipping of a medical clinic, the construction and grading of roads, and the building of ablution facilities. Additionally, military engineers repaired sections of the Ed Damazin-Dindirou-Kurmuk road to assist the return of refugees from Ethiopia. The UN military also provided a group of local youths with vocational training.[49] All these activities were undertaken by the Troop Contributing Countries.

The CPA provision related to the demarcation of the boundary of Abyei progressed from 2007. The report of Abyei Boundaries Commission (ABC) sought to define and demarcate the Abyei Area, but the report was rejected by both the parties who claimed that the ABC crossed the limit of their mandate in the report. As a result, both the parties referred the matter to the Permanent Court of Arbitration (PCA) in the Hague through an Agreement on July 7, 2008.[50] PCA gave its ruling on July 9, 2009 and defined the boundary of Abyei Area.[51] Both the parties accepted the ruling and a committee was then appointed for demarcation of the boundary.[52] A history of the Abyei border agreements is illustrated in map at Appendix 4.[53]

The Sudan People's Liberation Movement suspended its participation in the Government of National Unity in October 2007, mentioning their dissatisfaction with implementation of the CPA.[54] This happened due to a difference of opinion between the two leaders of the north and the south. However, with the involvement of the UN the issue was resolved. In 2008, a serious violation of the ceasefire occurred in May, in Abyei, involving fighting between the two armies.[55]

From 2007 to 2009, the mission continued its mandated tasks and priority gradually shifted towards preparation for the referendum instead of efforts in state-building. The author's experience in Sudan from 2009 to 2010 bears testimony to the state-building efforts of the government being directed towards the North rather than the South, though the mission was focusing its efforts on the South as mandated.[56] However, he witnessed a contrasting scenario when he went to a remote northern rural place Muglad (map at Appendix 5), which was north of Abyei and about 850 kilometres south-west of Khartoum, to identify projects for the population. The author noticed the people were living below the poverty line; the population's livelihood depended on donkeys with no road network and few basic amenities. He faced difficulty in prioritizing projects as the local population needed everything and everything was a priority.

Similarly, only glimpses of state-building efforts in the South were visible with poor infrastructure as well as inefficient civil service officials. Southern Sudan did not have any university or major hospitals. Its people relied on the north for education and healthcare. Several times the author went to the states of Southern Sudan, namely Rumbek, Yei, Yambio, Torit, and Wau (map at Appendix 6) and found no sign of development, limited primary health care facilities, and only basic education institutes. The only modern state infrastructure was in the capital Juba. The land of

110 The United Nations Peace Operations in Sudan

Southern Sudan is fertile, agriculture and livestock are the livelihood, but the population does not have any training related to modern technical know-how.

The December 2010 Report of the Secretary-General on the UN Mission in Sudan indicated success stories of voter registration as well as considerable progress in preparations for the Southern Sudan referendum scheduled for January 9, 2011. But little progress was made on the establishment of the Abyei Referendum Commission.[57] The security environment in Southern Sudan had nonetheless shown significant improvement, with only routine allegations of border incursion by both forces. The parties identified five contested areas along the January 1, 1956 border and agreed that physical demarcation could start immediately in other areas, with the UN missions' technical and logistical assistance. As per CPA, technical preparations for the popular consultations in Southern Kordofan were in process, whereas in Blue Nile the preparations were behind schedule.[58]

Wealth sharing remained a major issue and thus the CPA addressed the sharing of wealth judiciously.[59] Delay in sharing oil revenue was a source of major frustration for the SPLM.[60] Hilde Johnson noticed, "Southern Sudan's ninety-eight percent income was from oil. Apart from a significant shortfall between 2005 and 2008, it received its share of fifty percent of net revenue."[61] During 2010 wealth sharing made a major progress when the national government transferred US$ 522.53 million in oil revenues to the Government of Southern Sudan, resulting in a cumulative total of US$ 1.82 billion between January and September 2010. The oil producing states and Abyei also received their shares in the same period: Unity State (US$ 18.04 million), Upper Nile State (US$ 36 million), Southern Kordofan State (US$ 12.63 million), and Abyei (US$ 860,000).[62] Oil revenue accounted for more than ninety percent of the Government of the South Sudan's income, of which forty percent was spent on the army.[63] Due to huge income from oil revenue, Southern Sudan did not develop other sectors to generate revenue.

The UN mission also supported the development of the Southern Sudan Police Service. The UN police provided training on referendum security and assistance with the preparation of referendum security plans. By 2010, the UN police had trained 25,840 Southern Sudan Police Service personnel, including 2,254 female officers.[64] In order to ensure a special focus on the protection of civilians and an appropriate response to disruptions in law and order, the UN police provided training to 1,448 officers of the UN formed police unit. Additionally, the UN police supported the development of a three-year strategic plan for the service, which was approved by the Minister of the Interior.[65]

The mission stepped up its protection activities in 2010 through joint civil-military patrols and initiatives to foster local-level reconciliation – part of a broader strategy pertaining to the protection of civilians.[66] Despite these efforts, 450 civilians were killed and at least 40,000 displaced in Southern Sudan in 2010.[67] However, South Sudan, Africa's second new state in the post-Cold War era, achieved its independence on July 9, 2011 after 99.57 percent of southerners voted for self-determination.[68]

The United Nations Peace Operations in Sudan **111**

Assessments on UN Mission in Sudan

The mandate of UN Mission in Sudan (UNMIS) was clear, and the CPA partly addressed the issues of the sources of conflict. The entire CPA period focused on "reaching the moment of referendum and its defining expression of Southern self-determination."[69] UNMIS attempted to address a number of causes of conflict by hosting meetings between tribal leaders to talk about the seasonal migration of people through farming areas. These discussions led to agreements, decreased tensions in Abyei and southern Sudan.[70] The failure to fully tackle aspects of border demarcation between the North and the South nonetheless generated uncertainty, tension, and violence.[71] The CPA attempted to promote wealth and power sharing in hope of preserving unity.[72] However, the outcome of UNMIS resulted in self-determination by South Sudan.

It was clear from the inception of the mission that the focus of different stakeholders, mainly the two governments, was not to make the unity of Sudan attractive. In fact, although UNMIS' mandate included a Chapter VII element, it was designed and resourced to act more as a Chapter VI mission, monitoring the implementation of the peace agreement and facilitating the delivery of humanitarian assistance between two factions trying to pull away from conflict. "Threats and spoilers to the peace agreement were expected to be addressed to by political means only."[73] Additionally, the implementation of the CPA "lagged in some cases, due to lack of capacity as well as lack of commitment."[74]

In Southern Sudan, disarmament was an effort to bring some groups under the control of the state, both by removing weapons from some groups and by authorizing the use of arms by others. Communities were reluctant to disarm and in some cases the government authorized some groups in Western Equatoria (maps at Appendix 3 and 6) to hold weapons to counter the threat of the Lord's Resistance Army. Moreover, in Lakes State (maps at Appendix 3 and 6) the government authorized the use of weapons to a group of cattle guards. In fact, "disarmament was targeted along ethnic lines, which in turn intensified local divisions."[75]

Neither of the parties felt secure in the presence of the UN, with understrength forces of about 10,000 personnel deployed over a huge area, and under-resourced. Speaker of the house of the Government of South Sudan, James Wani Igga, once commented that the UN in Sudan "was a leopard without teeth. Once the sheep know this, they will play around."[76] The capability of the UN was never enhanced during the entire period despite serious tribal clashes in Malakal (2008) and Abyei (2009).

Giving almost six years' time in the CPA to implement mandated obligations looked like a mockery, a waste of time and money. Nearly every CPA stipulation was delayed or only partially implemented, except one event, the referendum.[77] A referendum under the UN arrangement within one to two years (2006–7) could have been conducted and if the result of the referendum was in favour of self-determination of the South, the UN could have supported a state-building mission in the South from the outset.

112 The United Nations Peace Operations in Sudan

The provisions of Joint/Integrated Units (JIU) in the CPA looked like a maverick idea. During the implementation phase of the CPA, UN focused on the JIUs, which did not work. The maximum size of the JIUs reached eighty-three percent of the mandated strength by 2009, and by 2010 the size has reduced to seventy-three percent.[78] The reality, as the interim period unfolded, was that neither side took the JIUs particularly seriously, and JIUs became a security threat in most of the areas where they were deployed, rather than a provider of security.[79] While UN mission and other international partners supported various training programmes and efforts to adequately equip the forces, the fundamental problem of integration was never solved.[80] The JIUs were largely considered to be dysfunctional, as well as a serious risk to north-south stability.[81] The better option could have been to keep two armies intact to develop and remain on their in respective sides. After the referendum, if unity was preferred by the population, then two armies could have been merged.

In fact, neither the North nor the South tried for unity of Sudan despite the provisions of the CPA. Johnson argued that "the interim period failed to make the unity attractive – many international bodies emphasized that the South was unready – a few African leaders also advised more time."[82] Arguably, the North wanted more delay for the loss of significant oil revenue and the South waited for their right to self-determination. The author's impression as the Chief of Civil-Military Coordination (CIMIC) section of UNMIS (2009–10), and while working with the government officials both at the national and state level, was that the preference for self-determination was always foremost. However, local populations seemed to be looking for a united Sudan. Additionally, in the North, due to an efficient civil administration who knew their job as well, who understood the functioning of the UN and benefited from the presence of strong security intelligence, the UN mission had difficulties in terms of freedom of movement. Anything and everything had to be processed through the Government of Sudan in Khartoum.

Although the CPA committed both sides to working for unity, secession became the primary aim of the Sudan People's Liberation Movement (SPLM). "The SPLM therefore began building a strong army made up of southern militias who were offered more money than their northern Sudan counterparts. Loyalty was rewarded with a license to commit fraud, and corrupt practices became commonplace."[83] The leadership of the SPLM and Government of South Sudan did not build trust and legitimacy with the public and Southern Sudan as a whole.[84]

Hilde Johnson argued that "the interim CPA period was not used to strengthen the foundations on which the country could be built."[85] During the implementation phase of the CPA, the mission directed most of its attention to capacity and institution building to the South.[86] But these were slow and rendered insignificant so far as developing state institutions and capacity building of the Sudan People's Army (SPLA) is concerned. The SPLA was poorly equipped, and its officers lacked basic education as they were in the bush for thirty years. The Chief of CIMIC section of UNMIS[87] worked with the Minister of the State Ministry of Education of Government of Southern Sudan. The minster highlighted that the main

The United Nations Peace Operations in Sudan **113**

problem of the SPLA officers and soldiers was primary education. Thus, he involved one international NGO to work with the ministry in order to start planning and educating military personnel. Additionally, the entire population lacked education and there were limited number of schools; children were educated under the trees. As a small initiative the Chief of the CIMIC section took up a project to construct ten schools in ten states for non-formal education through the international NGO. Details of these projects related to civil-military coordination for the assistance with national-level state-building are also discussed in this chapter.

In summary, the successful completion of the Southern Sudan self-determination referendum was a significant achievement of the mission. The major focus of the mission was the elections and the referendum. However, the UN mission obscured local dynamics of Southern Sudan and that ultimately hold the key to a sustainable peace.[88] However, the referendum demonstrated how the peace and security work was effective. Despite the achievement, several key issues contained in the CPA remained unresolved or incomplete. The issues included but not limited to addressing the question of Abyei's future status, the popular consultations in Blue Nile and Southern Kordofan States, and security issues related to the disposition of armed forces along the border.[89] A UN Security Council Resolution closed the UN Mission in Sudan and opened new peace operations in South Sudan as UN Mission in South Sudan and in Abyei as UN Interim Security Force in Abyei from July 11, 2011.[90] South Sudan was not ready for independence and still needed help with state-building. Consequently, after independence the state institutions crumbled leading to renewed conflict within South Sudan in 2013.

Civil-Military Coordination (CIMIC) in the UN Mission in Sudan

The UN Mission in Sudan (UNMIS) operated from March 24, 2005 to July 9, 2011 with 14,699 personnel comprising military, police and civilians.[91] The area of operations of UNMIS was divided into six sectors comprising military forces mostly from Bangladesh, Egypt, India, Kenya, Pakistan, and Zambia. CIMIC in the UNMIS followed principles and core tasks as stipulated in the 2002 UN Department of Peacekeeping Operation Policy.[92] UNMIS also integrated humanitarian aspects of the CIMIC policy of the Office for the Coordination of Humanitarian Affairs, developed in 2003 and 2008 respectively.[93] Thus, any interaction between humanitarian and military actors was guided by "principles of mutual respect, interdependence, and the primacy of the humanitarian organizations in humanitarian work."[94] The responsibility for coordination with national, state, and local authorities was with the respective Office for the Coordination of the Humanitarian Affairs or Resident Coordinator's Support Office involving the relevant UN-CIMIC section. Such arrangements facilitated the implementation process of the Comprehensive Peace Agreement (CPA).

114 The United Nations Peace Operations in Sudan

Liaison arrangements and clear lines of communication were established by the 2008 UN-CIMIC Guidelines for Sudan.[95] In practice, coordination and liaison arrangements functioned regularly between UN military, development partners, and humanitarian organizations at the state and national level, and were conducted through coordinating bodies such as the Office for the Coordination of the Humanitarian Affairs/the Resident Coordinator's Support offices (as applicable). The UN-CIMIC section was the focal point for the military at different levels in such coordination. Additionally, considerations were given to involve female military personnel, if available, in order to address issues of cultural sensitivity and to aid with the effectiveness of assistance, whenever necessary.[96]

The UN mission in Sudan indicated the variety of information to be provided by the humanitarian stakeholders to the military forces in 2005. According to UN-CIMIC Guidelines for Sudan, the broad areas covered information relevant to the security of civilians and humanitarian staff, plans and information on humanitarian activities. Similarly, information provided by the military to the humanitarian community included any information that might have a direct impact on the security of humanitarian personnel or operations, the need of humanitarian assistance arising from patrol reports, and planned humanitarian activities of the military.[97]

In practice, information was shared jointly between the UN-CIMIC and humanitarian/ development partners at the level of the state/area Office for the Coordination of Humanitarian Affairs or Resident Coordinator's Support Office. This was usually done through weekly meetings/briefing sessions and sharing daily/weekly reports (as applicable). CIMIC activities (civil assistance activities) of the military and the civilian components of the mission were coordinated and approved under arrangements established by the Resident/Humanitarian Coordinator.

The UN Mission in Sudan faced challenges upon its establishment in 2005 with respect to CIMIC. The 2005 October Six Monthly Report of the mission raised a number of concerns in this regard, including an insufficient depth of understanding by each of the humanitarian and development communities and by the military pillar of each other's vital interests, and an insufficient CIMIC capacity at the headquarters level to manage appropriate military responses to individual issues in CIMIC. The mission mitigated these concerns by having an additional staff officer trained in CIMIC in dealing with the humanitarian and development community at the headquarters level.[98] However, such challenges persisted throughout the duration of the mission.

The UN-CIMIC section undertook a few activities to support the mandate of the peace operation from 2005. However, CIMIC activities gradually geared up. During 2009–10, such activities were in full swing as the referendum of South Sudan for self-determination or unification with Sudan was approaching. These activities served as a tool and contributed to the implementation of the 2005 Comprehensive Peace Agreement (CPA) and thereby assisted in national-level state-building. The main endeavour of CIMIC was to display the presence of the

The United Nations Peace Operations in Sudan **115**

UN even to the most remote areas, and not restrict its good work only to accessible areas. CIMIC components were more or less successful in their aims and carried out a number of activities for local populations. A summary of broad CIMIC activities in Sudan from 2005 to June 2010 is furnished in the following paragraphs after studying corresponding UN mission reports obtained from archival research (locations are shown in maps at Appendix 5 and 6 respectively).[99]

Troop contributing countries (TCCs) provided regular medical support to the local population in deployment locations. This included, but was not limited to, the establishment of occasional medical camps/clinics in remote locations, the support of the outpatient departments of hospitals in the absence of doctors and medical staff in Malakal area, and the accompaniment of patrols to provide medical support to populations in remote places. Additionally, medical assistance was provided to government departments and select UN agencies during national- or state-level programmes/campaigns. For instance, the National Polio Surveillance Project, National Immunization Day, HIV/AIDs awareness, outbreaks of dengue and yellow fever in Kadugli area, cholera outbreaks in Wau area all received CIMIC assistance.[100]

TCCs repaired roads, bridges, culverts, runways in Wau, jetties in Malakal, hand pumps, generators, and power supply lines. They also established water points and provided a continuous supply of water to UN agencies and NGOs in selected areas. Additionally, construction was undertaken for roads in different locations; outpatient clinics in Juba; classrooms, offices, toilets at the university in Ed Damazin; and electric poles were installed in Kadugli.[101]

CIMIC personnel collaborated with the UN High Commissioner for Refugees, World Food Programme, and NGOs to ensure the safe passage of returnees, and provide supervision for cholera camps in Southern Sudan. The veterinary team of Kadugli, from the Indian military units, provided veterinary-related support, including establishing a hospital in Kadugli and camps. They also supported livestock owners, covering surgical operations. Additionally, the team rendered assistance during the cattle plague epidemic in Kadugli region.

TCCs military forces provided assistance to Joint/Integrated Units (JIUs) and Joint/Integrated Police Units (JIPUs) for their capacity building programmes as per the provision of the CPA. This assistance included training on child protection, emergency medical response, carpentry, the English language, medical and surgical emergencies for the medical staff, and agricultural support. Assistance also covered mentoring in different fields, organizing sports activities, donating medicines to hospitals, and aid with transport, water, general plumbing and electrical works, medical services, the erection of tents, and other related activities. Such efforts directly contributed to the implementation of the CPA and offered a "bottom-up" approach to assisting state-building programmes.

Bangladeshi units provided agricultural expansion programmes with the help of NGOs in Juba, Torit, Yei, and Maridi, including assistance to livelihood programmes through agro-based projects as shown in Figure 4.1.[102] Other CIMIC activities included, but were not limited to, providing humanitarian assistance with convoy escorts,

FIGURE 4.1 A glimpse of CIMIC activities in 2009–10: Agro-based project in Southern Sudan by Bangladesh military unit.

as well as occasional transport support to World Food Programme and UN Children's Fund. Additionally, training on mine awareness to local NGOs and training on the English language in nursing schools were provided. Football matches between the UN military and Joint/Integrated Units, university students, street children, and national teams were also organized from time to time to keep populations away from conflict.

Donation programmes covered providing stationery and reading materials to schools, drugs to hospitals, drugs and clothes to prisons, foods to orphanages, and sewing machines to earn a livelihood. Other assistances included setting up assembly points and the provision of basic needs, such as water, for returning Internally Displaced Persons (IDPs); undertaking cleanliness drives in schools, hospitals, sports complexes, and other common places; and assisting civil and local administration in preparing for the celebration of important international and national days.

These above-mentioned CIMIC activities mainly emerged from the initiatives of TCCs military forces, where UN-CIMIC at the sector or local levels engaged in the coordination process. The UN-CIMIC section oversaw activities of the sectors and in turn kept the hierarchy officially informed (through weekly briefing sessions and periodic reports) about the role of CIMIC entities in implementing the CPA at the local level. The UN-CIMIC section also introduced the inclusion of a small paragraph covering brief CIMIC activities in the weekly report of the mission headquarters destined for UN headquarters in 2009.[103] In summary, CIMIC activities attempted to display the presence of the UN and arguably assisted in country- and community-level state-building.

These CIMIC activities were applied unevenly by TCCs. Asian contingents such as Bangladesh, India, and Pakistan were often involved in community assistance-related CIMIC activities. The Chinese contingent was seldom involved in CIMIC activities and were mostly engaged in donation programmes and repairing of roads and culverts. Not all African TCCs undertook CIMIC activities.

From the list of above-mentioned CIMIC activities, the Chief of CIMIC section discovered that by rendering medical support to local populations, CIMIC activities by the military forces were more focused, and saw more dividends. However, these efforts were not coordinated with UN agencies and concerned ministries of the host government. This medical service was rendered independently by TCCs medical elements without coordinating with any UN agencies, government offices, or other humanitarian actors. The host government was not much aware of these medical services rendered for local populations. Thus, the Chief of CIMIC section approached the most difficult coordination mechanism of providing medical support involving all concerned stakeholders including the ministries of the host government and thereby greatly assisted in national-level state-building efforts.[104]

A model of coordination by CIMIC to assist in state-building in the health sector

Troop Contributing Countries (TCCs) of the UN Mission in Sudan deployed medical doctors and paramedics in most of the states of Southern Sudan, Southern Kordofan, Blue Nile, and Abyei (map at Appendix 3) right from the beginning of the mission. There were as many as twenty-three different categories of UN medical hospitals – Level I (seventeen), Level II (five), and Level III (one) – according to the size of the area of operations, vis-à-vis the number of UN personnel who needed the medical support. Therefore, Level I medical hospitals were at the contingent level, Level II hospitals were at the sector level, and the Level III hospital was to support all UN personnel. In addition to their UN duties, the TCC medical facilities provided services to the local population, on humanitarian grounds, and on a routine basis as part of CIMIC activities. These services were not a mandated task. For instance, in 2009 alone, TCCs provided medical treatment to 7,012 Sudanese all over Sudan.[105] Additionally, a good number of medical camps/clinics were established from time to time in remote areas based on the humanitarian needs of the local population. The host government and UN agencies remained ignorant about the services provided by the UN military.[106]

To facilitate the coordination of TCCs' voluntary medical services to the Sudanese, the Chief of CIMIC section started working to collaborate with the concerned ministry of health within UNMIS deployment areas and other health officials at the state level. As a first step of coordination, a pilot project was planned by UN-CIMIC section and was discussed with the Under-Secretary Ministry of Health Southern Sudan on January 13, 2010, and subsequent bilateral consultative meetings were held with officials of the UN Children's Fund Southern Sudan Area Office. The informal approach was followed by a letter from the Chief CIMIC Section to the State Ministry of Health of the Government of Southern Sudan on January 18, 2010.[107] The pilot project involved working together on an "Assistance to Child Survival Initiative (ACSI) Programme," i.e., the vaccination of children on the National Immunization Day in Yei, a Southern Sudan state (map at Appendix 6). This programme was intended to contribute to the wider stability and national-level state-building endeavours for war-affected populations in absence of capacity on the part of the host government. Accordingly, from January 21–26, 2010, UN-CIMIC personnel, TCC medical personnel, including military observers, and other stakeholders (UN Children's Fund, medical staff from the State Ministry of Health, concerned community leaders) all joined together for the programme. Prior to that, the local officials reached out to the community to urge them to bring their children for vaccination. The programme drew children for vaccination as shown in Figure 4.2.

This programme clearly demonstrated the capability of TCC medical personnel as well as UN agency and the state government officials, but the lack of capacity was noticed amongst the health workers at the state level – they did not have doctors and adequate qualified medical staff to support such a programme. Therefore, this ACSI programme became a platform for UN-CIMIC section to draw up action plans for a greater involvement all over Sudan. The success of this collaboration became the basis for rolling out similar support in other states. A detailed coordination plan was essential at the national and state level, with the Ministry of Health at the federal and state level, UN agencies, and other partners.

FIGURE 4.2 Assistance to Child Survival Initiative (ACSI) programme, Yei, Southern Sudan, January 21–26, 2010.

The United Nations Peace Operations in Sudan 119

It then became a challenge to convince the leadership of the UN mission at different tiers, before engaging the leadership of the host government. The leadership of the mission was hesitant as the medical service was not a mandated task but part of voluntary contribution by the TCCs. It was difficult at the initial stage but the Chief of CIMIC section eventually convinced the UN leadership. The mission Chief of Staff (Farid Zarif, a former Afghan diplomat and later head of UN missions in Kosovo and Liberia) assisted the Chief of CIMIC section in this regard. The Chief of CIMIC section moved on to discussions with federal government officials. Thereafter, he met the Under-Secretary of the Federal Ministry of Foreign Affairs and discussed the details of the coordination mechanism. He highlighted the benefits to local populations vis-à-vis the capacity of the TCC medical support and the lack of capacity to provide such support at the central as well as the state level. The minister agreed and was happy about such a gesture from the UN. Later the mission headquarters approached the Federal Ministry of Foreign Affairs officially on February 8, 2010, indicating a willingness to render medical services to the local populations through a coordinated approach.[108] It included coordination involving UN agencies, and all other government and non-government stakeholders as described in the following paragraphs.

Voluntary medical support to local populations by TCC medical units in the areas where UN military was deployed continued, subject to the availability of medical staff and the approval of the applicable TCC commanding officer. However, such service would not involve any financial obligation or involvement with respect to patients or organizations, or any liability for medical services provided by the UN. TCC medical staff would work with local medical staff as part of 'capacity building' and to 'add value' to the local health services. In such cases, the respective ministries would provide general and emergency medical supplies, while UN Children's Fund would provide necessary maternal–child-health related supplies.

Additionally, TCC medical outfits would support Campaign-based programmes like National Immunization Days, ACSI, child/school health days, and malaria control programmes, as well as routine immunization activities, in order to 'add value' to the programmes. Moreover, provision was made for the training of local medical staff in the use of medical equipment available in the military medical facilities as part of 'capacity building' in the health sector.

Upon sending an official request by the mission, the Chief of CIMIC section undertook extensive meetings with the officials of the federal ministries of foreign affairs and health. This resulted in the Federal Ministry of Health issuing clearance.[109] Therefore, the Federal Ministry of Foreign Affairs officially conveyed its consent to the mission headquarters on April 20, 2010 to improve the health conditions in the rural areas.[110] However, it required the registration of the medical staff to be authenticated by the Sudanese Medical Council in order to avoid legal complications in providing medical treatment to local populations.

This unique coordination by the CIMIC section took three months to organize and marked a historic development involving the hierarchy of the host

120 The United Nations Peace Operations in Sudan

government, state government, mission leadership, and UN agencies. It can serve as a model of CIMIC in UN peace operations to assist in state-building in the nation-wide health sector and to support local populations. The UN-CIMIC section along with TCCs also played their part by undertaking different QIPs to assist in national-level state-building.

CIMIC activities by TCCs through undertaking Quick Impact Projects in Sudan

Quick Impact Projects (QIPs) undertaken in Sudan by TCCs as part of CIMIC activities also contributed towards the implementation of the CPA. There is a difference between the QIPs undertaken by the Western military forces conducting counter insurgency operations in conflict-ridden areas and the QIPs implemented under a UN mandate. The Western militaries' QIPs are a function of the combat commander's budget for utilization in CIMIC activities. For instance, arguably, some projects undertaken in Iraq and Afghanistan by the Western militaries were not generally part of a coherent national development strategy. In contrast, QIPs by the UN are civilian-led and controlled from the mission headquarters through a policy. The funds are allotted from the UN headquarters to the field missions on a yearly basis.

In Sudan, according to the 2008 Quick Impact Projects Administrative Instructions, the preference of QIPs was given to projects that supported or enabled activities related to socially oriented projects. These projects included but were not limited to conflict management/conflict resolution, electoral/referendums, improving the basic social environment, protection of civilians, logistical support/repair/maintenance of civil infrastructure, sports activities, and emergency medical services.[111] The coordination process for QIPs followed by the mission was reviewed and developed by the Chief of CIMIC section in order to establish a better coordination and a "user friendly" process. It may be noted here that until 2008 the mission was facing challenges in processing QIP proposals, implementing QIPs within a timeframe, and utilizing funds available for undertaking QIPs. Therefore, a new process was followed from 2009, as shown in Figure 4.3. The process worked well, and within a short time QIP proposals came to the mission headquarters. The process also made the UN-CIMIC section and sector CIMIC officers more involved and the UN-CIMIC section could also undertake and implement QIPs rapidly within a record timeframe. The Annual Evaluation Report (July 1, 2009 - June 30, 2010) for QIPs in UNMIS by the QIPs Management Team (August 2010), indicated that different components of the UNMIS undertook projects in the fields of education, health, agriculture, police empowerment, water and sanitation, support to IDPs and returnees, women's empowerment, community empowerment, governance and justice, youth empowerment, media promotion, food security, and support to elections.[112] These projects contributed to national-level state-building.

From 2005 to 2008, UN military forces were aware of serious lack of education and health facilities in Southern Sudan after thirty years of civil war. As a

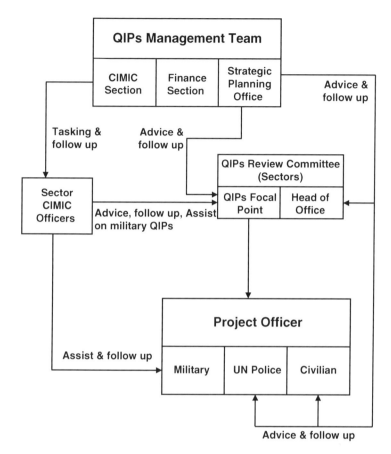

FIGURE 4.3 QIP coordination flow chart in the UNMIS.
Prepared by the Chief of CIMIC section, UNMIS, September 2010.

consequence, TCCs military forces focused attention towards undertaking QIPs in the education and health sectors, apart from other sectors, to assist with national-level state-building. A glimpse of the QIPs, undertaken by TCCs from 2005 to 2009 are outlined in table 4.1 (locations are shown in maps at Appendix 5 and 6).[113]

QIPs in Sudan by the UN-CIMIC Section in 2009–10

The UN-CIMIC in Sudan undertook a number of QIPs, which remained a model of assistance in national-level state-building during 2009–10. QIPs targeted the key areas – education, agriculture, health, sports, and energy according to the needs of local populations, mostly in Southern Sudan. The projects were broad in nature and matched a people-centric approach as recommended later by the UN High-Level Independent Panel on Peace Operations in 2015.[114] The author's personal experience as the Chief of CIMIC section in 2009–10 offered an important opportunity to witness, document, and study the latest ideas of the UN-CIMIC in practice. The Chief of

122 The United Nations Peace Operations in Sudan

TABLE 4.1 QIPs undertaken by TCCs through CIMIC in Sudan (2005–09).

Year	QIPs
2005	• The repair/renovation of primary schools in Kadugli and Kassala.
	• The construction of a bus stand in Kadugli.
2006	• The repair/renovation of a primary school in coordination with UN High Commission for Refugees in Kassala, an orphanage in Malakal, a hospital in Ed Damazin, and a teachers' training institute with a school in Juba.
	• The provision of furniture for a children's school in Juba.
	• The repair of two culverts in Malakal.
2008	• The repair/renovation of a resource centre in Maridi, a primary and secondary schools, a hospital in Abyei, the provision of medical instruments to the Torit hospital, a women's centre, and a school with two classrooms and toilets.
	• The provision of new textbooks for eight basic schools, four kindergartens, and two co-ed secondary schools near Khartoum.
	• Construction of two pit latrines in a school and an IDP Camp in Omdurman, a low-cost toilet complex for the Joint/Integrated Units, a passenger shed in an airstrip in Maridi, police posts for local police and the Joint Integrated Police Units in Abyei, and a potable water pipe distribution system in East Khartoum.
2009	• Construction of public toilets in Yambio.

Source: UNMIS, Khartoum, "UNMIS Military Update: The Force Commander's Monthly Military Report-November 2005, January 2006, May 2006, July 2006, August 2006"; UNMIS CIMIC, "UNMIS CIMIC Activities Summary-2008", Yearly report (Khartoum, 20 January 2009). (Developed by the author)

CIMIC section took a lead role in planning, assisting in approval processes, and implementing the projects. These projects were funded from the QIPs funds, coordinated with the Office for the Coordination of Humanitarian Affairs, donors, government offices, and UN agencies, and implemented by different stakeholders – military, international and local NGOs, and private sectors. The Chief of CIMIC section was the project officer for all eight projects: one in the agricultural field, two in the education sector, one in the health sector, one in sports, two in the energy sector, and one in basic services. The idea behind such initiatives was to set an example to contribute in national-level state-building, addressing a few of the roots of conflict, and thus assisting in implementing the CPA.

Project 1: Health sector

War-torn Southern Sudan was seriously lacking in the health sector. The people were deprived of basic medical services, despite the efforts from different stakeholders including TCC medical elements. The renovation of the Wau Eye Clinic (location of Wau is at map, Appendix 6), for example, through partnership with the UN-CIMIC section, the World Health Organization, the Kenyan Battalion and a private company, addressed the dire necessity of treating patients suffering from river blindness.[115]

The Wau Teaching Hospital was established in 1909 as a district hospital for Bahr el Ghazal state. The capacity of the hospital was 558 beds, in which twelve beds belonged to an eye clinic. However, they were not enough beds in the eye clinic for a highly populated region like Bahr el Ghazal. The hospital was the only referral hospital for four states: Western Bahr el Ghazal, Northern Bahr el Ghazal, Lakes, and Warrap (map at Appendix 3 and 6).

Greater Bahr El-Ghazal had alarming rate of blindness. Historically, river blindness and cataracts were the major causes of blindness in the region. The blind and their families were, therefore, socially and economically affected. As such, blindness in this region posed a major health concern. Therefore, constant functioning of the eye clinic in Wau, the state capital, was essential.

The eye clinic consisted of an eye ward, an operation theatre, a reception room, a refraction room and a specialist room. The eye clinic was very old, with worn out windows and doors. The eye ward was supposed to have nine beds, but it had only one. The roofs were old and leaking. There were cracks in the walls, and no lights or fans were available. The condition of the wiring had deteriorated. The false ceiling was also damaged in various places. The operation theatre was outdated and could hardly serve the purposes of patients. Latrines and bathrooms were in a pathetic state.[116]

The author, as Chief of CIMIC section, along with his deputy (Major Janie Desjardins from Canada), met with the Country Director of the World Health Organization (WHO) to discuss a possible collaboration between the mission and WHO to support local populations through a QIP. The Country Director informed them about the above-mentioned situation at the eye clinic, and intimated that the WHO had already procured all the necessary equipment for it. But the WHO could not

FIGURE 4.4 A glimpse of the Wau Eye Clinic before renovation.

install the equipment, due to the condition of the clinic. Renovations were not within their mandate, which only covers the provision of technical assistance. The Country Director also assured the provision of an ophthalmologist by the WHO for the clinic. The Chief of CIMIC section immediately assured him of collaboration, and thus the project was planned.

The project involved the renovation of the Wau Eye Clinic by the UN Mission and a donation of equipment from the WHO, which was worth US$ 78,066. The renovation cost of US$ 25,000 included both new furniture and repair work: thirty hospital beds, six tables and fourteen chairs for doctors and staff, electrical fittings, a water network, the repair of five pit latrines, and the installation of false ceilings.[117]

The project was jointly supervised by the Sector 2 Civil Affairs Officer (Mev Bardiqi, an Australian UN Volunteer) and the CIMIC Officer of Sector 2 (Major Bakari Kotea from the Kenyan army). The furniture was manufactured by Al-Gourashi Steel Manufacturing Factory and was transported to Wau by Mbili for Transport and Contracting Company Limited. UN-CIMIC section undertook the air transportation of the eye clinic equipment through UN cargo flights. This transportation arrangement also addressed the mandate gap of the WHO.

Projects 2 and 3: Energy sector

Abyei was one of the most contested areas during the civil war in Sudan. According to the Comprehensive Peace Agreement (CPA), the Abyei Area (maps at Appendix 4

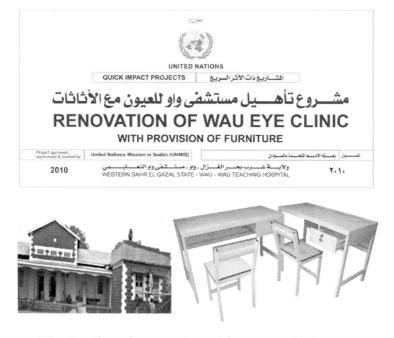

FIGURE 4.5 Wau Eye Clinic after renovation and furniture provided.

and 5) was considered a special administrative area governed directly under the institution of the presidency. In the absence of electricity in Abyei, two projects – a solar power system for the hospital and the secretariat of social services, and a separate solar power system for three schools in Abyei were planned. The project partnered the UN-CIMIC section with the Ministry of Science and Technologies, the Government of Sudan's Energy Research Institute, and the Zambian Battalion. The projects were aimed to improve Abyei's health services, education, and office management by providing solar power systems. This, in turn, would improve the basic services in the area with an intent to prevent conflict and assist in socio-economic development.

The project involved the Energy Research Institute (ERI), a governmental institution established in 1972 as an implementing partner. The mandate of ERI was to promote the adoption of renewable energy technologies to support rural development with energy-based services. ERI established a pilot line to manufacture solar power system modules. It had previously undertaken the successful commissioning and installations of solar systems in rural areas.[118]

The first project's cost was US$ 25,000, and it was supervised by the CIMIC Officer of Sector 6 (Lt Colonel John Ndhlovu from the Zambian army). The project was intended to serve a total population of about 750,000 in Abyei, also with an intent to prevent conflict and assist in socio-economic development. A glimpse of the project is shown in Figure 4.6:

FIGURE 4.6 Solar power system for the hospital and the secretariat of social services in Abyei.

As part of socio-economic development in the education sector, the second project aimed at improving education services in the three main schools in Abyei – the Abyei Secondary School, the Abyei Girls School, and the ECS Basic School – by providing solar power systems for classrooms, computers, and offices in these schools, which did not have electricity. The lack of education services compared to other part of the country were a source of conflict. The project would also assist in conducting night classes for the students at the secondary level. About 1,000 students in the Abyei area would be the direct beneficiaries of this project.

The cost of the project was US$ 25,000. Similar to the previous project, this project was also supervised by the Sector 6 CIMIC Officer. A glimpse of the project is shown in Figure 4.7.

Project 4: Sports sector

The purpose of "sport for peace" initiatives was to harness the power of sport to support the four central peacebuilding activities: building relationships, connecting individuals to communities, using sport as a communications platform, and creating a space for dialogue.[119] As Shimon Peres said, "you don't wait for

FIGURE 4.7 Solar power system for schools in Abyei.

The United Nations Peace Operations in Sudan **127**

peace in order to use sport for peace. You can use sport to achieve peace."[120] Sports alone cannot prevent conflict or build peace. But they can contribute to broader, more comprehensive efforts in a range of important ways.[121]

Sports are one of the ways to keep people engaged in order to prevent armed conflict. The Sudanese are football lovers, which the Chief of CIMIC section observed during his familiarization visits to different parts of Sudan from June to July 2009. These visits encouraged a realization that sports could be a tool for conflict prevention/resolution, as well as an approach to peacebuilding. Participation in regular sports activities could encourage and facilitate the reintegration of people affected by war. When the Chief of CIMIC section discussed the matter of supporting the community through sports activities with the officials of the Sudan Football Association, he was informed that due to the prolonged civil war, the Association faced difficulty in supporting communities with sports equipment.[122]

The Sudan Football Association is an organization which promotes football in the country. It has fifty-seven local associations throughout Sudan. The associations at the state level organize sports in their respective states. It was quickly apparent that by providing footballs to all the football associations for the IDPs and disadvantaged populations, the UN would assist in minimizing socio-ethnic differences (a source of conflict) greatly throughout the mandated areas, and thereby assist in the implementation of the CPA. The project took all affected states into consideration, and therefore, contributed to build peace through sports.

The project, Sports for peace – supporting IDPs and disadvantages populations – involved providing 610 high quality footballs (Adidas-Europass), approved by the Sudan Football Association, with a cost of US$ 24,355. It involved a partnership with UN-CIMIC, the Sudan Football Association, and a private company. The balls were purchased by a private company and transported to the Northern and Southern states. Where the UN sectors were operating, the balls were distributed by the UN and the rest of the balls were handed over to the respective local affiliates of the Sudan Football Association.[123]

It was estimated by the Sudan Football Association that almost 1,000 youths from the areas of conflict, displacement, reintegration, and rehabilitation would directly benefit as football team members. Additionally, it was anticipated that the benefit of the football matches would affect over 10,000 spectators over the year according to the population of targeted areas. As a whole, the engagement of the youth in sports would minimize or prevent their engagement in counterproductive activities that could lead to conflict.

Projects 5 and 6: Education sector

Due to decades of conflict in Sudan, thousands of children were recruited as soldiers or were associated with armed groups. These children were at a higher risk of

FIGURE 4.8 Handing over ceremony of the project: Sports for Peace.

dropping out from schools and needed assistance to reintegrate into society. Considering the devastating situation in Southern Sudan, the main challenge was to build capacity and develop the infrastructure in the education sector.

The project to build ten schools and create a sustainable environment free from exploitation and war involved a partnership between the UN-CIMIC, the UN Children's Fund, the Government of Southern Sudan, and an international NGO (Building Resources Across Communities, BRAC). BRAC was selected as an implementing partner. It obtained a license from the Government of Southern Sudan to provide non-formal education through a

The United Nations Peace Operations in Sudan   **129**

curriculum approved by the Ministry of Education.[124] BRAC's non-formal approach to education was considered a way of targeting children who were facing difficulty in getting an education. In addition, children in remote locations, and those whose lifestyles were not easily accommodated (such as poor children, street children, nomads, child soldiers) to the routines of formal schools, also needed to be educated. Moreover, the non-formal model was cost effective. The project involved the construction of ten schools in five states of Southern Sudan as illustrated in table 4.2:[125]

TABLE 4.2 Location and number of schools in Southern Sudan states.

States	County (location and number of schools)-map at Appendix 6
Central Equatoria	Yei – 5
Jonglie	Bor – 2
Lakes	Rumbek – 3

Source: Data adapted from UNMIS CIMIC QIP Proposal January 7, 2010.

The schools were also to be treated as community centres, which would be places of socialization, adolescent development and training, and community sensitization. For each school, a piece of land was provided by the local community. Under the financial support from UNMIS (US\$ 24,375) in each of the ten spots, a 24`x 14`x 8` (feet) structure was constructed for this purpose.[126] The schools were utilized for the provision of non-formal education to eight to fourteen-year-old poor or disadvantaged children, who had dropped out from schools. Additionally, the schools provided life skills and livelihood training to adolescent girls aged fifteen to twenty-four, and a space for indoor games for youths. A total of ten female facilitators/teachers were recruited and trained to conduct the school activities. Additionally, a ten-member parents' committee was formed for the management and maintenance of the school. The community utilized the space as a community centre to build a culture of peace.

The project was supervised by three designated Sector CIMIC officers according to their areas of operation – Sector 1, Bangladesh (Major Dilip Kumar) covering Juba, Torit, and Yei – Sector 2, Kenya (Major Bakari Kotea) covering Rumbek – Sector 3, India (Major Asthana) covering Bor. These officers, along with the Chief of CIMIC section, undertook the initial site visit, developed the project proposal in coordination with BRAC, monitored the progress of the project, and finally closed the project, within three months. UN Children's Fund provided books and writing materials for the students. A few of the completed schools are shown in Figure 4.9:[127]

FIGURE 4.9 A glimpse of a few completed schools of the project.

Another project in the education sector involved seating support for the school at Hai Elrahma village near Khartoum, which targeted Internally Displaced Persons (IDPs) and local populations. It was undertaken through partnership with UN-CIMIC, UN Children's Fund, the local NGO, and the Government of Sudan's Disarmament, Demobilization and Reintegration Commission.

Hai Elrahma is a village located in Khartoum State, West Omdurman, about thirty-two kilometres from Khartoum in Umbada province, Dar Alsalam. There were forty-six different tribes living together in the same area from war affected areas in the southern and western parts of the country. Because of the civil war, the IDPs notably increased in the village and thus it became one of the most densely populated areas in the province.[128] The large population of IDPs in one place with a shortage of basic needs became a source of continued clashes. Therefore, supporting basic needs and reintegrating IDPs into the society would promote peaceful coexistence between different tribes and ethnicities. This would also address minimizing socio-ethnic differences, which was one of the sources of conflict in Sudan.

The basic services that would be availed by IDPs would also directly and indirectly benefit the wider population in the area. In particular, supporting education-related programmes would keep the children away from conflict. This attempt would result in having a safer society with an improved security situation.

Only one primary school was in Hai Elrahma locality, which consisted of sixteen classes – eight for girls, and eight for boys. The number of students was 1313–754 in the boys' section, and 559 in the girls' section. There were ten teachers and nine part-timers.[129] The students and teachers did not have seats or desks in the school, as shown in the Figure 4.10:

FIGURE 4.10 Conditions of classrooms before starting the project.

The project was initiated by the North Sudan Disarmament, Demobilization and Reintegration Commission Sudan, and the Director of Administration, Hai Elrahma School. It involved providing three hundred twenty benches with worktables, fifteen chairs for teachers, fifteen desks for teachers, and two cupboards, with a cost of US $24,850. The project proposal was submitted on August 20, 2009 and the implementing partner was the Director of Hai Elrahma School, who involved the Al Gourashi Steel Factory, Khartoum as an executing agency. The UN Children's Fund provided books and writing material through the Government of Sudan. The project was handed over to the school authorities on November 3, 2009. Figure 4.11 show a glimpse of the furniture after the completion of the project.[130]

Project 7: Agricultural field

Southern Sudan was a food deficient country, where vegetable production systems and practices could not meet the food needs of the population.[131] As a result of the civil war, all the existing farms and croplands were damaged, and farming activities stopped. South Sudanese were also still ploughing manually, devoting a lot of time to farming. But the land of Southern Sudan is fertile, and Building Resources Across Communities (BRAC),[132] an international NGO, marked its presence in Southern Sudan with its goal to eradicate hunger and poverty through livelihood programmes.

The project, which was to provide food security, along with enhanced mechanical ploughing, was achieved through partnership with UN-CIMIC section, the UN Food and Agricultural Organization, BRAC, and a private company.

FIGURE 4.11 A glimpse of furniture upon completion of the project.

The United Nations Peace Operations in Sudan **133**

This project, with a cost of US$ 24,850, took place in four states of Southern Sudan and benefitted approximately 1,000 farmers. The UN mission provided funding for a tractor, BRAC hired a driver and provided a salary and fuel for the tractor, the UN Food and Agricultural Organization rendered technical assistance, and a multi-national company (SUTRAC) covered the cost to transport the tractor along the 1500-kilometre-long Khartoum-to-Juba river route. The entire affair was coordinated by the Chief of CIMIC section and supervised by the Sector CIMIC officer, Sector 1 (Major Dilip Kumar from Bangladesh), based in Juba.

The objective of the project was to provide assistance to 1,000 farmers – each farming one acre of land through a committee formed by the community – and to build their capacities in land preparation, cultivation, ploughing, sowing, and harvesting. The purpose of the project was also to increase the utilization of fallow land and to enhance food production. This project involved poor and unemployed farmers, most of them returnees, so that they could generate income. Once the project was implemented, a cross-section of people would likely remain busy, and at the same time hunger-free. This would facilitate UN efforts to keep them away from conflicts.

The details of the area covered, including number of beneficiaries (farmers) under the project, are appended in Table 4.3 (locations are shown in map at Appendix 6):[133]

In this project, BRAC provided assistance by training the farmers in agricultural practices, which commenced in April 2010. BRAC, in collaboration with the UN Food and Agricultural Organization, provided seeds of different crops and tools for cultivation and farming. Community members became the owners of the tractor through a committee (consisted of three to four members from each "payam").[134] Other communities of selected payam(s) could use the tractor through BRAC. In the first year, BRAC would bear all the expenses, including the driver's salary. But from the second year the committee would operate the tractor and would charge for ploughing to recover the expenses.[135]

TABLE 4.3. Areas and beneficiaries by providing mechanical ploughing in Southern Sudan.

State	County	Payam	Land (acre)	Beneficiaries (Farmers)
Jonglei	Bor	Bor	300	300
Central Equatoria	Juba	Northern Bari, Mangala, Rejaf	250	250
Central Equatoria	Yei	Yei	250	250
Eastern Equatoria	Torit	Nyong	200	200

Source: Data adapted from United Nations Mission in Sudan, "Memorandum of Understanding between United Nations Mission in Sudan and BRAC Southern Sudan," March 31, 2010. (Report was prepared by the author)

134 The United Nations Peace Operations in Sudan

FIGURE 4.12 BRAC official handing over tractor to the local community in Southern Sudan.

Project 8: Basic services

Al-Muglad is located near the contested area of Abyei (map at Appendix 5). The locality was one of the largest and most underserved localities in Sudan, inhabited by about 35,000 people of different ethnic groups. The area witnessed a tremendous increase in population during the civil war, during which large numbers of tribes affected by the war moved in. The area also witnessed another migration from the western states of Darfur due to the war. Additionally, oil exploration activities attracted more and more people to the area. The influx of people resulted in huge pressure on social services, health, water, and education. Most of the population earned their livelihood through animals and crops. During the civil war, the area was conflict-ridden, but during the implementation phase of the Comprehensive Peace Agreement (CPA), peace prevailed. Therefore, the security situation became conducive to undertaking socio-economic development as well as minimizing socio-ethnic differences.

During the period of May 25–27, 2010, the Chief of CIMIC section along with representatives from the Civil Affairs Section of the mission headquarters, visited Al-Muglad. Their goal was to prioritize and unify the position of local government officials and community leaders on a number of QIPs offered by the Deputy Special Representative of the Secretary General of the mission during his visit to

The United Nations Peace Operations in Sudan 135

Muglad in early March 2010. The team took along the Deputy Commissioner of Muglad's locality, community leaders, and the local representative of youth for determining and prioritizing their essential needs so that the mission could undertake viable QIPs. After detailed discussions and a site visit, the main priorities were identified as the health, sanitation, education, and water sectors.

In the health and sanitation fields, a slaughterhouse was found to be an open area lacking simple hygienic measures and therefore a serious health concern. Additionally, the locality did not have a waste management system, requiring at least a truck for the transportation of the waste to a designated place. The team noticed only a single water source was available in the area both for humans and animals – another grave health concern. Thus, a project was required to provide pure water sources for humans and animals. Moreover, the team visited one of the higher secondary schools for girls which was found to be very congested, with a huge number of students in each class without adequate furniture. The school also needed renovation work. A glimpse of these locations is shown in Figure 4.13.[136]

The project proposal of QIPs in Muglad involved a joint initiative of UNMIS CIMIC and Civil Affairs. The projects proposed were safe sanitation through the construction of a new slaughterhouse,[137] hygienic water in a water-yard through the separation of human and animal water sources,[138] waste management through the provision of a waste disposal truck,[139] and the provision of furniture and rehabilitation of the girls' school.[140] The proposal of these projects was later submitted for approval. As my tenure as the Chief of CIMIC terminated in July 2010, I handed over responsibilities to my successor to follow up on the project.

Assessment of QIPs through CIMIC in Sudan

A review of the CIMIC section's state-building projects in Sudan reveals how important it was to be proactive in overcoming the complicated post conflict operating environment. The difficulties and challenges of undertaking QIPs from 2005–2008 included (but were not limited to) the scarcity of trusted and reliable implementing partners; the non-involvement of the CIMIC personnel down to sectors' CIMIC; the non-involvement of the UN military as an implementing partner because it did not have a UN "index number,"[141] nor was it connected to mission's banking system; not following up with the projects from the mission headquarters and sector headquarters; a failure to keep all relevant stakeholders onboard. These aspects were clear from the "UNMIS QIPs tracking sheet dated August 23, 2009" – a total of twenty QIPs (US $ 400,045, out of US$ 2 million) were approved in 2007–08, but only eight projects were completed. In 2008–09, six projects (US$ 124,220 out of US$ 2 million) were approved, and only two projects were completed on time.[142]

Despite these difficulties, deliberate discussions with UN agencies, in order to study their mandate and as well as possible engagement in QIPs – revealed how the UN-CIMIC section could address the gaps in the mandate of UN agencies. In this regard, the Chief of CIMIC section's participation in training on "UN civil-military

FIGURE 4.13 Images showing state of slaughterhouse, water point and school complex.

The United Nations Peace Operations in Sudan **137**

coordination" by the Office for the Coordination of Humanitarian Affairs in Nairobi, Kenya in November 2009 helped him to understand the stakeholders, like UN agencies and NGOs. It may be mentioned here that the mission's military leadership was not willing to send him to the course, which was stipulated as a requisite qualification for the CIMIC officers. Later, due to the good office of the Deputy Special Representative of the Secretary General/Resident Coordinator/ Humanitarian Coordinator (Ms. Ameerah Huq), the Chief of CIMIC section took part in the 5-day training.

From the success story of QIPs, it was clear that appropriate selection and constant monitoring by the project officer remained the key to timely completion of a project. Additionally, frequent liaising between a project officer, the QIP focal point, and the finance focal point was essential to guide a project towards its completion. Disbursing the QIPs' funds to the account of the project officer (in this case, the author) who had the index number took much less time, and this arrangement was very convenient for implementing partners, as they got their payment instantly. The involvement of the entire UN-CIMIC apparatus – CIMIC section at the headquarters and sector CIMIC entities – paid dividends in projecting the UN all over Sudan through a well-orchestrated plan of QIPs. This process helped to assist with the implementation of the CPA, enhanced effectiveness, resulted a positive impact of CIMIC for populations in Sudan, and ultimately contributed to addressing sources of conflict by mostly engaging in national-level state-building efforts, and occasionally minimizing socio-ethnic differences.

Conclusions

Sudan gained independence from the British in 1956, and the DRC achieved independence in 1960 from the Belgians. Both the countries had colonial legacies that provided sources of conflict. For Sudan, the sources of conflict arose from slavery as well as socio-ethnic, economic, and infrastructure differences between the North and the South. This ultimately resulted in prolonged civil war from 1963 to 2004.

Sudan's conflict was due to North-South rivalry. The North suppressed and subjugated the South in all spheres of activities be it wealth sharing or state-building. However, the South lacked unity of approach due to poor leadership, which was later institutionalized from 1983. The North never wanted federal status for the South. However, the CPA changed the scenario and from 2005 to 2011, both the North and the South did not focus on unity of Sudan. Thus, the South seceded through a referendum in 2011. Separation took place while a host of major problems remained unresolved.[143]

The mission in Sudan undertook civil-military coordination tasks in different forms. In Sudan, state-building was a focus in the South, but proved inadequate to stand the country on its own after independence. CIMIC sections, UN agencies, and development partners helped to build or rebuild that local community capacity that developed nations take for granted but that had been denied in so many parts of Sudan by years of colonial underdevelopment and war. The author's direct

138 The United Nations Peace Operations in Sudan

experience and observations while serving as the Chief of CIMIC section in Sudan revealed the importance of leadership and coordination of medical support involving all stakeholders. That set of medical programmes offer an important model of UN-CIMIC coordination in the field of UN-CIMIC for national-level state-building. The approach of undertaking QIPs by section in different fields (education, health, energy, sports, agriculture, and livelihood) – taking sources of conflict into consideration – and keeping all the CIMIC apparatus and stakeholders onboard – may remain an example for peace operations to follow. Therefore, UN-CIMIC entities, if active and dynamic, can ensure that security duties and CIMIC go side by side and remain an effective tool to support the populations. CIMIC activities thus can serve the purpose of national-level state-building as well as employing a "bottom-up" approach to delivering state-building programmes.

Notes

1 United Nations, "Award in the Arbitration Regarding the Delimitation of the Abyei Area between the Government of Sudan and the Sudan People's Liberation Movement/Army", 22 July 2009, 195, legal.un.org/riaa/cases/vol_XXX/145–416.pdf.
2 United Nations Security Council, "UN Security Council Resolution 1590 (2005): Establishment of the UN Mission in Sudan" (United Nations, 24 March 2005), http://www.un.org/en/ga/search/view_doc.asp?symbol=S/RES/1590(2005).
3 Matthew Arnold and Matthew LeRiche, *South Sudan: From Revolution to Independence* (Oxford University Press, 2013), 121.
4 UNMIS, Khartoum, "Monthly Update: The Force Commander's Monthly Military Report-May 2006", Monthly Report (Khartoum, 18 June 2006), 11–12.
5 "Conflict in Darfur affected international peace and security greatly. Thus, the UN and African Union jointly launched a hybrid operation since 2007. The mission came into existence when the UN mission in Sudan was ongoing"; "UNAMID", UNAMID, accessed 30 January 2018, https://unamid.unmissions.org/.
6 United Nations Security Council, "UN Security Council Resolution 1590 (2005): Establishment of the UN Mission in Sudan".
7 Scott Straus, *Making and Unmaking Nations: War, Leadership, and Genocide in Modern Africa* (Ithaca, UNITED STATES: Cornell University Press, 2015), 232, http://ebookcentral.proquest.com/lib/unb/detail.action?docID=3138725.
8 United Nations, "Award in the Arbitration Regarding the Delimitation of the Abyei Area between the Government of Sudan and the Sudan People's Liberation Movement/Army", 195.
9 UNDP, "Leadership, Trust and Legitimacy in Southern Sudan's Transition after 2005", in *Capacity Is Development*, 2010, 7, https://www.undp.org/content/dam/aplaws/publication/en/publications/capacity-development/drivers-of-change/leadership/leadership-trust-and-legitimacy-in-southern-sudan-transition-after-2005/Leadership_trust%20and%20legitimacy%20in%20Southern%20Sudan%20transition%20after%202005.pdf. The 2008 census indicated that Dinka make up around thirty-seven percent of the south "s population, Nuer nineteen percent, Azande six percent, and other tribes smaller amounts. These figures are disputed but are indicative of the tribal shares.
10 United Nations, "Award in the Arbitration Regarding the Delimitation of the Abyei Area between the Government of Sudan and the Sudan People's Liberation Movement/Army", 195.
11 Yousif Elsamani, "Minerals Potential and Resources in Sudan," UNCTAD, November 23, 2015, http://unctad.org/meetings/en/Presentation/17OILGASMINE%20Dr%20Yousif%20Elsamani%20S1.pdf.

The United Nations Peace Operations in Sudan   139

12 Hilde F. Johnson, *South Sudan: The Untold Story from Independence to the Civil War* (I.B. Tauris, 2016).
13 Christophe R. Rossi, "The International Community, South Sudan, and the Responsibility to Protect", *International Law and Politics* 49, no. 129 (n.d.): 159.
14 Johnson, *South Sudan*.
15 Arenas-Garcia, "The UNMIS in South Sudan: Challenges & Dilemmas", 10. Although Islam was adopted as state religion, Christianity and other indigenous beliefs, mainly practised in the South, were permitted. Additionally, southern militias would be dismantled, integrating fighters into a national army.
16 Marina Ottaway and Mai El-Sadamy, "Sudan: From Conflict to Conflict," The Carnegie Papers, Middle East, no. May (2012): 5; Centre for Conflict Resolution, "Stabilising Sudan: Domestic, Sub-Regional, and Extra-Regional Challenges," Policy Advisory Group Seminar Report (South Africa, August 23, 2010), 14. Oil in commercial quantity was discovered in 1978 by Chevron near the towns of Bentiu and Heglig, close to the North-South boundary. The discovery made it all the more important for the North to maintain control, while providing added incentives to the southern rebels to fight for control of the territory.
17 Rossi, "The International Community, South Sudan, and the Responsibility to Protect", 159.
18 Joshua S. Goldstein, *Winning the War on War: The Decline of Armed Conflict Worldwide* (New York: Plume, 2012), 151.
19 Johnson, *South Sudan*. Hilde Johnson was a minister of international development for Norway and was deeply involved in the negotiations that led to the CPA in 2005. She was the Special Representative of the Secretary-General in the UN Mission in South Sudan (2011–14).
20 Arenas-Garcia, "The UNMIS in South Sudan: Challenges & Dilemmas", 11.
21 "CPA between The Government of The Republic of The Sudan and The Sudan People's Liberation Movement/Sudan People's Liberation Army", 2005, 4, https://pea ceaccords.nd.edu/sites/default/files/accords/SudanCPA.pdf.
22 "CPA", 21.
23 "CPA", 20.
24 "CPA", 21–44.
25 "CPA", 48.
26 "CPA", 54.
27 United Nations, "Award in the Arbitration Regarding the Delimitation of the Abyei Area between the Government of Sudan and the Sudan People's Liberation Movement/Army", 199.
28 "CPA", 63–69.
29 "CPA", 71–75.
30 Aly Verjee, "Sudan's Aspirational Army: A History of the Joint Integrated Units," *CIGI SSR Issue Papers* 2, no. May (2011): 4; "The Comprehensive Peace Agreement between The Government of The Republic of The Sudan and The Sudan People's Liberation Movement/Sudan People's Liberation Army," 77–90.
31 Arnold and LeRiche, *South Sudan*, 126.
32 Verjee, "Sudan's Aspirational Army: A History of the Joint Integrated Units", 4–5.
33 United Nations Security Council, "The United Nations Security Council Resolution 1590 (2005) " (United Nations, 24 March 2005), http://www.un.org/en/ga/search/view_doc.asp?symbol=S/RES/1590(2005).
34 Johnson, *South Sudan*, 21.
35 Johnson, 33.
36 Ottaway and El-Sadamy, "Carnegie Endowment for International Peace", 4.
37 Jair van der Linj, "To Paint the Nile Blue: Factors for Success and Failure of UNMIS and UNAMID", *Clingendael Institute and Radboud University Nijmegen*, 2008, 8.
38 Arnold and LeRiche, *South Sudan*, 116.

140 The United Nations Peace Operations in Sudan

39 United Nations Security Council, "Report of the Secretary-General on the Sudan", Quarterly (New York, 21 December 2005), 1, www.un.org/en/ga/search/view_doc.asp?symbol=S/2005/821.

40 United Nations Security Council, 7.

41 United Nations, "Award in the Arbitration Regarding the Delimitation of the Abyei Area between the Government of Sudan and the Sudan People's Liberation Movement/Army", 162.

42 United Nations Security Council, "Report of the Secretary-General on the Sudan", 2.

43 United Nations Security Council, 3.

44 United Nations Security Council, "The January 2007 Report of the Secretary-General on the Sudan," Quarterly (New York, 25 January 2007), 1, http://www.un.org/en/ga/search/view_doc.asp?symbol=S/2007/42.

45 UNMIS, Khartoum, "Monthly Update: The Force Commander's Monthly Military Report-May 2006", 1.

46 Linj, "To Paint the Nile Blue: Factors for Success and Failure of UNMIS and UNAMID," 11; Richard Saunders, "Strengthening International Support for Peacekeeping in Sudan: Lessons from UNMIS," 2007, 6, https://yorkspace.library.yorku.ca/xmlui/bitstream/handle/10315/7151/SAUNDERS%20-%20UNMIS%20in%20Sudan%20(Dec%202007)-2.pdf?sequence=1&isAllowed=y.

47 United Nations Security Council, "The January 2007 Report of the Secretary-General on the Sudan", 4.

48 UNMIS, Khartoum, "Monthly Update: The Force Commander's Monthly Military Report-May 2006", 11–12.

49 United Nations Security Council, "The January 2007 Report of the Secretary-General on the Sudan", 7.

50 "Arbitration Agreement between The Government of Sudan and The Sudan People's Liberation Movement/ Army on Delimiting Abyei Area", 7 July 2008, https://pca-cpa.org/wp-content/uploads/sites/175/2016/02/Arbitration-Agreement-between-The-Government-of-Sudan-and-The-Sudan-People "s-Liberation-Movement_Army-on-Delimiting-Abyei-Area-July-7-2008.pdf.

51 Arnold and LeRiche, *South Sudan*, 123.; United Nations, "Award in the Arbitration Regarding the Delimitation of the Abyei Area between the Government of Sudan and the Sudan People's Liberation Movement/Army", 413–15.

52 Department of Public Information, "United Nations Peace Operations 2009: Year in the Review", January 2010, 35.

53 "Sudan: SAS on Heglig & Abyei", The Arabist, accessed 22 January 2019, https://arabist.net/blog/2012/4/30/sudan-sas-on-heglig-abyei.html.

54 Johnson, *South Sudan,* 45.

55 Johnson, 78.

56 "The author was the Chief of CIMIC section in UNMIS in 2009–10."

57 United Nations Security Council, "The December 2010 Report of the Secretary-General on the Sudan", Quarterly (New York, 31 December 2010), 1, http://www.un.org/en/ga/search/view_doc.asp?symbol=S/2010/681.

58 United Nations Security Council, 4.

59 Centre for Conflict Resolution, "Stabilising Sudan: Domestic, Sub-Regional, and Extra-Regional Challenges," 16.

60 Arnold and LeRiche, *South Sudan*, 127.

61 Johnson, *South Sudan,* 102.

62 United Nations Security Council, "The December 2010 Report of the Secretary-General on the Sudan", 5.

63 Arnold and LeRiche, *South Sudan*, 129.

64 United Nations Security Council, "The December 2010 Report of the Secretary-General on the Sudan," 7.

65 United Nations Security Council, 8–9.

66 Hakan. Edstrom, *Political Aspirations and Perils of Security Unpacking the Military Strategy of the United Nations* (Basingstoke: Palgrave Macmillan, 2013).; United Nations Security Council, "The December 2010 Report of the Secretary-General on the Sudan", 10.

67 Edstrom, *Political Aspirations and Perils of Security Unpacking the Military Strategy of the United Nations,* 45.

68 Johnson, *South Sudan,* 124.

69 Arnold and LeRiche, *South Sudan*, 120.

70 Linj, "To Paint the Nile Blue: Factors for Success and Failure of UNMIS and UNAMID", 12–13.

71 Arenas-Garcia, "The UNMIS in South Sudan: Challenges & Dilemmas", 12.

72 Rossi, "The International Community, South Sudan, and the Responsibility to Protect", 157.

73 Arenas-Garcia, "The UNMIS in South Sudan: Challenges & Dilemmas", 16.

74 Johnson, *South Sudan,* 131.

75 Arenas-Garcia, "The UNMIS in South Sudan: Challenges & Dilemmas", 11.

76 Linj, "To Paint the Nile Blue: Factors for Success and Failure of UNMIS and UNAMID," 12.

77 Arnold and LeRiche, *South Sudan*, 121.

78 Verjee, "Sudan's Aspirational Army: A History of the Joint Integrated Units," 5; United Nations Security Council, "The December 2010 Report of the Secretary-General on the Sudan," 8.

79 Arnold and LeRiche, *South Sudan*, 126.

80 Verjee, "Sudan's Aspirational Army: A History of the Joint Integrated Units", 9.

81 Verjee, 2.

82 Johnson, *South Sudan,* 143.

83 Amanda Lucey, "Practical Pathways to Peace: Lessons from Liberia and South Sudan", n.d., 5.

84 UNDP, "Leadership, Trust and Legitimacy in Southern Sudan's Transition after 2005", 5.

85 Johnson, *South Sudan,* 146.

86 Linj, "To Paint the Nile Blue: Factors for Success and Failure of UNMIS and UNAMID", 13.

87 "The Chief of CIMIC in UNMIS was the author, who worked in UNMIS from 9 June 2009 to 8 July 2010."

88 Arenas-Garcia, "The UNMIS in South Sudan: Challenges & Dilemmas", 17.

89 United Nations Security Council, "The April 2011 Report of the Secretary-General on the Sudan", Quarterly (New York, 12 April 2011), 21–24, http://www.un.org/en/ga/search/view_doc.asp?symbol=S/2011/239.

90 Edstrom, *Political Aspirations and Perils of Security Unpacking the Military Strategy of the United Nations.*; United Nations Security Council, "The United Nations Security Council Resolution 1997 (2011)", 11 July 2011, http://www.un.org/en/ga/search/view_doc.asp?symbol=S/RES/1997(2011).

91 "UNMIS Facts and Figures – United Nations Mission in the Sudan", accessed 27 February 2019, https://peacekeeping.un.org/sites/default/files/past/unmis/facts.shtml.

92 UN Department of Peacekeeping Operations, "The United Nations Civil-Military Coordination Policy 2002' (United Nations, 9 September 2002).

93 Office for the Coordination of Humanitarian Affairs (OCHA), *Civil-Military Coordination Handbook* (Geneva: OCHA, 2003); OCHA, "Civil-Military Coordination Guidelines for Sudan" (OCHA, 1 April 2008).

94 Office for the Coordination of Humanitarian Affairs (OCHA), *Civil-Military Coordination Handbook*; OCHA, "Civil-Military Coordination Guidelines for Sudan".

95 UNMIS Resident and Humanitarian Coordinator, "United Nations Civil Military-Coordination Guidelines for Sudan", 23 April 2008.

142   The United Nations Peace Operations in Sudan

96 "Author's observation from UNMIS. There were a few female peacekeepers in UNMIS. Efforts were made to utilize them in the role to accompany patrols from time to time."

97 UNMIS Resident and Humanitarian Coordinator, "United Nations Civil Military-Coordination Guidelines for Sudan".

98 UNMIS, Khartoum, "UNMIS Military Update: The Force Commander's Six-Monthly Military Report: March-September 2005", 12.

99 UNMIS, Khartoum, "UNMIS Military Update: The Force Commander's Six Monthly Military Report: March-September 2005"; UNMIS, Khartoum, "UNMIS Military Update: The Force Commander's Monthly Military Report-October 2005", Monthly Report (Khartoum, 14 November 2005); UNMIS, Khartoum, "UNMIS Military Update: The Force Commander's Monthly Military Report-November 2005", Monthly Report (Khartoum, 5 December 2005); UNMIS, Khartoum, "UNMIS Military Update: The Force Commander's Monthly Military Report-January 2006", Monthly Report (Khartoum, 8 February 2006); UNMIS, Khartoum, "UNMIS Military Update: The Force Commander's Monthly Military Report-May 2006", Monthly Report (Khartoum, 18 June 2006); UNMIS, Khartoum, "UNMIS Military Update: The Force Commander's Monthly Military Report-July 2006", Monthly Report (Khartoum, 9 August 2006); UNMIS CIMIC, "UNMIS CIMIC Activities Summary-2008", Yearly report (Khartoum, 20 January 2009); UNMIS Military, "Agro Based Project by Military" (Southern Sudan, 1 September 2009).

100 UNMIS, Khartoum, "UNMIS Military Update: The Force Commander's Six Monthly Military Report: March-September 2005"; UNMIS, Khartoum, "UNMIS Military Update: The Force Commander's Monthly Military Report-October 2005"; UNMIS, Khartoum, "UNMIS Military Update: The Force Commander's Monthly Military Report-November 2005"; UNMIS, Khartoum, "UNMIS Military Update: The Force Commander's Monthly Military Report-January 2006"; UNMIS, Khartoum, "UNMIS Military Update: The Force Commander's Monthly Military Report-May 2006"; UNMIS, Khartoum, "UNMIS Military Update: The Force Commander's Monthly Military Report-July 2006"; UNMIS CIMIC, "UNMIS CIMIC Activities Summary-2008"; UNMIS Military, "Agro Based Project by Military".

101 UNMIS, Khartoum, "UNMIS Military Update: The Force Commander's Six Monthly Military Report: March-September 2005"; UNMIS, Khartoum, "UNMIS Military Update: The Force Commander's Monthly Military Report-October 2005"; UNMIS, Khartoum, "UNMIS Military Update: The Force Commander's Monthly Military Report-November 2005"; UNMIS, Khartoum, "UNMIS Military Update: The Force Commander's Monthly Military Report-January 2006"; UNMIS, Khartoum, "UNMIS Military Update: The Force Commander's Monthly Military Report-May 2006"; UNMIS, Khartoum, "UNMIS Military Update: The Force Commander's Monthly Military Report-July 2006"; UNMIS CIMIC, "UNMIS CIMIC Activities Summary-2008"; UNMIS Military, "Agro Based Project by Military".

102 UNMIS Military, "Agro Based Project by Military".

103 "CIMIC activities were not reported to the main mission report destined for UN headquarters before 2009. The Chief of CIMIC section ensured the inclusion of appropriate content in the mission report as such".

104 "The author (a Lieutenant Colonel from Bangladesh Army) worked as Chief of CIMIC section in UNMIS headquarters from June 9, 2009 to July 8, 2010."

105 UNMIS, Khartoum, "Note Verbale from UNMIS to Ministry of Foreign Affairs, Government of Sudan on 'UNMIS Provision of Basic Medical Services to Local Populations'", Note Verbale: OCOS/PCR/01.02/MD/10.01, 8 February 2010.

106 "The author (a Lieutenant Colonel from Bangladesh Army) worked as Chief of CIMIC section in UNMIS headquarters from June 9, 2009 to July 8, 2010."

107 Chief CIMIC Section, UNMIS, "Correspondence between UNMIS CIMIC Section and State Ministry of Health Government of Southern Sudan", Formal, 18 January 2010.

108 UNMIS, Khartoum, "Note Verbale from UNMIS to Ministry of Foreign Affairs, Government of Sudan on UNMIS Provision of Basic Medical Services to Local Populations".

109 Directorate General International Health, "Letter from Federal Ministry of Health, Republic of Sudan to Federal Ministry of Foreign Affair", Formal letter, 13 April 2010.

110 National Mechanism, Ministry of Foreign Affairs Office, Republic of Sudan, "Note Verbale from Ministry of Foreign Affairs to UNMIS", Note Verbale: MFA/PHD/23/2/295, 20 April 2010.

111 UNMIS, Khartoum, "United Nations Mission in Sudan: Quick Impact Projects Administrative Instructions" (UNMIS, 1 February 2008).

112 UNMIS QIPs Management Team, "Annual Evaluation (July 1, 2009 – June 30, 2010) QIPs in UNMIS", Yearly report (Khartoum, August 2010), https://mail.yahoo.com/d/folders/1/messages/30476?.intl=ca&.lang=en-CA&.partner=none&.src=fp.

113 UNMIS, Khartoum, "UNMIS Military Update: The Force Commander's Monthly Military Report-November 2005", 10–11; UNMIS, Khartoum, "UNMIS Military Update: The Force Commander's Monthly Military Report-January 2006", 12–13; UNMIS, Khartoum, "UNMIS Military Update: The Force Commander's Monthly Military Report-May 2006", 11–12; UNMIS, Khartoum, "UNMIS Military Update: The Force Commander's Monthly Military Report-July 2006"; UNMIS CIMIC, "UNMIS CIMIC Activities Summary-2008".

114 United Nations, "Report of the High-Level Independent Panel on Peace Operations", Review on Peace Operations (New York, 16 June 2015), 14, https://peaceoperationsreview.org/wp-content/uploads/2015/08/HIPPO_Report_1_June_2015.pdf.

115 "River blindness, also known as onchocerciasis, is a parasitic infection that can cause severe skin irritation, itching and, over time, visual impairment", "What Is River Blindness? NTDs Protecting Sight", *Sightsavers* (blog), accessed 10 March 2019, https://www.sightsavers.org/protecting-sight/ntds/what-is-river-blindness/.

116 UNMIS CIMIC, "Quick Impact Project: Renovation of the Wau Eye Clinic-Contract Deed" (UNMIS, 16 February 2010).

117 UNMIS CIMIC, "Quick Impact Project: Renovation of Wau Eye Clinic-Project Closure Report", 20 March 2010.

118 UNMIS CIMIC, "Quick Impact Proposal: Solar Power System for Hospital and Secretariat of Social Services in Abyei", 12 February 2010.

119 United Nations, "Sport and Peace: Social Inclusion, Conflict Prevention and Peace-Building" (New York: United Nations), 206–8, accessed 28 February 2019, https://www.un.org/sport/sites/www.un.org.sport/files/ckfiles/files/Chapter6_SportandPeace.pdf.

120 United Nations, Sports and Peace, 220.

121 United Nations, Sports and Peace, 206.

122 UNMIS CIMIC, "Quick Impact Project Proposal: Sports for Peace – Supporting Internally Displaced Persons and Disadvantage Populations", 22 December 2009.

123 UNMIS CIMIC, "Quick Impact Project Closure Report: Sports for Peace – Supporting Internally Displaced Persons and Disadvantage Population through Sudan Football Association", Project Closure Report (Khartoum, 24 February 2010).

124 "Memorandum of Understanding between BRAC Southern Sudan and Ministry of Education, Government of Southern Sudan", 1 October 2009.

125 UNMIS CIMIC, "UNMIS QIP Proposal: School to Build a Sustainable Environment Free from Exploitation and War", 7 January 2010.

126 Sirocco Mayom Biar Atem, "UN CIMIC Gives BRAC 58,500 SDG for School Construction" (Juba Post, 14 June 2010).

127 UNMIS CIMIC, "UNMIS QIP: Project Closure Report-School to Build a Sustainable Environment Free from Exploitation and War", Final Report (Khartoum, 30 May 2010).

128 UNMIS CIMIC, "Quick Impact Project Proposal: Seating Support for the School", 20 August 2009.

144 The United Nations Peace Operations in Sudan

129 UNMIS CIMIC.
130 UNMIS CIMIC, "Quick Impact Project Closure Report: Seating Support for the School in Hai Elrahma", Project Closure Report (Khartoum, 24 October 2009).
131 Sirocco Mayom Biar Atem, "BRAC Extending Agriculture and Food Security in Southern Sudan", *The Juba Post*, 15 March 2010.
132 Shine Theme, "BRAC in South Sudan", BRAC, accessed 27 January 2019, http://www.brac.net/south-sudan?view=page.
133 United Nations Mission in Sudan, "Memorandum of Understanding between United Nations Mission in Sudan and BRAC Southern Sudan", 31 March 2010.
134 United Nations Mission in Sudan.
135 UNMIS CIMIC, "UNMIS QIP Completion Report", 29 June 2010.
136 UNMIS CIMIC, "Quick Impact Project Proposal: Hygienic Water in Water-Yard through Separation of Human and Animal Water Source", 1 June 2010; UNMIS CIMIC, "Quick Impact Project Proposal: Rehabilitation of a Girls School and Providing Furniture", 1 June 2010; UNMIS CIMIC, "Quick Impact Project Proposal: Safe Sanitation through Construction of Slaughter House in Al-Muglad", 1 June 2010; UNMIS CIMIC, "Quick Impact Project Proposal: Waste Management through Providing Waste Disposal Truck in Al-Muglad", 1 June 2010.
137 UNMIS CIMIC, "Quick Impact Project Proposal: Safe Sanitation through Construction of Slaughter House in Al-Muglad".
138 UNMIS CIMIC, "Quick Impact Project Proposal: Hygienic Water in Water-Yard through Separation of Human and Animal Water Source".
139 UNMIS CIMIC, "Quick Impact Project Proposal: Waste Management through Providing Waste Disposal Truck in Al-Muglad".
140 UNMIS CIMIC, "Quick Impact Project Proposal: Rehabilitation of a Girls School and Providing Furniture".
141 "Index numbers are allotted to the UN staff officers and military observers, who receive pay and allowances directly from the UN headquarters financial system. Contingent members are not issued with index number and they receive pay and allowances through respective government financial system."
142 UNMIS Strategic Planning Office, "UNMIS QIPs: Tracking Sheet", 23 August 2009.
143 Ottaway and El-Sadamy, "Carnegie Endowment for International Peace", 2.

CONCLUSION

Introduction

The roots of conflict in the Democratic Republic of Congo (DRC) and Sudan mostly relate to the economic exploitation of resources, socio-ethnic differences, and a failure to address state-building. In the case of Sudan (and South Sudan since independence in 2011) and the DRC the roots of conflict and instability still exist. Recent UN-CIMIC activities were mostly engaged in "bottom-up approach" of state-building in those two long-suffering countries. Though the United Nations (UN) effort was far from perfect, the actions of the UN-CIMIC assisted with conflict resolution better than anything tried before. Moreover, the UN has developed a more sophisticated and better supported approach to peace and stability operations. Sudan and the DRC are proof of that.

The establishment of the UN Relief and Rehabilitation Administration (UNRRA) in 1943, was the first step for "United Nations" to assist with state-building for countries affected by the Second World War. After the creation of the UN in 1945, UN agencies continued in the footsteps of UNRRA. The UN itself first experimented with the art of stabilization through its peace operations after the Suez Crisis (UN Emergency Force – UNEF I: 1956–67). State-building was directly addressed by undertaking UN civilian operations in the Congo (ONUC: 1960–64). These two peace operations became the models for undertaking subsequent operations in Africa in 1989 after the Cold War ended. During the 1990s, UN tested new conflict resolution methods in a series of operations in Namibia, Mozambique, Angola, Sierra Leone, and Liberia, in the process developing a new pattern of UN assistance to nations emerging from conflict.

UN efforts in the Congo from 1960–67 and in other African conflict zones after the Cold War were driven by the goal of strategic level state-building. These efforts were "top-down" strategies which bore similarities to foreign imposed

DOI: 10.4324/9781003275404-6

146 Conclusion

colonial methods of state-building instead of partnerships with the host government. Later UN missions sought to partner and assist in state-building efforts by other agencies rather than to lead it.

The key to recent UN success appears to be state building from the "bottom up" through more focussed and assertive CIMIC operations. In the 1990s, Civil-military coordination (CIMIC) was in a stage of evolution and officially appeared in UN peace operations in the 2000s. CIMIC was applied, for instance, in the DRC (1999–2010), Sudan (2005–2011), Ivory Coast (2004–2016), and Liberia (2003–2018). These UN-CIMIC in peace operations were indirectly involved with addressing the sources of conflict related to socio-ethnic differences and state-building. Such CIMIC efforts offered a "bottom-up" solution to delivering state-building programmes at the country- and community-level.

By 2008 the UN Capstone Doctrine acknowledged that, "UN peace operations are neither designed for nor equipped to engage in long-term development, nor in capacity-building efforts."[1] However, due to the inability of other actors to take the lead in the immediate aftermath of hostilities and violence, UN peace operations could initiate or prepare the ground for longer-term institution- and capacity-building efforts through CIMIC.[2] This assistance is rendered as part of community assistance initiatives according to the 2002 and 2010 UN-CIMIC policy to support local populations due to the inadequate capacity of humanitarian stakeholders in conflict-ridden areas. After all, in an integrated UN mission, the nexus of UN peace operations components, development partners, and humanitarian stakeholders makes a strategic partnership.

CIMIC is all about sharing burdens to ensure collaboration between stakeholders in a specific context at the country- and community-level. Thus, in the DRC (UN operation: 1999–2010) and Sudan (UN mission: 2005–2011), CIMIC entities assisted in addressing the aspects-related to state-building by reaching out to populations through rebuilding livelihoods, supporting the health and education fields, and improving communal relationships. Several CIMIC activities and projects were linked to the apparatus of state-building – agriculture, education, health, and energy sectors – and assisted in instilling "local ownership" in Sudan. CIMIC activities were assumed by Troop Contributing Countries (TCCs), in addition to Quick Impact Projects (QIPs). TCCs from Asia such as Bangladesh, India, and Pakistan were mostly involved and proactive in undertaking CIMIC activities that reached out to populations in both missions. Joshua Goldstein argued that "South Asian countries have both the capacity and competence to provide more soldiers to undertake the complex integrated missions."[3] Bangladeshi peacekeepers were also "humanitarian peacekeepers and contributed a lot for local populations in Sierra Leone."[4] Not only in these missions, but also in other UN peace operations, South Asian countries remained involved in CIMIC activities on their own initiative.

Peace dividend measures (discussed in Chapter III), recommended by the "UN Panel of Experts on the illegal exploitation of natural resources and other forms of wealth from the DRC,"[5] elaborated on the importance of trust and confidence-related activities and QIPs. In the DRC, these measures were part and parcel of CIMIC activities. But these efforts require appropriate linkage with strategic and

Conclusion 147

national level planning, which was missing in the DRC. However, as a whole, this study suggests that CIMIC entities contributed to state-building at the national level and reached out to populations in the DRC and Sudan.

The 2015 High-Level Independent Panel on Peace Operations (HIPPO)[6] recommended that there be "more people-centric UN peace operations." This demanded more focused attention on community-related activities and support for national initiatives for rural and local development.[7] However, these activities needed to form part of a well-articulated strategy at the strategic and national level in any UN peace operation, with national/state level plans at the country/community level and with the UN Sustainable Development Goals (SDGs) 2030 at the strategic level. An appropriate structure to deal with issues related to CIMIC at the UN headquarters was missing. Therefore, CIMIC related aspects lacked strategic direction and follow up when requests were made from mission headquarters to UN headquarters.

Africa and Bottom-Up State-Building

This study finds that Africa is particularly receptive to bottom-up state-building. Its colonial legacy – of exploitation, arbitrarily imposed boundaries that cut across indigenous cultural, ethnic, and linguistic lines, and the limited local state-building commitments made by retreating colonial powers created or aggravated many fractures. Solutions have likewise been local and particular. One of the key roots of conflict in the DRC and Sudan have been discussed in Chapter I: a failure to address state-building. However, Cold War rivalry fueled the conflict, which greatly affected the Congo during the UN operation there in 1960–64. Internal dynamics of both the countries in terms of communal violence (in the DRC and Southern Sudan) remain a potential source of conflict.

In UN peace operations, CIMIC entities attempted to take these sources of conflict into consideration, while undertaking activities or projects for local populations. Being aware of these considerations helped CIMIC entities manage conflict resolution through directed activities and support to local populations. The failure of state-building in the DRC and Southern Sudan remains the most important source of conflict. The DRC bore testimony to the inadequate attention towards state-building during the colonial era and experienced total state collapse during 1965–97. Similarly, right from the colonial era until 2004, state-building was not addressed in Southern Sudan: leadership was not developed at different tiers, socio-economic development was lacking, people remained uneducated, health care became a serious concern, and agricultural development did not take place despite the presence of fertile lands. These factors consequently became affairs of UN peace operations.

In the Congo, the UN peace operation of 1960–64 was a model of strategic level state-building for a newly independent country. After the UN withdrew, this socio-economic development did not last long due to the corruption and inefficiency of Joseph Mobutu and his failure ultimately led to state collapse. When the

148 Conclusion

second UN peace operation was launched in 1999, the mission was engaged with ensuring a secure environment during its initial years. The mission addressed sources of conflict related to the involvement of neighbouring countries and to the exodus of refugees and of internally displaced persons. CIMIC entities in the DRC were involved in several activities, including QIPs for local populations, and thus contributed to state-building at the national level.

Comparison of CIMIC activities and QIPs in Sudan and the DRC

The policy of the UN-CIMIC was applied in both peace operations in Sudan and in the DRC. CIMIC also followed the established principles and core tasks integrating humanitarian considerations, as delineated by UN policy. The mandate of the mission in the DRC emphasized improving security situations, and thus CIMIC took time to gear up, though respective TCCs such as Bangladesh, India, Indonesia, and Nepal took initiatives to support local populations. Similarly, the CIMIC section was involved at the community level mostly because of the initiative of the TCCs' military units in Sudan.

In both missions, UN-CIMIC entities were understaffed and undertrained. UN-CIMIC staff in Sudan at the headquarters underwent institutional training, but sector CIMIC personnel were trained by the mission as and when necessary. In contrast, UN-CIMIC staff in the DRC lacked institutional training. Both the missions faced challenges related to knowledge of CIMIC by the leadership at different tiers. However, the direct involvement of the Special Representative to the Secretary-General in the DRC from the US, William Lancy Swing (2003–2007),[8] assisted in implementing QIPs and thereby played a role in promoting peace as well as state-building.

The approach of CIMIC, as well as the undertaking of QIPs by TCC military forces in both missions, helped to reach out to local populations. These efforts, though short-term, helped communities with their immediate needs. However, such efforts would yield more dividends, if they were integrated into long-term national plans. Therefore, the plan of CIMIC activities and QIPs need to be based on a yearly plan – effectively integrated with the relevant plans of the host government. Though the allocation of funds in QIPs was not enough to create an impact in a wider context, a well-articulated integration with other donors and international financial institutes would contribute to the efforts of sustained peace and development. After all, QIPs contribute to the local economy as well as to the capacity building of the local implementing partners, executing agencies and thereby assist in national-level state-building.

CIMIC activities were applied in Sudan and the DRC according to the situation, and therefore their application and effects were wide-ranging depending on the TCCs, the leaders involved, and the nature of the conflict. Both the missions in Sudan and the DRC customized respective policies on CIMIC according to the structure of the mission. In the DRC, the Office for the Coordination of Humanitarian Affairs (OCHA) and CIMIC unit jointly developed their policy,[9] but the

UNMIS policy of CIMIC was developed separately by the OCHA and CIMIC section[10]. MONUC's policy established joint protection working groups comprising UN agencies, NGOs, and UN military units at the provincial level. Thus, MONUC followed a more decentralized approach to CIMIC activities and QIPs.

The CIMIC unit at the MONUC headquarters did not involve brigade CIMIC officers at the country-level to undertake CIMIC activities. In contrast, in Sudan CIMIC section involved sector CIMIC officers to undertake broad-based projects. TCCs military units independently undertook CIMIC activities in the DRC. Thus, in MONUC, unlike UNMIS, CIMIC activities were left to TCCs without coordination. However, in MONUC, CIMIC units supported two key national-level state-building tasks – DDRRR and the electoral process. The CIMIC section in Sudan assisted in elections but was not involved in assistance with Disarmament, Demobilization, and Reintegration (DDR) related task. There DDR was mainly the responsibility of the host government and the UN mission established a separate entity to deal with issues related to DDR.[11]

In the DRC, CIMIC units assisted the Congolese army in its capacity-building programme, which was a part of security sector reform. In contrast, CIMIC sections in Sudan did not work with Sudan Armed Forces/South Sudan People's Liberation Army, but rather rendered assistance to Joint/Integrated Units and Joint Integrated Police Units to implement the Comprehensive Peace Agreement.

In Sudan, CIMIC section established a nation-wide coordination in 2010 to render medical support to local populations by TCC military forces through coordination with host governments, UN agencies, and other partners. In the DRC, TCCs' medical support to local populations was unevenly provided without much coordination with relevant health organizations.

QIPs undertaken in Sudan in 2009–10 was broad-based, encompassing several fields of state-building – education, health, agriculture, sports, and energy. On the other hand, MONUC undertook a huge number of QIPs for local populations without much linkage to broader state-building efforts. As a whole, CIMIC activities in Sudan focused on assisting in country- and community-level state-building in 2009–10, whereas in the DRC CIMIC activities assisted such state-building activities by default.

The Sudan Model and Best Practices

In Sudan, the UN peace operation gradually paid attention to state-building in the South as a measure of implementing the Comprehensive Peace Agreement (CPA). The UN peace operation in Sudan worked to develop state institutions, and a community assistance programme was undertaken in different fields of state-building. During 2009–10, several CIMIC activities and projects were linked with long-term socio-economic development initiatives. For instance, Quick Impact Projects (QIPs) for the agricultural, educational, health, and energy sectors were undertaken in line with government policies to promote socio-economic development, thus instilling "local ownership." This, in turn, assisted with national-level state-building.

150 Conclusion

CIMIC activities endeavoured to address other sources of conflict, such as socio-ethnic difference, which were prevalent in Sudan. Projects for internally displaced persons targeted the coexistence of local inhabitants of Northern Sudan with internally displaced persons from Southern Sudan through education in the same school (Chapter IV). Projects for the underserved Muglad area (map at Appendix 5) attempted to address minimizing socio-ethnic difference amongst the communities (a good number of whom were internally displaced persons who moved in during the civil war) by targeting the needs of these populations. These projects offered basic services to all, regardless of whether they were internally displaced persons or Indigenous Africans.

In UN peace operations, CIMIC activities are context-dependent with respect to the stage of the mission. The type and intensity of CIMIC activity also varies according to the security situation.[12] Therefore, areas for civil-military collaboration relate to different phases in UN peace operations and the prevailing security situation. However, the core tasks of UN-CIMIC – liaison and information-sharing – remain applicable in any security situation. Gaps in the mandate of UN agencies, vis-a-vis UN missions, can be bridged by liaising and sharing of information through CIMIC. For instance, in UN peace operations in Sudan attendance in weekly meetings of the UN Country Team and Humanitarian Country Team at the different levels by the CIMIC officers assisted in liaison and information-sharing.

An effective CIMIC results from shared understanding, which is accrued through training together. It is important to foster mutual understanding between civilian and military actors. This means providing comprehensive training on the applications of CIMIC related to humanitarian stakeholders for the military prior to deployment. Similarly, humanitarian actors should acquire an understanding of the military's objectives and culture. In Sudan, humanitarian organizations hardly trained their personnel on understanding the military's role and culture – it was the UN military forces who were proactive in organizing training on humanitarian subjects. In general, "responsibilities and lines of authority of NGOs are unclear, which creates competing agendas and overly complex sets of relationships."[13] Moreover, "with a few exceptions, humanitarian actors rarely have experience of dealing with their military counterparts, and do not have intimate knowledge of civil–military guidelines, doctrines or procedures established by the UN."[14] Though this argument was based on the scenario in South Sudan in 2013, it remains valid for any UN peace operation.

Training together remains the key to breaking the barriers of organizational culture. The training should focus on instilling a shared understanding of the situation and its problems and should coordinate efforts by all stakeholders to achieve a unity of effort. Training organized by the Office for the Coordination of Humanitarian Affairs on CIMIC was very useful to develop a shared understanding between the stakeholders (Chapter IV).[15] Additionally, this model was effective for the training of UN civil and military personnel, to equip them for the role of CIMIC officers in the military as well as humanitarian entities.

Conclusion **151**

A consistency of approach of CIMIC activities is essential across the UN mission. It was convenient for CIMIC section in Sudan to coordinate CIMIC activities and undertake QIPs with a few of the contingents from Bangladesh, India, and Pakistan. However, the Egyptian, Kenyan, and Zambian military outfits were less responsive and reactive. Thus, CIMIC activities were applied unevenly in the mission area. Arguably, the experiences of these three Asian countries in handling low intensity conflict or counter-insurgency operations gave them the required knowledge to undertake "pacification" projects for local populations. The study of UN peace operations (2001–2011) found significant problems with the training level of African military outfits in handling CIMIC activities and QIPs.

Lessons learnt

An efficient CIMIC organizational structure with qualified personnel greatly helps any UN peace operation engaged in trust and confidence building activities with the local populations. In Sudan this ensured a clear concept of CIMIC's roles and resulted in a successful outcome in its assistance with national-level state-building and the achievement of UN objectives. For instance, in UNMIS headquarters Sudan, CIMIC section had only three positions in 2009–10: Chief J9/CIMIC, Deputy J9/CIMIC, and an administrative assistant.[16] Obviously, the outfit was understaffed. Ensuring training of CIMIC personnel also remained a continuous challenge in any UN peace operation. In Sudan, two officers received institutional training on CIMIC and therefore, despite the shortage of manpower, they took CIMIC to new heights in 2009–10. Each sector had only one CIMIC officer (a Major from their respective armies) and a clerk. Below the sector level, UN military observers represented CIMIC in addition to their routine responsibilities. In UN operation in the DRC, according to Coning, "the CIMIC section was located within an operational support branch and underrepresented."[17]

The study of practice of CIMIC in Sudan and the DRC revealed that TCC military forces were needed to operate in the "humanitarian space" in conflict-ridden areas. Although humanitarian stakeholders, especially NGOs, continue to resist military forces undertaking activities related to supporting local populations, the military operates in their space from time to time. For instance, in Sudan, in 2006, one of the renowned NGOs, Doctors Without Borders/Médecins Sans Frontières (MSF), was assisting in the outpatient department of the only children's hospital in Malakal (map at Appendix 6) by providing specialist doctors, medics, and medicines. The sudden withdrawal of MSF from Malakal created a void in humanitarian coverage in the whole area. Thereafter, a Level II medical hospital Sector 3 from India took charge of the department with three doctors, including specialists, to fill the capability gap left by MSF's doctors.[18] There is no denying the fact that UN peace operations' components reached out to local populations as and when necessary, especially through their voluntary medical service.

The practice of CIMIC suggested that the best and noblest way to assist local populations in UN peace operations was to engage in medical support. The medical coordination arrangements (Chapter IV) orchestrated by CIMIC section in Sudan engaged TCC medical outfits in supporting local populations.[19] It involved coordination with ministries of the host government, the World Health Organization, the UN Children's Fund, and other stakeholders for the provisions of basic medical services to local populations. In this context, TCCs' military forces had the capacity to support local populations. In contrast, for humanitarian stakeholders it was a huge burden to support such medical services and for them it was also not practical, nor feasible, to acquire the capacity. Thus, this arrangement of coordination to support basic medical services for populations may serve as a model for future UN peace operations.

CIMIC activities and QIPs did not receive adequate budgets in Sudan and the DRC. Therefore, TCCs mostly utilized funds from their own resources to undertake CIMIC activities. Proper planning and execution of CIMIC sections' activities required a budget. CIMIC activities undertaken in Sierra Leone, Sudan, Ethiopia-Eritrea, Liberia, Ivory Coast, and the DRC, utilized funds and stores from the TCCs' own sources. For instance, military units were provided with national funds for CIMIC activities (Bangladesh in Sierra Leone, Liberia, Sudan, Ivory Coast, and DRC; China in Sudan; Egypt in Sudan; Finland in Ethiopia-Eritrea). Additionally, funds were collected from the soldiers for community support activities (e.g., Nigeria in Liberia, Uruguay in the DRC[20]), and the military shared its own stores with the communities (Pakistan in Liberia and the DRC).[21] India also deployed a specialized veterinary team in Sudan along with the infantry unit for the sole purpose of aiding local populations.[22] India also constructed a veterinary hospital in Kadugli, Sudan (supervised by the same veterinary team), from their national funds.[23] The introduction of a budget for CIMIC's activities would help CIMIC entities to meet the needs of local populations. Additionally, corporate social responsibility-related funds of private companies can be obtained through CIMIC section's efforts and thereby render befitting assistance to local populations. For instance, the transportation cost of a tractor for a QIP (Chapter IV) in Southern Sudan was provided by SUTRAC, a private company, who bore the expenditure by using their corporate social responsibility-related funds.[24]

UN peace operations assisted in developing the capacity of an implementing partner and at the same time depended on them to steer a project for local populations. In a conflict-ridden area, it was difficult to select a local NGO to implement a project. Therefore, CIMIC was a tool to involve the UN military as an efficient implementing partner, and to undertake QIPs to support local populations. After all, funds were essential to reach out and create an impact amongst local populations. Military involvement in QIPs does not mean that the military was neglecting its primary responsibility – maintaining secure environments so that others could operate in the areas of operation. The experiences of Sudan and the DRC suggested that in both missions, the UN military could be involved in CIMIC activities and QIPs without neglecting their core tasks. There was a concern in Sudan that the utilization of military engineering assets would hamper the engineering units' ability to undertake mission-essential tasks. But the military

Conclusion   **153**

engineers' capability to undertake versatile repair, renovation, and construction work had multiple benefits. Due to their expertise, military engineering assets remained an important tool to undertake any project within the shortest possible timeframe. However, these assets were needed to be utilized in QIPs in coordination with the Director Mission Support/Integrated Support Services of the mission headquarters in order to ensure mission-essential tasks were not hampered.

A joint approach of addressing challenges and difficulties of CIMIC activities and undertaking QIPs helped to keep all stakeholders on board while a UN peace operation was ongoing. In Sudan, a joint visit to areas of operation (sectors) was undertaken from July 23 to August 10, 2009, by the Strategic Planning Office – the QIP focal point and the Chief of CIMIC section. The visit aimed at ascertaining the difficulties and challenges faced by the stakeholders in the field of CIMIC as well as QIPs, and to determine future courses of action by the mission headquarters. During the visit the team interacted with different stakeholders – military, civil affairs, UN agencies, select NGOs, and government ministries – and suggested that the military take up more QIPs as an efficient and trusted implementing partner. It may be noted here that military outfits and personnel usually undertake a one-year tour of duty in UN peace operations. Thus, their involvement raises questions as to the sustainability of a project. Appropriate handing/taking over of the responsibility of the military outfits, and a couple of days of overlap between the outgoing and incoming CIMIC/project officer, may be a solution to this issue. The same issue applies to the civilian international staff (the project officers for QIPs), who, for instance, went on annual leave from Sudan. However, in both cases the handing/taking of responsibilities would be essential. Other recommendations of the joint report were adopted and followed in Sudan subsequently.[25] The following paragraphs discuss the recommendations and lessons of the joint team and continue with the analysis offered in Chapter IV.

According to the joint report, one of the requirements for successful QIPs was the involvement of an efficient implementing partner. The CIMIC section in Sudan found that NGOs are usually the reliable and efficient implementing partners for QIPs. For instance, Building Resources Across Communities (BRAC) Southern Sudan, an international NGO, helped in undertaking two QIPs (the provision of a tractor for mechanical ploughing and construction of ten schools for non-formal education) on time by duly assessing the need of local populations.[26] BRAC had efficient project management skills – identification of the project, preparation of the proposal, supervision, financial management, and implementation of the project – which are essential requisites for a successful QIP. The NGO aligned their projects with the plan of the state government, which targeted the needs of local populations and assisted in national-level state-building. They were also conversant with the UN system of project management. Additionally, because of the partnership with a private company, this company covered the transportation cost (US$ 3,500) of a tractor.[27] Moreover, the Energy Research Institute, a government establishment in the energy sector, also implemented two QIPs in the conflict-ridden Abyei area in Sudan,[28] and thus proved an efficient implementing partner.

154 Conclusion

Similarly, the appropriate selection of an executing agency was also essential for the durability and sustainability of the project. For instance, the Al Gourashi Steel Manufacturing Factory of Khartoum, Sudan, provided high quality and cost-effective furniture for the QIP in the Wau eye clinic and in a school near Khartoum in 2009–10 (Chapter IV).[29] It was the responsibility of the implementing partner to ensure the selection of the executing agency. Upon selection of this factory, the CIMIC section along with officials of the implementing partner, visited the factory to assess the capacity of the workshop. Upon satisfaction, a Memorandum of Understanding was signed. This approach helped not only with the completion of the project on time, but also assisted in the monitoring of the project and the delivery of good quality products to the clients.[30]

Addressing socio-economic development remained a key component of state-building at the national level. CIMIC section assisted in socio-economic development in Sudan. For instance, the above-mentioned executing agency had a minimum capacity and production in 2009. When CIMIC section's projects (the provision of furniture to a school and eye clinic) were underway in the factory, it had an 800 square metre area and twelve workers, with a production capacity of 300 sets of school furniture per month. Through furniture projects at the school and eye clinic, the CIMIC section changed the design and material of the furniture in order to make it more cost effective and durable. The factory came into the limelight upon completion of the projects and continued to increase its capacity. After nine years (as of January 31, 2019), the factory has increased its area and capacities to a 2,400 square metre area, with forty-five workers and with an increased capacity of 3,500 sets of school furniture per month, incorporating modern technology and equipment.[31] Therefore, CIMIC section's efforts sustained the field of socio-economic development and assisted in national-level state-building.

The "CIMIC team" approach served the purpose of envisioning a strategic idea and implementing that idea effectively at the tactical level. Thus, in turn, the presence of such a team in the mission was felt. The involvement of CIMIC personnel as the project officers in QIPs worked well in Sudan as a model for the QIP's management. The QIP of the construction of ten schools in Southern Sudan involved three sector CIMIC officers from Bangladesh, India and Kenya;[32] the project of providing a tractor for mechanical ploughing involved a sector CIMIC officer from Bangladesh;[33] the projects of solar power systems in Abyei involved a sector CIMIC officer from Zambia;[34] the project of providing furniture to a school near Khartoum involved the Deputy Chief of CIMIC section, a female officer from Canada.[35] Thus, following this model, the CIMIC section of mission headquarters of any UN peace operation can plan and initiate projects for the entire area of operation in a wider context, and can assist in implementing mandates by utilizing sector CIMIC officers to supervise projects.

The study also revealed that basic strategies of CIMIC lay with coordination, which range from coexistence to cooperation.[36] Coordination arrangements for a successful QIP required a good understanding between the QIP focal points and CIMIC officers at different tiers. Colocation of these two persons in the same

Conclusion 155

office, for better coordination and management, helped in this regard. Such colocation arrangements were practiced in Sector 3 of UN mission in Sudan, where the Sector CIMIC officer from India and the QIP focal point shared the same office.[37] This arrangement promoted a better understanding, and from the mission headquarters it was convenient to deal with Sector 3 regarding CIMIC activities and QIP affairs.

CIMIC was crucial to developing partnerships between different stakeholders in order to sustain projects. Undertaking QIPs through a CIMIC section-UN agency partnership paid dividends in Sudan, and thus its QIPs were more likely to be sustained. Additionally, the partnership between the mission and a UN agency/private company/local community worked well in Sudan. For instance, the project of renovating the eye clinic in Wau involved a partnership with World Health Organization;[38] the project of the construction of ten schools for imparting nonformal education featured a partnership with the State Ministry of Education and NGO;[39] the project of providing a tractor was partnered with the local community and NGO;[40] and the project of providing furniture to a school had a partnership with UN Children's Fund and the school authorities.[41] All these partnerships were undertaken for sustainability and instilled local ownership. Additionally, these establishments, including the designated international and local NGOs, developed a good understanding with CIMIC officers. The UN mission in Sudan could therefore reach out to local populations with more visibility.

A CIMIC entity-Civil Affairs partnership helped to engage with local communities more intimately and thereby greatly assist in implementation of the mandate. This partnership helped the governance and civil administration components connect with the stabilization and development process through CIMIC. A joint visit to identify QIPs by a CIMIC officer, a civil affairs officer, and concerned QIP focal points assisted in the correct identification of a project and its subsequent follow up. For instance, the joint visit to Muglad in Sudan by the Chief of CIMIC section was with two civil affairs officers (local staff with adequate ground knowledge, who understood the needs of the population), and community leaders.[42] Therefore, it was easy to reach a consensus on the right projects. As a result, upon identification of four QIPs for Muglad, the Chief of CIMIC section volunteered to become the project officer, and one of the civil affairs officers also offered to assist.

The barrier of organizational culture was minimized through effective engagement of CIMIC and involvement of UN agencies in peacekeeping. The CIMIC section in Sudan was able to bridge the organizational gap with respect to "blue UN" and "black UN" through undertaking QIPs with UN agencies. The leadership and knowledge of their mandates by the CIMIC section played a significant role in this regard. Similarly, the involvement of UN agencies in QIPs, as per their mandate and expertise, assisted in steering projects in the right direction. For instance, the UN Food and Agricultural Organization rendered technical assistance in an agricultural project,[43] and the UN Children's Fund provided books and writing materials for schools.[44] All this assistance rendered the QIPs very effective.

156 Conclusion

CIMIC assisted in addressing the "mandate gap" of UN agencies. UN agencies were established with respective mandates to render technical expertise and assistance in different fields of state-building. A UN agency depends on other partners to undertake a broad-based project. Therefore, CIMIC outfits assisted UN agencies by filling gaps in their mandates to realize a project. For instance, the World Health Organization procured equipment for the Wau eye clinic in South Sudan but could not undertake renovation of the clinic or provide hospital beds and other furniture, due to a gap in their mandate. Therefore, the CIMIC section filled that gap and undertook renovation works and provided hospital beds and other furniture for the eye clinic as a QIP. The clinic was therefore functional upon completion of the QIP.[45]

The involvement of CIMIC section in Sudan in any project facilitated ownership by the host government/local community. Ley Reychler in his 2010 article "Peacemaking, Peacekeeping, and Peacebuilding," argues that "Local ownership helps to achieve conflict resolution and management of conflict by involving locals in the peace processes."[46] However, projects may not be sustained if the host government or concerned local stakeholder does not monitor and support the project. For instance, the Wau eye clinic was handed over to the authority of the Government of Southern Sudan in 2010.[47] While writing this book, there was an inquisitiveness on the part of the author to check the continued sustainability of this project. Coincidentally, a Bangladeshi infantry battalion was deployed in Wau under the UN Mission in South Sudan (UNMISS) in February 2019. Upon request by the author, the CIMIC officer of the unit went to the clinic and submitted two signed reports by the administrator of the clinic and the Head of Office of the Office for the Coordination of Humanitarian Affairs Sub Office, Wau. These reports covered the status of the clinic with images.[48] According to the report, this hospital had been facing lots of difficulties since the independence of South Sudan in 2011, especially after the commencement of civil war in December 2013. The clinic was using the same furniture and equipment, although it was not in good condition due to lack of maintenance. The eye clinic faced a shortage of doctors, equipment, and medicine. At the time of reporting there was no doctor available, though on average fifty patients visit the clinic daily and are cared for by two medical assistants and two nurses, and the operation theatre was functional. A glimpse of the eye clinic (as of February 2019) is shown in Figure 5.1.

CIMIC remained an excellent area where the leadership skills of a person could be demonstrated. Jean-Pierre Lacroix, the Under Secretary-General of the Department of Peace Operations, UN Headquarters, observed during an interview with the author that, "CIMIC is all about the leadership of a person on the ground. There are policies in place, which need understanding and effective implementation. But the leader puts these into practice with his innovations."[49] However, "the mission's engagement in civil-military relations begins and ends with the leadership."[50] Sudan was thus a place to demonstrate the leadership potential of the Chief of CIMIC section. According to the statistics of UN Intranet Global, CIMIC entities as a whole undertook twelve out of two-hundred forty-

FIGURE 5.1 A glimpse of the Wau Eye Clinic, South Sudan as of February 2019. Colonel AKM Majharul Haque, Contingent Commander, "Email: Report on Present Status of the Wau Eye Clinic by Bangladesh Infantry Battalion (UNMISS)," February 13, 2019, https://mail.yahoo.com/d/folders/1/messages/29279?.intl=uk&.lang=en-GB&.partner=none&.src=fp.

seven QIPs in all eight UN peace operations from 2017–18.[51] In contrast, the CIMIC section completed seven QIPs within three to eight months in a single UN peace operation in Sudan (the details are discussed in Chapter IV). This achievement demonstrated the practice of appropriate leadership skills for successful QIPs. Additionally, medical support coordination to provide basic medical services to local populations, involving all relevant stakeholders, was an example of leadership acumen in a UN peace operation. The Chief of CIMIC section never looked at his military rank (Lieutenant Colonel), status or protocol, but mixed with all tiers of different stakeholders, including local populations, to get the job done. The involvement of UN agencies, NGOs, private companies, government establishments, and a sports organization in QIPs bears testimony to the leadership potential of the CIMIC personnel. The leadership of the Special Representative of the Secretary General in the DRC (2004–7) helped to undertake a good number of QIPs during a three-year period.

Mentoring, at times, became a responsibility of the CIMIC section, to keep concerned officials in the loop and to assist in implementing the mandate. The Chief of CIMIC section in Sudan got an opportunity to demonstrate his accrued leadership skills when he mentored a Civil Affairs Officer/ QIP focal point of Sector 2 (an Australian female, UN Volunteer) and a Sector 2 Civil Engineer (a Chinese female, UN international staff). Both were members of the QIP Review Committee of Sector 2 in Sudan. They had not handled QIPs during their tenure;

158 Conclusion

thus, they apparently were not comfortable with forwarding QIPs to mission headquarters. The Chief of CIMIC section was aware of this fact and went to Sector 2 in Wau before initiating the project, "Renovation of the Wau Eye Clinic." Taking along the Sector 2 CIMIC Officer, he met with these two officers separately and discussed the project with them at length. Apparently, they were convinced, and he decided to stay in Wau during New Year's Eve. They then completed the project proposal and arranged a meeting of the QIP Review Committee of Sector 2. The committee approved the project and submitted it to mission headquarters for final approval. The civil affairs officer/QIP focal point for Sector 2 volunteered to jointly assist in the supervision of the QIP, along with the Sector 2 CIMIC officer. The Chief of CIMIC section carried the approved QIP proposal with him and left for Khartoum, assisted in convening the QIPs Management Committee at the UNMIS headquarters, obtained approval, became project officer, and completed the project on time.[52]

Finally, the gamut of QIPs demanded the establishment of a QIP management cell at the headquarters of the mission. In Sudan, QIPs were implemented from the mission's inception in 2005, though there had been slow progress and non-completion/follow up of projects until mid-2009. Beginning in September 2009, the Office of the Chief of Staff at the mission headquarters had to take on the responsibility of integrating QIPs with the CIMIC unit.[53] The importance of QIPs in promoting peace in post-conflict communities cannot be understated, given that QIPs are implemented within a short time frame to ensure confidence-building and to demonstrate the early dividends of stability to the population. Therefore, the UN mission in Sudan felt it necessary to establish a QIP management cell within the mission in order to better manage QIPs. The mission Strategic Planning Office suggested a separate "QIP section" (with CIMIC entities) in 2010 in order to provide effective and efficient programme management in mission headquarters and in sectors.[54]

The study found that the QIP programme management cell may be established with the following staff: one programme coordinator, one CIMIC officer, two project officers, one finance assistant, one language assistant, and one project assistant for each sector (local/national staff). Based on lessons learned from Sudan, a QIP's coordination mechanism is suggested for UN peace operations in Figure 5.2, by taking CIMIC entities onboard.

The lessons and good practices of CIMIC activities, and the involvement of CIMIC personnel in QIPs in Sudan, can serve the purpose of steering CIMIC's involvement with assistance in national-level state-building and local outreach. CIMIC activities and QIPs undertaken in the DRC and Sudan remain examples for assistance with state-building at the country- and community-level.

The appropriate identification, efficient management, and sustainment of CIMIC activities were essential in a wider context in order to assist with national-level state-building. A strong monitoring system needs to be introduced to ensure the implementation of projects. If needed, the military or humanitarian patrols' programme would be integrated to include visits to project sites. When undertaking a project, gender issues need to be addressed, considering the cultural

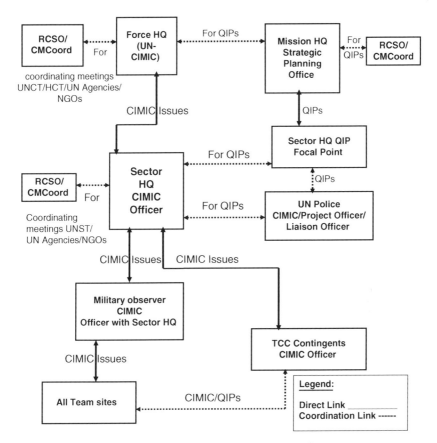

FIGURE 5.2 Suggested coordination mechanism for QIPs management in UN peace operations.
Developed by the Chief of CIMIC section, UN Mission in Sudan, April 2010.

dimensions of local populations. Locations and types of projects need to be determined from national or state plans, or other plans related to the UN Development Assistance Framework and to the UN Sustainable Development Goals (SDGs) 2030. This approach would contribute greatly to the 2019 reforms initiative of the UN. Thus, CIMIC projects and QIPs should be termed "CIMIC projects for *trust and confidence building*," because these endeavours result in assistance with state-building at the national level and outreach to local populations.

Recommendations

The study found that there was value in promoting the unity of efforts between UN peace operation components and UN agencies. UN agencies remain committed to the long-term goal of sustainable peace in conflict-ridden countries. Such

160 Conclusion

agencies have no official mandate of peacekeeping, but functionally and organizationally become involved in peacekeeping or peacebuilding in the broader sense.[55] These agencies are not directly under the chain of command of UN headquarters. In Sudan, CIMIC section's liaison were routed through the Resident Coordinator's Support Office, which is the office of the Deputy Special Representative of the Secretary-General/Resident Coordinator/ Humanitarian Coordinator, who wears three hats. The Deputy Special Representative of the Secretary-General/ Resident Coordinator/Humanitarian Coordinator remains responsible for the coordination of both humanitarian operations and the UN country team, and for maintaining links with governments and other parties and donors.[56] Moreover, the same individual again reports to three different UN entities based in New York. In multi-dimensional UN peace operations managing such a gamut of coordination with humanitarian and development entities remained a huge challenge for a single person. Moreover, Cedric De Coning argued, "The most serious concerns raised to date relate to the perceived loss of humanitarian independence when the Humanitarian Coordinator becomes one of the Deputy Special Representatives of the Secretary- General."[57] Recently the UN attempted to address the issue and strengthened the Resident Coordinator's office during a process of reforms in 2018–19.[58] However, the same individual would continue to wear three hats at the UN mission level.

CIMIC activities and challenges emerging from UN peace operations remain unaccounted for at the strategic level. Other than the UN-CIMIC policy, UN peace operations did not receive any strategic guideline related to CIMIC due to absence of a dedicated structure at the UN headquarters. Additionally, CIMIC-related issues were reported by the force commander to the Department of Peace Operations at the UN headquarters. These issues were also not followed up subsequently due to the absence of a dedicated entity at the Department of Peace Operations. Although CIMIC issues remained the responsibility of the Deputy Military Adviser of the Department of Peace Operations, there was no staffing.[59] As at the field mission level, the CIMIC outfit's role has been defined for the military and humanitarian components of CIMIC, therefore, the establishment of an entity at the strategic level (UN headquarters in New York) to coordinate with the Office for the Coordination of Humanitarian Assistance/Emergency Relief Coordinator and the Development Operations Coordination Office on CIMIC matters became a necessity. This was acknowledged by the Under-Secretary General of the Department of Peace Operations during his interview with the author on May 25, 2018, and with the Chief of Current Military Operations Service of the Department of Peace Operations on August 3, 2018, respectively.[60] According to the letter of the UN Secretary-General to the member states on launching reform of the UN,

> With the start of the [New Year], four new departments came into being: the Department of Management Strategy, Policy and Compliance, the Department of Operational Support, the Department of Political and Peacebuilding

Affairs and the Department of Peace Operations. We also launched a reinvigorated Resident Coordinator system, served by a newly-fortified Development Coordination Office, thus opening a new era in the way we support efforts to advance sustainable development.[61]

The study found that CIMIC related entities have not been addressed in the context of the reform of the UN,[62] which became effective from January 1, 2019.[63] The study of CIMIC structure revealed that the following Figure 5.3 may serve as a coordination link at the strategic level between the Department of Political and Peacebuilding Affairs, the Peacebuilding Support Office, the Department of Peace Operations, the Department of Operational Support, the Emergency Relief Coordinator, and the Development Operations Coordination Office.

Here the CIMIC cell may remain responsible for providing strategic direction to UN peace operations through the Department of Peace Operations/Department of Political and Peacebuilding Affairs and also for receiving information from UN peace operations through the same departments, and in turn may follow up/coordinate with the Emergency Relief Coordinator/Development Operations Coordination Office (as applicable). The suggested CIMIC cell, as a minimum, may be composed of one colonel (P5 level), one lieutenant colonel for CIMIC activities (P4 level), one lieutenant colonel as the QIPs focal point (P4 level), and one general assistant.[64] These personnel need experience of UN peace operations in

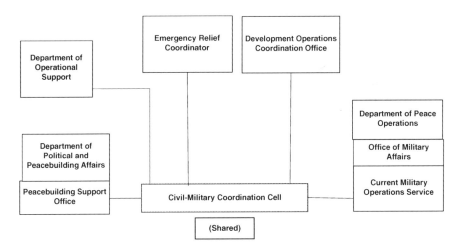

FIGURE 5.3 Establishment of CIMIC cell at UN headquarters and coordination link with different departments and offices.
Prepared by the author in consultation with Nedialko Kostov, Special Assistant to the Assistant Secretary-General, Department of Peace Operations (April 2-3, 2019); Md Arifur Reza, Deputy Chief Current Military Operations Service, and S M Asadul Haque, Peacekeeping Affairs Officer, Current Military Operations Service, Department of Peace Operations, UN Headquarters (February 4-5, 2019). (Developed by the author)

162 Conclusion

CIMIC outfits, with requisite qualification in CIMIC for the military, development partners, and humanitarian stakeholders.

Inclusion of dedicated CIMIC outfits in UN peace operations assisted in both Sudan and the DRC with an efficient undertaking of CIMIC activities and QIPs. Such outfits are embedded with Western armies to undertake CIMIC projects in operational areas. In the past couple of decades, specific CIMIC military units have been formally recognized to facilitate military-civilian cooperation in some of the armies within NATO. In Rwanda, a Canadian CIMIC unit worked closely with a lead civilian agency and the UN Development Programme to coordinate the delivery of humanitarian relief supplies to Rwandan refugees.[65] Canada also deployed a CIMIC unit in Afghanistan.[66] The inclusion of CIMIC officers in select UN agencies also resulted in better coordination with UN peace operations, bridging the gap of organizational cultures. Apart from CIMIC outfits in UN peace operations, for instance, the World Food Programme in Sudan had a staff assigned as CIMIC officer, who helped to coordinate CIMIC activities with the UN mission.

Jean-Luc Marrett argues that "The theme of CIMIC should focus on a UN objective with common agendas, synergy in efforts, and shared burdens to achieve tasks."[67] Civil assistance – mission support and community support – remained one of the important tools for CIMIC outfits to assist in state-building. Community support projects – a people-centric approach – are undertaken through QIPs and CIMIC activities, to instill trust and confidence amongst the local populations. Through these activities/projects UN peace missions assisted in state-building at the national level for sustained peace and development. TCC military forces remained responsible to help secure a safe environment on the ground and at the same time through CIMIC activities assisted in state-building. These military forces have the capacity and capability to offer assistance to complete a project within the shortest possible timeframe. However, according to Ashraf Ghani and Clare Lockhart, "a random series of efforts to 'win hearts and minds' through projects often occur that instead cause frustration and resentment."[68] They further contend that "local populations in Afghanistan often stated that the QIPs designed to 'win their hearts and minds' were disappointing in their quality."[69] Therefore, QIPs in UN peace operations should be broad in nature with appropriate funding, targeting assistance to state-building endeavours.

Final Thoughts

In conclusion, the UN can develop increased capacity for bottom-up state-building in post-colonial societies. Many parts of Africa remain at risk from political instability, economic insecurity, and armed conflict, aggravated by climate pressures. Building peace and stability there requires more than security and policing operations. The sources of conflict-related to address state-building can be overcome. A strong CIMIC complement in UN peace operations worked in Sudan and DRC at reinforcing local solutions and capacity to overcome unique local challenges. It may very well work elsewhere to enable African nations to shape their own future.

Conclusion   163

Notes

1 UN Department of Peacekeeping Operations and Department of Field Support, *United Nations Peacekeeping Operations: Principles and Guidelines* (New York: United Nations, 2008), 28–29.
2 UN Department of Peacekeeping Operations and Department of Field Support, 28–29.
3 Joshua S. Goldstein, *Winning the War on War: The Decline of Armed Conflict Worldwide* (New York: Plume, 2012), 126.
4 MONUC Deputy Special Representative of the Secretary-General, Deployment of Bangladeshi peacekeepers in the Eastern Congo, Discussion with Bangladesh Team, 22 April 2003.
5 United Nations Security Council, "UN Panel of Experts on the Illegal Exploitation of Natural Resources and Other Forms of Wealth from the DRC", UN Documents, 23 October 2003, 20, https://www.undocs.org/S/2003/1027.
6 United Nations, "Report of the High-Level Independent Panel on Peace Operations", Review on Peace Operations (New York, 16 June 2015), 14, https://peaceoperationsreview.org/wp-content/uploads/2015/08/HIPPO_Report_1_June_2015.pdf. The HIPPO held its Regional Consultation for Asia Pacific in Bangladesh in January 2015. The author was the Director Overseas Operations at the Army Headquarters. He took personal initiative to organize the forum and presented a keynote paper, "Challenges and Way Ahead for UN peace operations: Experience of Bangladesh." A few issues were addressed in the final report of the HIPPO from the paper.
7 United Nations, 39.
8 "Thousands of Congolese Benefitting from MONUC"s Quick Impact Projects – Democratic Republic of the Congo", ReliefWeb, accessed 18 January 2019, https://reliefweb.int/report/democratic-republic-congo/thousands-congolese-benefitting-monucs-quick-impact-projects.
9 MONUC CIMIC Unit and OCHA, "Guidelines for Interaction between MONUC Military and Humanitarian Organizations" (MONUC, Kinshasa, 8 June 2006), 19.
10 UNMIS Strategic Planning Office, "UNMIS QIPs: Tracking Sheet", 23 August 2009.
11 "These observations were obtained from relevant policies and guidelines on CIMIC and QIPs of the UNMIS and MONUC respectively."
12 Michael Brzoska and Hans-Georg Ehrhart, "Civil-Military Cooperation in Post-Conflict Rehabilitation and Reconstruction: Recommendations for Practical Action", *Stiftung Entwicklung Und Frieden (SEF)/ Development and Peace Foundation*, no. Policy paper 30 (November 2008): 1–12.
13 Ashraf Ghani and Clare. Lockhart, *Fixing Failed States: A Framework for Rebuilding a Fractured World* (Oxford; Oxford University Press, 2008), 176, http://public.eblib.com/choice/publicfullrecord.aspx?p=415309.
14 Wendy Fenton and Sean Loughna, "The Search for Common Ground: Civil–Military Coordination and the Protection of Civilians in South Sudan" (Humanitarian Policy Group and Overseas Development Institute, London, December 2013), 1, https://www.odi.org/sites/odi.org.uk/files/odi-assets/publications-opinion-files/8784.pdf.
15 OCHA, "Agenda for the 95th UN-CMCoord Course, Nairobi, Kenya, November 8–13, 2009", 28 October 2009.
16 Cedric de Coning, "Civil-Military Coordination Practices and Approaches Within United Nations Peace Operations", *Journal of Military and Strategic Studies* 10, no. 1 (1 September 2007): 14, https://jmss.org/article/view/57636.
17 Coning, 15.
18 UNMIS, Khartoum, "UNMIS Military Update: The Force Commander's Monthly Military Report-May 2006", Monthly Report (Khartoum, 18 June 2006), 12.
19 National Mechanism, Ministry of Foreign Affairs Office, Republic of Sudan, "Note Verbale from Ministry of Foreign Affairs to UNMIS", Note Verbale: MFA/PHD/23/2/295, 20 April 2010.

164 Conclusion

20 Colonel Gonzalo Mila (Retired), Former Commander, Uruguay Infantry Battalion in MONUC, CIMIC Practice by Uruguayan Units in UN Peace Operations, Discussion on involvement of Uruguayan units in CIMIC activities, 5 April 2019.

21 Coning, "Civil-Military Coordination Practices and Approaches Within United Nations Peace Operations", 19. The author's personal experience also suggests that South Asian countries spent their own funds to undertake CIMIC activities in UN peace operations.

22 Coning, 19.

23 "The Chief of CIMIC section in UNMIS (2009–10) was the author." The veterinary hospital project was supervised by the veterinary team of the Indian Outfit in UNMIS. Chief of CIMIC section visited the construction site during his tenure in UNMIS. This was a dire necessity for the populations, who earned their livelihood through livestock.

24 BRAC Southern Sudan, "Quick Impact Project Proposal: Providing Food Security Through Enhanced Mechanical Ploughing", Project proposal (Khartoum: UNMIS, CIMIC, 10 February 2010).

25 Saleem Ahmad Khan and Mirwais Durrani, "Joint Visit Report on CIMIC and QIP by the Strategic Planning Office and Chief CIMIC", Joint Report (Khartoum, 12 August 2009).

26 BRAC Southern Sudan, "Quick Impact Project Proposal: Providing Food Security Through Enhanced Mechanical Ploughing"; UNMIS CIMIC, "UNMIS QIP: Project Closure Report-School to Build a Sustainable Environment Free from Exploitation and War", Final Report (Khartoum, 30 May 2010).

27 BRAC Southern Sudan, "Quick Impact Project Proposal: Providing Food Security Through Enhanced Mechanical Ploughing".

28 UNMIS CIMIC, "Quick Impact Proposal: Solar Power System for Hospital and Secretariat of Social Services in Abyei", 12 February 2010; UNMIS CIMIC, "Quick Impact Project: Solar Power System for Three Schools in Abyei", 17 March 2010.

29 UNMIS CIMIC, "Quick Impact Project: Renovation of the Wau Eye Clinic-Contract Deed" (UNMIS, 16 February 2010); UNMIS CIMIC, "Quick Impact Project Proposal: Seating Support for the School", 20 August 2009.

30 UNMIS CIMIC, "Quick Impact Project Closure Report: Seating Support for the School in Hai Elrahma", Project Closure Report (Khartoum, 24 October 2009); UNMIS CIMIC, "Quick Impact Project: Renovation of Wau Eye Clinic-Project Closure Report", 20 March 2010.

31 Mutaz Gourashi, "CIMIC as a Tool for Socio-Economic Development in Sudan", 1 February 2019; *Present state of Al Gourashi Steel Factory*, Video file, 3 vols (Khartoum, Sudan, 2019). Coincidently, the mobile phone number of Mutaz Gourashi was found in the contract deed of the projects. The author called him after nine years and obtained three video files through the "Whatsapp" on current status of the factory.

32 UNMIS CIMIC, "UNMIS QIP: Project Closure Report-School to Build a Sustainable Environment Free from Exploitation and War".

33 BRAC Southern Sudan, "Quick Impact Project Proposal: Providing Food Security Through Enhanced Mechanical Ploughing".

34 UNMIS CIMIC, "Quick Impact Proposal: Solar Power System for Hospital and Secretariat of Social Services in Abyei"; UNMIS CIMIC, "Quick Impact Project: Solar Power System for Three Schools in Abyei".

35 UNMIS CIMIC, "Quick Impact Project Closure Report: Seating Support for the School in Hai Elrahma".

36 Cedric De Coning, "Civil-Military Relations and U.N. Peacekeeping Operations", *World Politics Review*, 19 May 2010, 11.

37 Khan and Durrani, "Joint Visit Report on CIMIC and QIP by the Strategic Planning Office and Chief CIMIC". During the joint visit, it was observed that Sector 3 CIMIC officer and QIPs focal point were sharing the same office for better coordination and management of QIPs.

38 UNMIS CIMIC, "Quick Impact Project: Renovation of Wau Eye Clinic-Project Closure Report".

Conclusion 165

39 UNMIS CIMIC, "UNMIS QIP: Project Closure Report-School to Build a Sustainable Environment Free from Exploitation and War".

40 BRAC Southern Sudan, "Quick Impact Project Proposal: Providing Food Security Through Enhanced Mechanical Ploughing".

41 UNMIS CIMIC, "Quick Impact Project Closure Report: Seating Support for the School in Hai Elrahma".

42 UNMIS Civil Affairs, "UNMIS CIMIC-Civil Affairs Joint Report on Quick Impact Project in Muglad" (Khartoum, 30 May 2010).

43 BRAC Southern Sudan, "Quick Impact Project Proposal: Providing Food Security Through Enhanced Mechanical Ploughing".

44 UNMIS CIMIC, "UNMIS QIP: Project Closure Report-School to Build a Sustainable Environment Free from Exploitation and War".

45 UNMIS CIMIC, "Quick Impact Project: Renovation of Wau Eye Clinic-Project Closure Report".

46 Luc Reychler, "Peacemaking, Peacekeeping, and Peacebuilding", *Oxford Research Encyclopedia of International Studies*, 1 March 2010, https://doi.org/10.1093/acrefore/9780190846626.013.274.

47 UNMIS CIMIC, "Quick Impact Project: Renovation of Wau Eye Clinic-Project Closure Report".

48 Colonel AKM Majharul Haque, Contingent Commander, "Email: Report on Present Status of the Wau Eye Clinic by Bangladesh Infantry Battalion (UNMISS)," February 13, 2019 and Email from Major Fazle Rabbi, CIMIC officer of the unit covering reports from the administrator of the clinic dated April 16, 2019 and Yusuf Abdi Salah Head of Office OCHA Sub office, Wau, South Sudan dated May 8, 2019, https://mail.yahoo.com/d/folders/1/messages/29279?.intl=uk&.lang=en-GB&.partner=none&.src=fp, https://mail.yahoo.com/d/folders/1/messages/31007?reason=invalid_cred.

49 Jean-Pierre Lacroix, Interview with the UN Under-Secretary-General of the Department of Peace Operations on "The United Nations Peace Operations in Africa", 24 May 2018.

50 Wendy Fenton and Sean Loughna, "HPG Working Paper", 21.

51 The UN Intranet Global, "Quick Impact Projects (QIPs) | Iseek-External.Un.Org", Quick Impact Projects 2017–18, 10 December 2018, https://iseek-external.un.org/departmental_page/quick-impact-projects-qips.

52 UNMIS CIMIC, "Quick Impact Project: Renovation of Wau Eye Clinic-Project Closure Report".

53 Mekbib Kifle, "Report on Proposal for Quick Impact Projects Program Management Cell" (Khartoum: UNMIS, 1 June 2010).

54 Mekbib Kifle.

55 Lorraine Elliott, "The United Nations and Social Reconstruction in Disrupted States", in *From Civil Strife to Civil Society: Civil and Military Responsibilities in Disrupted States* (New York: United Nations University Press, 2003), 262.

56 UN Department of Peacekeeping Operations and Department of Field Support, *United Nations Peacekeeping Operations: Principles and Guidelines*, 69.

57 Cedric De Coning, "Civil-Military Coordination Practices and Approaches Within United Nations Peace Operations," *Journal of Military and Strategic Studies* 10, no. 1 (September 1, 2007): 27, https://jmss.org/article/view/57636.

58 Economic and Social Council General Assembly, "Repositioning the United Nations Development System to Deliver on the 2030 Agenda: Our Promise for Dignity, Prosperity and Peace on a Healthy Planet" (New York: United Nations, 21 December 2017), https://digitallibrary.un.org/record/1473546?ln=en.

59 Chief Current Military Operations Service Colonel Alexander Senchilin Department of Peace Operations, UN Headquarters, Civil-Military Coordination arrangements in UN Headquarters, One to one meeting, 30 August 2018.

60 Lacroix, Interview with the UN Under Secretary-General of the Department of Peace Operations on "The United Nations Peace Operations in Africa", Dhaka, 24 May 2018;

166 Conclusion

Colonel Alexander Senchilin, The United Nations Peace Operations in Africa: Role of Civil-Military Coordination, New York, 3 August 2018.

61 António Guterres, "United to Reform", Formal letter from the UN Secretary-General to Member States, 29 January 2019, 1, https://reform.un.org/.

62 UN DPPA-DPO Information Management Unit, "The 2019 Departments of Political and Peacebuilding Affairs and Department of Peace Operations" (United Nations, 1 January 2019), 1–2.

63 United Nations, "United to Reform |", United to Reform, 1 January 2019, https://reform.un.org/.

64 Md Arifur Reza, Discussion on CIMIC Cell at UN headquarters with Deputy Chief Current Military Operations Service, Department of Peace Operations, UN Headquarters, Telephone, 5 February 2019; S M Asadul Haque, Discussion on CIMIC Cell at UN headquarters with Peacekeeping Affairs Officer, Current Military Operations Service, Department of Peace Operations, UN Headquarters, Telephone and email, 4 February 2019.

65 Christopher Ankersen, *Civil-Military Cooperation in Post-Conflict Operations: Emerging Theory and Practice* (Routledge, 2007), 26.

66 Ankersen, 23. In UN peace operations, the psychological and information operations are not included within the functions of CIMIC.

67 Jean-Luc Marrett, "Complex Emergencies: Disasters, Civil-Military Relations, and Transatlantic Cooperation", in *Disaster Response, Complex Emergencies: Disasters, Civil-Military Relations, and Transatlantic Cooperation* (New York, 2010), 351–55, http://www.disastergovernance.net/study_groups/civil_military_relations/.

68 Ashraf Ghani and Clare. Lockhart, *Fixing Failed States: A Framework for Rebuilding a Fractured World* (Oxford; Oxford University Press, 2008), 5, http://public.eblib.com/choice/publicfullrecord.aspx?p=415309.

69 Ashraf Ghani and Clare. Lockhart, *Fixing Failed States: A Framework for Rebuilding a Fractured World* (Oxford; Oxford University Press, 2008), 178, http://public.eblib.com/choice/publicfullrecord.aspx?p=415309.

GLOSSARY

Civil Affairs. "The role of civil affairs is to engage and assist local civilian authorities and communities in efforts to consolidate peace by restoring the political, legal, economic and social infrastructures that support democratic governance and economic development. Broad range of professional backgrounds among civil affairs officers include political science, law, international relations, business administration, engineering, economics or a specific sectoral area pertinent to the needs of a mission, such as education, health and finance. Civil affairs officers are the civilian face of the mission to the local population." (Peacekeeping Best Practices Unit. "Handbook on United Nations Multidimensional Peacekeeping Operations". Department of Peacekeeping Operations and Department of Field Support, December 2003, https://peacekeeping.un.org/sites/default/files/peacekeeping-handbook_un_dec2003_0.pdf).

Civil-Military Coordination. "Civil-Military coordination (CIMIC) refers to the coordination mechanisms and procedures used by civilian partners and the UN military within the UN System. UN-CIMIC refers to the coordination mechanisms between the civilian partners and the UN military. UN-CMCoord refers to interaction or coordination for humanitarian purposes through the Office for the Coordination of Humanitarian

DOI: 10.4324/9781003275404-7

168 Glossary

Affairs (OCHA). Whilst UN-CIMIC refers to a military staff function to support UN Mission objectives, UN Humanitarian CIMIC (UN-CMCoord) refers more to a 'dialogue' and interaction for humanitarian purposes." (Department of Peacekeeping Operations, and Department of Field Support. "Policy: Civil-Military Coordination in UN Integrated Peacekeeping Missions (UN-CIMIC)". United Nations, 1 November 2010).

Integrated Mission. "An integrated mission is a strategic partnership between a multidimensional UN peace operation and the UN Country Team and Humanitarian Country Team." (Peacekeeping Best Practices Unit. "Handbook on United Nations Multidimensional Peacekeeping Operations". Department of Peacekeeping Operations and Department of Field Support, December 2003, https://peacekeeping.un.org/sites/default/files/peacekeeping-handbook_un_dec2003_0.pdf).

Millennium Development Goals (MDGs). "Adopted by the UN in 2000, the eight Millennium Development Goals (MDGs)– which range from halving extreme poverty rates to halting the spread of HIV/AIDS and providing universal primary education, all by the target date of 2015–form a blueprint agreed to by all the world's countries and all the world's leading development institutions." ("United Nations Millennium Development Goals", Accessed April 14, 2019, https://www.un.org/millenniumgoals/).

Multidimensional peacekeeping. "Multidimensional peace operations are composed of a range of components, including military, civilian police, political affairs, rule of law, human rights, humanitarian, reconstruction, public information and gender. There are also a number of areas, such as mission support and security and safety of personnel, that remain essential to peacekeeping regardless of a particular mission's mandate." (Peacekeeping Best Practices Unit. "Handbook on United Nations Multidimensional Peacekeeping Operations". Department of Peacekeeping Operations and Department of Field

	Support, December 2003, https://peacekeeping. un.org/sites/default/files/peacekeeping-handboo-k_un_dec2003_0.pdf).
Peace operations.	In 1992, the UN Agenda for Peace defined peace operations as a "field mission, usually involving military, police, and civilian personnel, deployed with the consent of the belligerent parties to monitor and facilitate the implementation of cea-sefires, separation of forces or other peace agree-ments." The 2015 High-level Independent Panel on Peace Operations (HIPPO) report strongly urged "the UN to embrace the term "peace operations" to signify the full spectrum of responses required. Thus, in 2019, the UN changed the name of the Department of Peacekeeping Opera-tions to the Department of Peace Operations." Boutros-Ghali, Boutros, "An Agenda for Peace: Preventive Diplomacy, Peacemaking and Peace-keeping," International Relations, 1992, 201–18; Cedric De Coning, "Civil-Military Coordination in United Nations and African Peace Operations," The African Centre for the Constructive Resolu-tion of Disputes (ACCORD), UN Complex Peace Operations, n.d., 48.
Quick Impact Projects.	Quick Impact Projects (QIPs) are "small-scale, low-cost projects, funded by UN missions, that are planned and implemented within a short timeframe. QIPs aim to build confidence in the mission, the mandate or the peace process and respond to the needs expressed by local communities." (United Nations, "United Nations Department of Peace-keeping Operations/Department of Field Support Policy on Quick Impact Projects". United Nations, 21 January 2013).
State-building.	"State-building is a primary means of sustaining peace and involves a focus on supporting national actors to build institutions and structures. The principles that guide state-building are regarded as key in con-temporary peace-building activities, such as the rule of law, governance, education, health. State-building is a truly inter-disciplinary activities involving social sciences, international relations, political studies, anthropology, economics, international development and security studies." (Amanda Lucey, "Practical

170 Glossary

Pathways to Peace Lessons from Liberia and South Sudan," n.d., 8; United Nations Security Council, "Security Council Unanimously Adopts Resolution 2282 (2016) on Review of United Nations Peacebuilding Architecture Meetings Coverage and Press Releases," Official, UN: Meetings coverage and press releases, April 27, 2016, https://www.un.org/press/en/2016/sc12340.doc.htm; Shinoda, "Peace-Building and State-Building from the Perspective of the Historical Development of International Society," 25–43, Zoe Scott, "Literature Review on State-Building," Governance and Social Development Resource Centre, May 2007, 18).

Sustainable Development Goals. "The 2030 Sustainable Development Goals (SDGs) were adopted by all UN Member States in 2015, provides a shared blueprint for peace and prosperity for people and the planet, now and into the future. At its heart are the 17 SDGs, which are an urgent call for action by all countries—developed and developing—in a global partnership. They recognize that ending poverty and other deprivations must go hand-in-hand with strategies that improve health and education, reduce inequality, and spur economic growth." (United Nations, "SDGs: Sustainable Development Knowledge Platform", Sustainable Development Goals Knowledge Platform, 2015, https://sustainabledevelopment.un.org/sdgs).

Traditional peacekeeping. "Traditional peacekeeping operations, model of a military operation deployed in support of a political activity. These operations involve military tasks such as monitoring ceasefires and patrolling buffer zones between hostile parties and are carried out by UN peacekeepers who may or may not be armed and who are widely known as "blue helmets" or "blue berets" because of their distinctive headgear." (Peacekeeping Best Practices Unit. "Handbook on United Nations Multidimensional Peacekeeping Operations". Department of Peacekeeping Operations and Department of Field Support, December 2003, https://peacekeeping.un.org/sites/default/files/peacekeeping-handbook_un_dec2003_0.pdf).

UN Development Assistance Framework.	"UN Development Assistance Framework (UNDAF) is a strategic, medium-term results framework that describes the collective vision and response of the UN system to national development priorities and results on the basis of normative programming principles. It describes how UN Country Teams will contribute to the achievement of development results based on a common country analysis and UN comparative advantage. The 2017 UNDAF guidance supports UN Country Teams to produce a new generation of UNDAFs that reflect the 2030 Agenda for Sustainable Development with SDGs at their core, and position them to provide quality support to member states in their aspiration to achieve the 2030 Agenda." (UN Sustainable Development Group, "UN Development Assistance Framework Guidance", 2017, https://undg.org/document/2017-undaf-guidance/).

APPENDIX 1

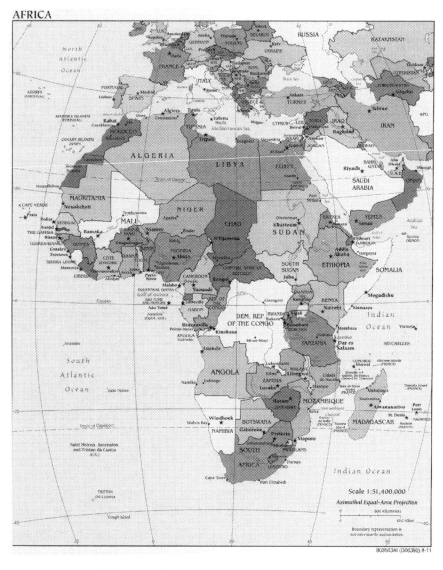

FIGURE A.1 Map of Africa as of 2011.
Source: http://legacy.lib.utexas.edu/maps/africa/txu-pclmaps-oclc-792930639-africa-2011.jpg, accessed on 30 June 2022.

APPENDIX 2

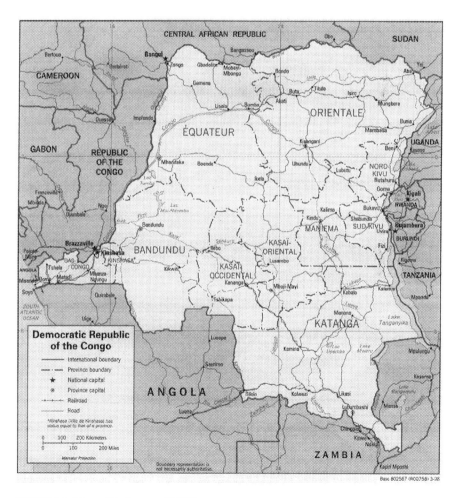

FIGURE A.2 Map of Sudan as of 2007.
Source: http://legacy.lib.utexas.edu/maps/africa/congo_demrep_pol98.jpg

APPENDIX 3

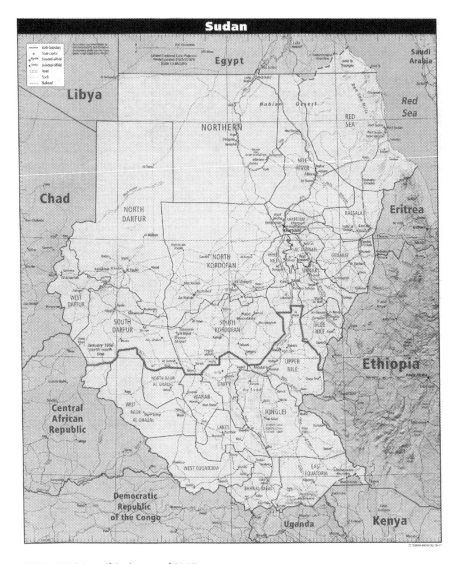

FIGURE A.3 Map of Sudan as of 2007.
Source: http://legacy.lib.utexas.edu/maps/africa/txu-oclc-219400066-sudan_pol_2007.jpg accessed on 30 June 2022.

APPENDIX 4

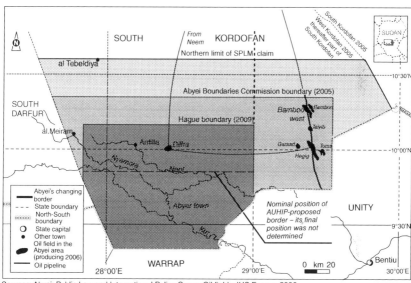

FIGURE A.4 A history of the Abyei border agreements.
Source: Small Arms Survey/Joshua Craze, 2011. Map created by MAPgrafix.
Craze, Joshua. 2011. *Creating Facts on the Ground: Conflict Dynamics in Abyei*. Human Security Baseline Assessment for Sudan and South Sudan, Working Paper No. 26. Geneva: Small Arms Survey.

APPENDIX 5

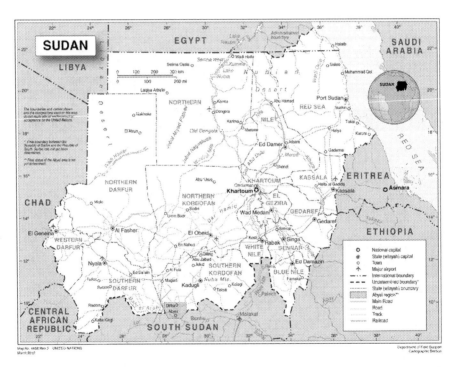

FIGURE A.5 Map of Sudan, encircled areas were the locations of UN deployment and CIMIC activities from 2005 to June 2010.

Source: Sudan | Geospatial, location data for a better world (un.org), accessed 01 July 2022.

APPENDIX 6

FIGURE A.6 Map of South Sudan (Erstwhile Southern Sudan)-encircled areas were the locations of UN deployment and CIMIC activities from 2005 to June 2010.
Source: South Sudan, Map No. 4450 Rev. 2, July 2020, United Nations, https://www.un.org/geospatial/content/south-sudan-1, accessed on 27 June 2022.

REFERENCES

Primary sources

Archives

Bureau of Technical Assistance, ONUC. 'Public Works Related Photos'. Photos on public works activities by ONUC Civilian Operations. Bukavu, October 1964. S-0728–0038, Box 38, File 1. United Nations Archives Records Management Section.

Chief Civilian Operations ONUC. Letter to Under Secretary Special Political Affairs, UN HQ, New York. 'Financial Guarantee of UNESCO Programme for Secondary Education by the Government of the Congo'. Letter to Under Secretary Special Political Affairs, UN HQ, New York, 22 June 1964. S-0728, Box 11, File 1. United Nations Archives Records Management Section.

Chief Civilian Operations ONUC. Letter to Under Secretary Special Political Affairs, UN HQ, New York. 'Financial Guarantee of UNESCO Programme for Secondary Education by the Government of the Congo'. Letter to Under Secretary Special Political Affairs, UN HQ, New York, 22 June Letter to Under Secretary in charge of civilian affairs, ONUC. 'Public Administration'. Letter to Under Secretary in charge of civilian affairs, ONUC, 12 December 1962. S-0728, Box 31, File 2. United Nations Archives Records Management Section.

Chief Civilian Operations ONUC. Letter to Under Secretary Special Political Affairs, UN HQ, New York. 'Financial Guarantee of UNESCO Programme for Secondary Education by the Government of the Congo'. Letter to Under Secretary Special Political Affairs, UN HQ, New York, 22 June Letter to Senior Adviser, Social Affairs, ONUC Leopoldville. 'Rural Development'. Letter to Senior Adviser, Social Affairs, ONUC Leopoldville, 1 December 1963. S-0728, Box 36, File 4. United Nations Archives Records Management Section.

Chief Civilian Operations ONUC. Letter to Under Secretary Special Political Affairs, UN HQ, New York. 'Financial Guarantee of UNESCO Programme for Secondary Education by the Government of the Congo'. Letter to Under Secretary Special Political Affairs, UN HQ, New York, 22 June. Formal Message No. ONUC 2391. 'UNESCO Programme for School Year 1964/65'. Formal Message No. ONUC 2391, 22 June 1964. S-0728, Box 11, File 1. United Nations Archives Records Management Section.

References **179**

Combined Civil Affairs Committee. 'United Nations Relief and Rehabilitation Administration', 11 August 1944. Series 0805, Box 2 and 4, File 2 and 14. United Nations Archive Records Management Section.

Deane, Philip. 'A UN Failure in Congo May Depose Hammarskjold'. *Toronto Global and Mail*. 2 February 1961. RG 25, Volume 5221. Library and Archives Canada, Government of Canada.

Deputy Chief Civilian Operations ONUC. Letter to Assistant Director, USAID. 'Agenda for Meeting on Public Works by ONUC Civilian Operations'. Letter to Assistant Director, USAID, 6 July 1963. S-0729, Box 1, File 16. United Nations Archives Records Management Section.

Executive Chairman Technical Assistance Board UN New York. '1964 Contingency Authorization – Public Health Advisory Services and Training – Congo', 6 January 1964. S-0728, Box 21, File 7. United Nations Archives Records Management Section.

FAO. *Progress Report December 1962: Agriculture*. Monthly Report. ONUC Civilian Operations. Leopoldville: FAO, January 1963. Series S-0844, Box 1, File 8 and S-0728, Box 1, File 1. United Nations Archives Records Management Section.

FAO ONUC. 'Need for FAO Experts in the Congo', 27 May 1963. S-0728, Box 1, File 1. United Nations Archives Records Management Section.

H. Kaufman, Acting civilian Affairs Officer, ONUC Stanleyville. Letter to S. Habib Ahmed, Chief Civilian Operations, ONUC Leopoldville. 'Police Advisory Services and Training'. Letter to S. Habib Ahmed, Chief Civilian Operations, ONUC Leopoldville, 5 June 1963. *S-0728*, Box 30, File 2. United Nations Archives Records Management Section.

International Monetary Fund. 'Currency Unification in the Congo', 1 July 1963. S-0728, Box 11, File 5. United Nations Archives Records Management Section.

Military Information. *Report on Communication Network: 1963*. Short Report. HQ ONUC. Leopoldville, 5 March 1963. S-0728, Box 6, File 4. United Nations Archives Records Management Section.

Nova Scotia Public Records. 'The Loyalist Collection, Papers Relating to the Negro Refugees: 1783–1839 and 1785–1853', n.d.

ONUC HQ. *An Interim Report – Congolese Civil Police Problems and Possible Solutions*. Leopoldville, 19 June 1963. *S-0728*, Box 30, File 2. United Nations Archives Records Management Section.

ONUC Public Administration Section. *Public Administration and Police Training*. Report of 1963. Leopoldville, 1963. S-0728, Box 31, File 2. United Nations Archives Records Management Section.

ONUC Staff New York. *Report of the United Nations Operation in the Congo as on May 1, 1963*. Yearly. New York: United Nations, 1 May 1963. MG 30, C241, Volume 32, Personal stuffs of John King Gordon, Senior Information Officer, United Nations. Library and Archives Canada, Government of Canada.

'Papers: 1785–1853. The Loyalist Collection'. Accessed 28 January 2018. https://loyalist.lib.unb.ca/node/4426.

Senior Consultant, Bureau of Social Affairs, ONUC. Letter to Senior Consultant Finance, ONUC Leopoldville. 'Social Research'. Letter to Senior Consultant Finance, ONUC Leopoldville, 14 December 1962. *S-0728*, Box 36, File 4. United Nations Archives Records Management Section.

United Nations Civilian Operations in the Congo. *Progress Report on United Nations Civilian Operations in the Congo (1–30 November, 1960)*. Monthly Report. Leopoldville, 12 May 1960. RG 25, Volume 5221. Library and Archives Canada, Government of Canada.

United Nations Press Services Office of Public Information. 'UN Civilian Operations in the Congo: The Largest Technical Assistance Operation Ever Undertaken'. Press Release.

180 References

New York, 1 March 1962. *MG* 30, C241, Volume 32, Personal stuffs of John King Gordon, Senior Information Officer, United Nations. Library and Archives Canada, Government of Canada.

United Nations, agencies, and field missions: documents, reports, and correspondence

'About UNICEF'. UNICEF. Accessed 18 October 2018. https://www.unicef.org/about/who/index_introduction.html.

'Africa Regional Perspective'. UNDP 50th Anniversary. Accessed 18 October 2018. http://50.undp.org/en/africa.

António Guterres. Formal letter from the UN Secretary-General to Member States. 'United to Reform'. Formal letter from the UN Secretary-General to Member States, 29 January 2019. https://reform.un.org/.

'Arbitration Agreement between The Government of Sudan and The Sudan Peoples' Liberation Movement/ Army on Delimiting Abyei Area', 7 July 2008. https://pca-cpa.org/wp-content/uploads/sites/175/2016/02/Arbitration-Agreement-between-The-Government-of-Sudan-and-The-Sudan-People's-Liberation-Movement_Army-on-Delimiting-Abyei-Area-July-7-2008.pdf.

BRAC Southern Sudan. 'Quick Impact Project Proposal: Providing Food Security Through Enhanced Mechanical Ploughing'. Project proposal. Khartoum: UNMIS, CIMIC, 10 February 2010.

Brahimi, Lakhdar. 'Letter Dated 17 August 2000 from the Chairman of the Panel on United Nations Peace Operations to the Secretary-General'. Report of the Panel on United Nations Peace Operations. New York, 17 August 2000.

Chief CIMIC Section, UNMIS. Formal. 'Correspondence between UNMIS CIMIC Section and State Ministry of Health Government of Southern Sudan'. Formal, 18 January 2010.

Department of Peacekeeping Operations. 'The United Nations Civil-Military Coordination Policy 2002'. United Nations, 9 September 2002.

Department of Peacekeeping Operations. 'The United Nations Civil-Military Coordination Policy 'United Nations Peacekeeping'. United Nations Peacekeeping. Accessed 13 February 2019. https://peacekeeping.un.org/en/node.

Department of Peacekeeping Operations. 'The United Nations Civil-Military Coordination Policy 'United Nations Peacekeeping Operations: Principles and Guidelines'. United Nations, 2008. https://peacekeeping.un.org/sites/default/files/capstone_eng_0.pdf.

Department of Peacekeeping Operations, and Department of Field Support. 'Policy: Civil-Military Coordination in UN Integrated Peacekeeping Missions (UN-CIMIC)'. United Nations, 1 November 2010.

Department of Peacekeeping Operations, and Department of Field Support. 'Policy: Civil-Military Coordination in UN Integrated Peacekeeping Missions (UN-CIMIC)'. United Nations, 1 November*United Nations Peacekeeping Operations: Principles and Guidelines*. New York: United Nations, 2008.

Department of Public Information. *UN Yearbook: 1946–47*. The Yearbook of the United Nations: The authoritative reference work on the UN System, 47 1946. https://www.unmultimedia.org/searchers/yearbook/page.jsp?bookpage=180&volume=1946-47.

Department of Public Information. *UN Yearbook: United Nations Peace Operations 2009: Year in the Review*, January 2010.

Directorate General International Health. Formal letter. 'Letter from Federal Ministry of Health, Republic of Sudan to Federal Ministry of Foreign Affair'. Formal letter, 13 April 2010.

References   181

DPPA-DPO Information Management Unit. 'The 2019 Departments of Political and Peace-building Affairs and Department of Peace Operations'. United Nations, 1 January 2019.

'Funds, Programmes, Specialized Agencies and Others', 18 November 2014. http://www.un.org/en/sections/about-un/funds-programmes-specialized-agencies-and-others/index.html.

General Assembly, Economic and Social Council. *Repositioning the United Nations Development System to Deliver on the 2030 Agenda: Our Promise for Dignity, Prosperity and Peace on a Healthy Planet.* New York: United Nations, 21 December 2017. https://digitallibrary.un.org/record/1473546?ln=en.

'History World Food Programme'. Accessed 18 October 2018. http://www1.wfp.org/history.

'History World Food Day, 16 October Food and Agriculture Organization of the United Nations'. Accessed 18 October 2018. http://www.fao.org/world-food-day/history/en/.

Khan, Saleem Ahmad, and Mirwais Durrani. *Joint Visit Report on CIMIC and QIP by the Strategic Planning Office and Chief CIMIC.* Joint Report. Khartoum, 12 August 2009.

Mekbib Kifle. *Report on Proposal for Quick Impact Projects Program Management Cell.* Khartoum: UNMIS, 1 June 2010.

'Memorandum of Understanding between BRAC Southern Sudan and Ministry of Education, Government of Southern Sudan', n.d.

MONUC. 'Resolutions of the Security Council on MONUC – United Nations Organization Mission in the Democratic Republic of the Congo'. MONUC: United Nations Organization Mission in the Democratic Republic of the Congo, 2010 1999. https://peacekeeping.un.org/sites/default/files/past/monuc/resolutions.shtml.

MONUC CIMIC Unit, and OCHA. *Guidelines for Interaction between MONUC Military and Humanitarian Organizations.* MONUC, Kinshasa, 8 June 2006.

'MONUC Facts and Figures – United Nations Organization Mission in the Democratic Republic of the Congo'. Accessed 27 February 2019. https://peacekeeping.un.org/sites/default/files/past/monuc/facts.shtml.

MONUC Force Headquarters. 'MONUC: Force Commander's Directive on CIMIC'. MONUC, 1 June 2003.

'MONUC Rehabilitating Two Important Buildings in Dungu MONUC'. Accessed 24 January 2019. https://monuc.unmissions.org/en/monuc-rehabilitating-two-important-buildings-dungu.

Mountain, Ross. Formal letter. 'Letter on Guidelines for Interaction between MONUC Military and Humanitarian Organizations from Humanitarian Coordinator, the DRC to UN Heads of Agencies, MONUC Heads of Offices, Heads of Sections, and NGOs'. Formal letter, 4 December 2006.

National Mechanism, Ministry of Foreign Affairs Office, Republic of Sudan. Note Verbale: MFA/PHD/23/2/295. 'Note Verbale from Ministry of Foreign Affairs to UNMIS'. Note Verbale: MFA/PHD/23/2/295, 20 April 2010.

Nations, Food and Agriculture Organization of the United. *Dimensions of Need: An Atlas of Food and Agriculture.* Food & Agriculture Org., 1995.

OCHA. 'Agenda for the 95th UN-CMCoord Course, Nairobi, Kenya, November 8–13, 2009', 28 October 2009.

OCHA. 'Agenda for the 95th UN-CMCoord Course, Nairobi, Kenya, November 8–13, 'Civil-Military Coordination Guidelines for Sudan'. OCHA, 1 April 2008.

'OCHA'. OCHA. Accessed 15 October 2018. https://www.unocha.org/node.

Office for the Coordination of Humanitarian Affairs (OCHA). *Civil-Military Coordination Handbook.* Geneva: OCHA, 2003.

Office for the Coordination of Humanitarian Affairs (OCHA). 'Guidelines on the Use of Military and Civil Defence Assets to Support United Nations Humanitarian Activities in

182 References

Complex Emergencies'. OCHA, 22 May 2017. https://www.unocha.org/publication/guidelines-use-military-and-civil-defence-assets-support-united-nations-humanitarian.

'ONUC'. Accessed 30 January 2018. https://peacekeeping.un.org/sites/default/files/past/onucB.htm.

QIPs Management Team, UNMIS. *Annual Evaluation (July 1, 2009 – June 30, 2010) QIPs in UNMIS*. Yearly report. Khartoum, August 2010. https://mail.yahoo.com/d/folders/1/messages/30476?.intl=ca&.lang=en-CA&.partner=none&.src=fp.

United Nations High Commissioner for Refugees. UNHCR Resources and Publications *Global Reports*. UNHCR. Accessed 11 October 2018. http://www.unhcr.org/resources-and-publications.html.

The Comprehensive Peace Agreement between The Government of The Republic of The Sudan and The Sudan People's Liberation Movement/Sudan People's Liberation Army, 2005. https://peaceaccords.nd.edu/sites/default/files/accords/SudanCPA.pdf.

UN Sustainable Development Group. 'UN Development Assistance Framework Guidance', 2017. https://undg.org/document/2017-undaf-guidance/.

UN Women. 'How We Work: UN System Coordination: Gender Mainstreaming'. UN Women. Accessed 28 January 2019. http://www.unwomen.org/en/how-we-work/un-system-coordination/gender-mainstreaming.

UNDP. 'Leadership, Trust and Legitimacy in Southern Sudan's Transition after 2005'. In *Capacity Is Development*, 1–18, 2010. https://www.undp.org/content/dam/aplaws/publication/en/publications/capacity-development/drivers-of-change/leadership/leadership-trust-and-legitimacy-in-southern-sudan-transition-after-2005/Leadership_trust%20and%20legitimacy%20in%20Southern%20Sudan%20transition%20after%202005.pdf.

'UNDP – United Nations Development Programme'. Accessed 18 October 2018. http://www.undp.org/content/undp/en/home.html.

'UNDP 50th Anniversary'. UNDP 50th Anniversary. Accessed 18 October 2018. http://50.undp.org/en/.

'UNICEF: 70 Years for Every Child'. Accessed 18 October 2018. https://www.unicef.org/about-us/70-years-for-every-child.

'UNICEF DR Congo – Our Programs'. Accessed 18 October 2018. https://www.unicef.org/drcongo/french/activities.html.

United Nations. 'Award in the Arbitration Regarding the Delimitation of the Abyei Area between the Government of Sudan and the Sudan People's Liberation Movement/Army', 22 July 2009. legal.un.org/riaa/cases/vol_XXX/145–416.pdf.

United Nations. 'Award in the Arbitration Regarding the Delimitation of the Abyei Area between the Government of Sudan and the Sudan People's Liberation Movement/Army', 22 July 'First United Nations Emergency Force (UNEF I) – Mandate'. Middle East-UNEF I Mandate. Accessed 28 October 2018. https://peacekeeping.un.org/sites/default/files/past/unef1mandate.html.

United Nations. 'Award in the Arbitration Regarding the Delimitation of the Abyei Area between the Government of Sudan and the Sudan People's Liberation Movement/Army', 22 July 'History of the United Nations'. Official. United Nations, 21 August 2015. http://www.un.org/en/sections/history/history-united-nations/.

United Nations. 'Award in the Arbitration Regarding the Delimitation of the Abyei Area between the Government of Sudan and the Sudan People's Liberation Movement/Army', 22 July 'ONUC Mandate'. UN peacekeeping. Republic of the Congo – ONUC, 14 July 1960. https://peacekeeping.un.org/sites/default/files/past/onucM.htm.

United Nations. 'Award in the Arbitration Regarding the Delimitation of the Abyei Area between the Government of Sudan and the Sudan People's Liberation Movement/Army', 22 July 'ONUMOZ'. Official. Mozambique, United Nations Operation in

Mozambique. Accessed 18 November 2018. https://peacekeeping.un.org/sites/default/files/past/onumoz.htm.

United Nations. 'Award in the Arbitration Regarding the Delimitation of the Abyei Area between the Government of Sudan and the Sudan People's Liberation Movement/Army', 22 July 'Report of the High-Level Independent Panel on Peace Operations'. Review on Peace Operations. New York, 16 June 2015. https://peaceoperationsreview.org/wp-content/uploads/2015/08/HIPPO_Report_1_June_2015.pdf.

United Nations. 'Award in the Arbitration Regarding the Delimitation of the Abyei Area between the Government of Sudan and the Sudan People's Liberation Movement/Army',22 July 'SDGs: Sustainable Development Knowledge Platform'. Sustainable Development Goals Knowledge Platform, 2015. https://sustainabledevelopment.un.org/sdgs.

United Nations. 'Award in the Arbitration Regarding the Delimitation of the Abyei Area between the Government of Sudan and the Sudan People's Liberation Movement/Army', 22 July 'Sport and Peace: Social Inclusion, Conflict Prevention and Peace-Building', 202–246. New York: United Nations. Accessed 28 February 2019. https://www.un.org/sport/sites/www.un.org.sport/files/ckfiles/files/Chapter6_SportandPeace.pdf.

United Nations. 'Award in the Arbitration Regarding the Delimitation of the Abyei Area between the Government of Sudan and the Sudan People's Liberation Movement/Army', 22 July 'Teaching about Decolonization'. Department of Public Information, 1991.

United Nations. 'Award in the Arbitration Regarding the Delimitation of the Abyei Area between the Government of Sudan and the Sudan People's Liberation Movement/Army', 22 July *The United Nations and the Congo: Some Salient Facts*. New York: United Nations, 1963.

United Nations. 'Award in the Arbitration Regarding the Delimitation of the Abyei Area between the Government of Sudan and the Sudan People's Liberation Movement/Army', 22 July 'UNAMIR'. Rwanda: United Nations Assistance Mission for Rwanda. Accessed 20 November 2018. https://peacekeeping.un.org/sites/default/files/past/unamir.htm.

United Nations. 'Award in the Arbitration Regarding the Delimitation of the Abyei Area between the Government of Sudan and the Sudan People's Liberation Movement/Army', 22 July 'United Nations Department of Peacekeeping Operations/ Department of Field Support Policy on Quick Impact Projects'. United Nations, 21 January 2013.

United Nations. 'Award in the Arbitration Regarding the Delimitation of the Abyei Area between the Government of Sudan and the Sudan People's Liberation Movement/Army', 22 July 'United Nations Operation in Somalia I (UNOSOM I)'. Somalia, UNOSOM I. Accessed 20 November 2018. https://peacekeeping.un.org/sites/default/files/past/unosomi.htm.

United Nations. 'Award in the Arbitration Regarding the Delimitation of the Abyei Area between the Government of Sudan and the Sudan People's Liberation Movement/Army', 22 July 'United Nations Organization Mission in the Democratic Republic of the Congo (MONUC)'. MONUC. Accessed 15 November 2018. https://peacekeeping.un.org/sites/default/files/past/monuc/index.shtml.

United Nations. 'Award in the Arbitration Regarding the Delimitation of the Abyei Area between the Government of Sudan and the Sudan People's Liberation Movement/Army', 22 July 'United to Reform '. United to Reform, 1 January 2019. https://reform.un.org/.

United Nations. 'Award in the Arbitration Regarding the Delimitation of the Abyei Area between the Government of Sudan and the Sudan People's Liberation Movement/Army', 22 July 'UNMEE: United Nations Mission in Ethiopia and Eritrea'. Accessed 20 November 2018. https://peacekeeping.un.org/sites/default/files/past/unmee/index.html.

United Nations. 'Award in the Arbitration Regarding the Delimitation of the Abyei Area between the Government of Sudan and the Sudan People's Liberation Movement/Army',

184 References

22 July 'UNOMSIL'. Sierra Leone, United Nations Observer Mission in Sierra leone, July 1998. https://peacekeeping.un.org/sites/default/files/past/unomsil/Unomsil.htm.

United Nations. 'Award in the Arbitration Regarding the Delimitation of the Abyei Area between the Government of Sudan and the Sudan People's Liberation Movement/Army', 22 July 'UNTAG'. Official. Namibia, United Nations Transition Assistance Group. Accessed 17 November 2018. https://peacekeeping.un.org/sites/default/files/past/untag.htm.

United Nations. 'Award in the Arbitration Regarding the Delimitation of the Abyei Area between the Government of Sudan and the Sudan People's Liberation Movement/Army', 22 July 'UNTAG'. Namibia-UNTAG. Accessed 17 November 2018. https://peacekeeping.un.org/sites/default/files/past/untagFT.htm.

United Nations. 'Award in the Arbitration Regarding the Delimitation of the Abyei Area between the Government of Sudan and the Sudan People's Liberation Movement/Army', 22 July 'United Nations Peacebuilding', Official, United Nations Peacebuilding, Accessed 26 March 2020, https://www.un.org/peacebuilding/.

'United Nations Millennium Development Goals'. Accessed 14 March 2019. http://www.un.org/millenniumgoals/.

United Nations Mission in Sudan. 'Memorandum of Understanding between United Nations Mission in Sudan and BRAC Southern Sudan', 31 March 2010.

'United Nations Relief and Rehabilitation Administration – UNARMS'. Accessed 11 October 2018. https://search.archives.un.org/united-nations-relief-and-rehabilitation-administration-1947.

United Nations Security Council. *Final Report of the Secretary-General on the UN Operation in Mozambique*. Final Report. New York, 23 December 1994. https://documents-dds-ny.un.org/doc/UNDOC/GEN/N94/515/76/PDF/N9451576.pdf?OpenElement.

United Nations Security Council. *Final Report of the Secretary-General on the UN Operation in Mozambique*. Final Report. New York, 23 December 1977. https://documents-dds-ny.un.org/doc/UNDOC/GEN/N97/234/17/IMG/N9723417.pdf?OpenElement.

United Nations Security Council. *Final Report of the Secretary-General on the United Nations Observer Mission in Liberia*. Final Report. New York, 12 September 1997. https://documents-dds-ny.un.org/doc/UNDOC/GEN/N97/234/17/IMG/N9723417.pdf?OpenElement.

United Nations Security Council. *Final Report of the Secretary-General on the UN Operation in Mozambique*. Final Report. New York, 23 December 'Report of the Independent Inquiry into the Actions of the United Nations during the 1994 Genocide in Rwanda [S/1999/1257]'. United Nations Peacekeeping, 15 December 1999. https://peacekeeping.un.org/en/report-of-independent-inquiry-actions-of-united-nations-during-1994-genocide-rwanda-s19991257.

United Nations Security Council. *Final Report of the Secretary-General on the UN Operation in Mozambique*. Final Report. New York, 23 December 'Report of the Secretary-General on the Sudan'. Quarterly. New York, 21 December 2005. www.un.org/en/ga/search/view_doc.asp?symbol=S/2005/821.

United Nations Security Council. *Final Report of the Secretary-General on the UN Operation in Mozambique*. Final Report. New York, 23 December 2004. https://documents-dds-ny.un.org/doc/UNDOC/GEN/N04/411/23/PDF/N0441123.pdf?OpenElement

United Nations Security Council. *Report of the Security Council Mission to West Africa, 20–29 June 2004*. Special Report. New York, 2 July 2004. https://documents-dds-ny.un.org/doc/UNDOC/GEN/N04/411/23/PDF/N0441123.pdf?OpenElement.

United Nations Security Council. *Final Report of the Secretary-General on the UN Operation in Mozambique*. Final Report. New York, 23 December 'Security Council Unanimously Adopts Resolution 2282 (2016) on Review of United Nations Peacebuilding Architecture Meetings Coverage and Press Releases'. Official. UN: Meetings coverage and press releases, 27 April 2016. https://www.un.org/press/en/2016/sc12340.doc.htm.

United Nations Security Council. *Final Report of the Secretary-General on the UN Operation in Mozambique*. Final Report. New York, 23 December 'Special Report of the Secretary-General on the UN Mission in Ethiopia and Eritrea'. Special Report. New York, 7 April 2008. https://documents-dds-ny.un.org/doc/UNDOC/GEN/N08/292/37/PDF/N0829237.pdf? OpenElement.

United Nations Security Council. *Final Report of the Secretary-General on the UN Operation in Mozambique*. Final Report. New York, 23 December 'Special Report of the Secretary-General on the United Nations Mission in Liberia'. Final Report. New York, 15 November 2016. https://unmil.unmissions.org/sites/default/files/special_unmil_sg_report_15_november_2016.pdf.

United Nations Security Council. *Final Report of the Secretary-General on the UN Operation in Mozambique*. Final Report. New York, 23 December 'The April 2011 Report of the Secretary-General on the Sudan'. Quarterly. New York, 12 April 2011. http://www.un.org/en/ga/search/view_doc.asp?symbol=S/2011/239.

United Nations Security Council. *Final Report of the Secretary-General on the UN Operation in Mozambique*. Final Report. New York, 23 December 'The December 2010 Report of the Secretary-General on the Sudan'. Quarterly. New York, 31 December 2010. http://www.un.org/en/ga/search/view_doc.asp?symbol=S/2010/681.

United Nations Security Council. *Final Report of the Secretary-General on the UN Operation in Mozambique*. Final Report. New York, 23 December 'The January 2007 Report of the Secretary-General on the Sudan'. Quarterly. New York, 25 January 2007. http://www.un.org/en/ga/search/view_doc.asp?symbol=S/2007/42.

United Nations Security Council. *Final Report of the Secretary-General on the UN Operation in Mozambique*. Final Report. New York, 23 December 'The United Nations Security Council Resolution 1590 (2005)'. United Nations, 24 March 2005. http://www.un.org/en/ga/search/view_doc.asp?symbol=S/RES/1590(2005).

United Nations Security Council. *Final Report of the Secretary-General on the UN Operation in Mozambique*. Final Report. New York, 23 December 'The United Nations Security Council Resolution 1997 (2011)', 11 July 2011. http://www.un.org/en/ga/search/view_doc.asp?symbol=S/RES/1997(2011).

United Nations Security Council. *Final Report of the Secretary-General on the UN Operation in Mozambique*. Final Report. New York, 23 December 'Thirty-First Report of the Secretary-General on the United Nations Organization Mission in the Democratic Republic of the Congo'. MONUC Mission Closing Report. New York, 30 March 2010. http://www.un.org/en/ga/search/view_doc.asp?symbol=S/2010/164.

United Nations Security Council. *Final Report of the Secretary-General on the UN Operation in Mozambique*. Final Report. New York, 23 December 'UN Panel of Experts on the Illegal Exploitation of Natural Resources and Other Forms of Wealth from the DRC'. UN Documents, 23 October 2003. https://www.undocs.org/S/2003/1027.

United Nations Security Council. *Final Report of the Secretary-General on the UN Operation in Mozambique*. Final Report. New York, 23 December 'UN Security Council Resolution 1279 (1999) – MONUC'. United Nations, 30 November 1999. http://www.un.org/en/ga/search/view_doc.asp?symbol=S/RES/1279(1999).

United Nations Security Council. *Final Report of the Secretary-General on the UN Operation in Mozambique*. Final Report. New York, 23 December 'UN Security Council Resolution 1457: UN Panel of Experts on the Illegal Exploitation of Natural Resources and Other Forms of Wealth from the DRC – Based on Actions on the Report Dated 15–10–2002'. United Nations, 24 January 2003. http://www.un.org/en/ga/search/view_doc.asp?symbol=S/RES/1457%282003%29.

186 References

United Nations Security Council. *Final Report of the Secretary-General on the UN Operation in Mozambique*. Final Report. New York, 23 December 'UN Security Council Resolution 1590 (2005): Establishment of the UN Mission in Sudan'. United Nations, 24 March 2005. http://www.un.org/en/ga/search/view_doc.asp?symbol=S/RES/1590.

United Nations Security Council. *Final Report of the Secretary-General on the UN Operation in Mozambique*. Final Report. New York, 23 December 'United Nations Security Council Resolution 1484 (2003): Authorization of Deployment of Interim Emergency Multinational Force in the Eastern DRC'. United Nations, 30 May 2003. www.un.org/en/ga/search/view_doc.asp?symbol=S/RES/1484%282003%29.

UNMIS CIMIC Section. *Quick Impact Project Closure Report: Seating Support for the School in Hai Elrahma*. Project Closure Report. Khartoum, 24 October 2009.

UNMIS CIMIC Section. *Quick Impact Project Closure Report: Seating Support for the School in Hai Elrahma*. Project Closure Report. Khartoum, 24 October *Quick Impact Project Closure Report: Sports for Peace – Supporting Internally Displaced Persons and Disadvantage Population through Sudan Football Association*. Project Closure Report. Khartoum, 24 February 2010.

UNMIS CIMIC Section. *Quick Impact Project Closure Report: Seating Support for the School in Hai Elrahma*. Project Closure Report. Khartoum, 24 October 'Quick Impact Project Proposal: Hygienic Water in Water-Yard through Separation of Human and Animal Water Source', 1 June 2010.

UNMIS CIMIC Section. *Quick Impact Project Closure Report: Seating Support for the School in Hai Elrahma*. Project Closure Report. Khartoum, 24 October 'Quick Impact Project Proposal: Rehabilitation of a Girls School and Providing Furniture', 1 June 2010.

UNMIS CIMIC Section. *Quick Impact Project Closure Report: Seating Support for the School in Hai Elrahma*. Project Closure Report. Khartoum, 24 October 'Quick Impact Project Proposal: Safe Sanitation through Construction of Slaughter House in Al-Muglad', 1 June 2010.

UNMIS CIMIC Section. *Quick Impact Project Closure Report: Seating Support for the School in Hai Elrahma*. Project Closure Report. Khartoum, 24 October 'Quick Impact Project Proposal: Seating Support for the School', 20 August 2009.

UNMIS CIMIC Section. *Quick Impact Project Closure Report: Seating Support for the School in Hai Elrahma*. Project Closure Report. Khartoum, 24 October 'Quick Impact Project Proposal: Sports for Peace – Supporting Internally Displaced Persons and Disadvantage Populations', 22 December 2009.

UNMIS CIMIC Section. *Quick Impact Project Closure Report: Seating Support for the School in Hai Elrahma*. Project Closure Report. Khartoum, 24 October 'Quick Impact Project Proposal: Waste Management through Providing Waste Disposal Truck in Al-Muglad', 1 June 2010.

UNMIS CIMIC Section. *Quick Impact Project Closure Report: Seating Support for the School in Hai Elrahma*. Project Closure Report. Khartoum, 24 October 'Quick Impact Project: Renovation of the Wau Eye Clinic-Contract Deed'. UNMIS, 16 February 2010.

UNMIS CIMIC Section. *Quick Impact Project Closure Report: Seating Support for the School in Hai Elrahma*. Project Closure Report. Khartoum, 24 October 'Quick Impact Project: Renovation of Wau Eye Clinic-Project Closure Report', 20 March 2010.

UNMIS CIMIC Section. *Quick Impact Project Closure Report: Seating Support for the School in Hai Elrahma*. Project Closure Report. Khartoum, 24 October 'Quick Impact Project: Solar Power System for Three Schools in Abyei', 17 March 2010.

UNMIS CIMIC Section. *Quick Impact Project Closure Report: Seating Support for the School in Hai Elrahma*. Project Closure Report. Khartoum, 24 October 'Quick Impact Proposal: Solar Power System for Hospital and Secretariat of Social Services in Abyei', 12 February 2010.

UNMIS CIMIC Section. *Quick Impact Project Closure Report: Seating Support for the School in Hai Elrahma*. Project Closure Report. Khartoum, 24 October 'United Nations Mission in Sudan: Weekly/Monthly/ Yearly CIMIC Report', 23 January 2010.

References **187**

UNMIS CIMIC Section. *Quick Impact Project Closure Report: Seating Support for the School in Hai Elrahma.* Project Closure Report. Khartoum, 24 October 'UNMIS CIMIC Activities Summary-2008'. Yearly report. Khartoum, 20 January 2009.

UNMIS CIMIC Section. *Quick Impact Project Closure Report: Seating Support for the School in Hai Elrahma.* Project Closure Report. Khartoum, 24 October 'UNMIS QIP Completion Report', 29 June 2010.

UNMIS CIMIC Section. *Quick Impact Project Closure Report: Seating Support for the School in Hai Elrahma.* Project Closure Report. Khartoum, 24 October 'UNMIS QIP: Project Closure Report-School to Build a Sustainable Environment Free from Exploitation and War'. Final Report. Khartoum, 30 May 2010.

UNMIS CIMIC Section. *Quick Impact Project Closure Report: Seating Support for the School in Hai Elrahma.* Project Closure Report. Khartoum, 24 October 'UNMIS QIP Proposal: School to Build a Sustainable Environment Free from Exploitation and War', 7 January 2010.

UNMIS Civil Affairs Section. *UNMIS CIMIC-Civil Affairs Joint Report on Quick Impact Project in Muglad.* Khartoum, 30 May 2010.

'UNMIS Facts and Figures – United Nations Mission in the Sudan'. Accessed 27 February 2019. https://peacekeeping.un.org/sites/default/files/past/unmis/facts.shtml.

UNMIS, Khartoum. 'Monthly Update: The Force Commander's Monthly Military Report-May 2006'. Monthly Report. Khartoum, 18 June 2006.

UNMIS, Khartoum. 'Monthly Update: The Force Commander's Monthly Military Report-May Note Verbale: OCOS/PCR/01.02/MD/10.01. Note Verbale from UNMIS to Ministry of Foreign Affairs, Government of Sudan on "UNMIS Provision of Basic Medical Services to Local Populations"'. Note Verbale: OCOS/PCR/01.02/MD/10.01, 8 February 2010.

UNMIS, Khartoum. 'Monthly Update: The Force Commander's Monthly Military Report-May 'United Nations Mission in Sudan: Quick Impact Projects Administrative Instructions'. UNMIS, 1 February 2008.

UNMIS, Khartoum. 'Monthly Update: The Force Commander's Monthly Military Report-May 'UNMIS Military Update: The Force Commander's Monthly Military Report-January 2006'. Monthly Report. Khartoum, 8 February 2006.

UNMIS, Khartoum. 'Monthly Update: The Force Commander's Monthly Military Report-May 'UNMIS Military Update: The Force Commander's Monthly Military Report-July 2006'. Monthly Report. Khartoum, 9 August 2006.

UNMIS, Khartoum. 'Monthly Update: The Force Commander's Monthly Military Report-May 'UNMIS Military Update: The Force Commander's Monthly Military Report-May 2006'. Monthly Report. Khartoum, 18 June 2006.

UNMIS, Khartoum. 'Monthly Update: The Force Commander's Monthly Military Report-May 'UNMIS Military Update: The Force Commander's Monthly Military Report-November 2005'. Monthly Report. Khartoum, 5 December 2005.

UNMIS, Khartoum. 'Monthly Update: The Force Commander's Monthly Military Report-May 'UNMIS Military Update: The Force Commander's Monthly Military Report-October 2005'. Monthly Report. Khartoum, 14 November 2005.

UNMIS, Khartoum. 'Monthly Update: The Force Commander's Monthly Military Report-May 'UNMIS Military Update: The Force Commander's Six Monthly Military Report: March-September 2005'. Six monthly report. Khartoum, 30 October 2005.

UNMIS Military. 'Agro-Based Project by Military'. Southern Sudan, 1 September 2009.

UNMIS Resident and Humanitarian Coordinator. 'United Nations Civil Military-Coordination Guidelines for Sudan', 23 April 2008.

UNMIS Strategic Planning Office. 'UNMIS QIPs: Tracking Sheet', 23 August 2009.

188 References

UNRRA, Division of Public Information. Fifty Facts About UNRRA. Washington, D.C., 1946.
'UNTSO'. United Nations Peacekeeping. Accessed 29 October 2018. https://peacekeeping.un.org/en/mission/untso.
'Where Global Solutions Are Shaped for You About UNOG The League of Nations (1919–1946)'. Accessed 20 February 2018. https://www.unog.ch/80256EDD006AC19C/(httpPages)/17C8E6BCE10E3F4F80256EF30037D733?OpenDocument.
'Where We Work: Sudan'. Accessed 18 October 2018. https://www.unicef.org/where-we-work.

Manuals

African Centre for the Constructive Resolution of Disputes (ACCORD). 'The African Civil-Military Coordination Programme 2006', 2006.
Department of Peacekeeping Operations & Department of Field Support. *United Nations Civil-Military Coordination (UN-CIMIC) Specialized Training Materials*. New York: Department of Peacekeeping Operations and Department of Field Support, 2014.
'Humanitarian Civil-Military Coordination: Publications OCHA'. Accessed 15 February 2018. https://www.unocha.org/legacy/what-we-do/coordination-tools/UN-CMCoord/publications.
Joanna Harvey Cedric de, ed. *Civil Affairs Handbook*. New York, NJ: United Nations, 2012.
Peacekeeping Best Practices Unit. 'Handbook on United Nations Multidimensional Peacekeeping Operations'. Department of Peacekeeping Operations and Department of Field Support, December 2003. https://peacekeeping.un.org/sites/default/files/peacekeeping-handbook_un_dec2003_0.pdf.

News media

Al Jazeera English. 'Russia in Africa: Inside a Military Training Centre in CAR Talk to Al Jazeera In The Field – YouTube'. Russia is back in the Central African Republic, 15 April 2019. https://www.youtube.com/watch?v=1tECHzB-uCM.
Atem, Sirocco Mayom Biar. 'BRAC Extending Agriculture and Food Security in Southern Sudan'. *The Juba Post*. 15 March 2010.
Atem, Sirocco Mayom Biar. 'BRAC Extending Agriculture and Food Security in Southern Sudan'. 'UN CIMIC Gives BRAC 58,500 SDG for School Construction'. *The Juba Post*, 14 June 2010.
'BBC – Manchester – Communities – It Began in Manchester'. Accessed 5 March 2018. http://www.bbc.co.uk/manchester/content/articles/2005/10/14/151005_pan_african_congress_feature.shtml.
CGTN Africa. Chinese Soldiers in South Sudan Improving the Livelihoods of IDPS. Wau, South Sudan, 2014. https://youtu.be/6Q4sZZhFTzQ.
Colonel AKM Majharul Haque. 'Report on Present Status of the Wau Eye Clinic by Bangladesh Infantry Battalion (UNMISS)', 13 February 2019. https://mail.yahoo.com/d/folders/1/messages/29279?.intl=uk&.lang=en-GB&.partner=none&.src=fp.
'Democratic Republic of Congo Profile'. *BBC News*, 6 December 2017, sec. Africa. http://www.bbc.com/news/world-africa-13286306.
Gourashi, Mutaz. 'CIMIC as a Tool for Socio-Economic Development in Sudan', 1 February 2019.
Gourashi, Mutaz. *Present state of Al Gourashi Steel Factory*. Video file. 3 vols. Khartoum, Sudan, 2019.

Shine Theme. 'BRAC in South Sudan'. BRAC. Accessed 27 January 2019. http://www.brac. net/south-sudan?view=page.

The China Africa Project. 'There Are a Lot More Chinese Soldiers in Africa Today... and Likely More to Come'. Accessed 10 March 2019. https://www.youtube.com/watch?v= 6Q4sZZhFTzQ.

The Times Digital Archive. 'Berlin Conference: 1884–85'. 25 March 1891. University of New Brunswick.

The Times Digital Archive. 'Berlin Conference: 'The Suez Canal'. 6 June 1877.

The UN Intranet Global. 'Quick Impact Projects (QIPs) Iseek-External.Un.Org'. Quick Impact Projects 2017–18, 10 December 2018. https://iseek-external.un.org/departmental_page/quick-impact-projects-qips.

TRT World. China's Base in Djibouti. Djibouti. Accessed 11 March 2019. https://www.youtube.com/watch?v=rPYGEm1v5D4.

Secondary sources

Articles

African Centre for the Constructive Resolution of Disputes (ACCORD). 'CIMIC and Peacebuilding Operations'. *African Journal of Conflict Resolution* 5, no. 2 (2005): 89.

Brown, Cindy. '"To Bury the Dead and to Feed the Living": Allied Military Government in Sicily, 1943'. *Canadian Military History*, Special Edition, The Sicily Campaign, 22, no. 3 (Summer 2013): 35–48.

Boutros-Ghali, Boutros, "An Agenda for Peace: Preventive Diplomacy, Peacemaking and Peace-keeping", *International Relations*, Volume 11, Issue 3, 1 December 1992, 201–218. http://journals.sagepub.com/doi/10.1177/004711789201100302.

Coning, Cedric De. 'Civil-Military Coordination Practices and Approaches Within United Nations Peace Operations'. *Journal of Military and Strategic Studies* 10, no. 1 (1 September 2007). https://jmss.org/article/view/57636.

Coning, Cedric De. 'Civil-Military Coordination Practices and Approaches Within United Nations Peace Operations'. 'Civil-Military Relations and U.N. Peacekeeping Operations'. *World Politics Review*, 19 May 2010, 9.

Wendy Fenton and Sean Loughna. 'The Search for Common Ground: Civil–Military Coordination and the Protection of Civilians in South Sudan'. Humanitarian Policy Group and Overseas Development Institute, London, December 2013. https://www.odi. org/sites/odi.org.uk/files/odi-assets/publications-opinion-files/8784.pdf.

Gallagher, Dennis. 'The Evolution of the International Refugee System'. *The International Migration Review* 23, no. 3 (1989): 579–598.

Rossi, Christophe R. 'The International Community, South Sudan, and the Responsibility to Protect'. *International Law and Politics* 49, no. 129 (n.d.): 129–180.

Books

Ahmad Alawad Sikainga. *Slaves into Workers: Emancipation and Labor in Colonial Sudan.* Accessed 28 June 2019. https://books.google.com.bd/books.

Akol, Lam. *Southern Sudan: Colonialism, Resistance and Autonomy*. Trenton, Asmara: The Red Sea Press Inc., 2007. Websites.

Centre for Conflict Resolution. *Stabilising Sudan: Domestic, Sub-Regional, and Extra-Regional Challenges*. Policy Advisory Group Seminar Report. Cape Town, South Africa, 23 August

190   References

2010. http://www.operationspaix.net/DATA/DOCUMENT/4597~v~Stabilizing_Sudan__ Domestic_Sub_Regional_and_Extra_Regional_Challenges__Policy_Advisory_Group_ Seminar_Report.pdf.

Channel Research, Belgium. *Joint Evaluation of Conflict Evaluation and Peacebuilding in the Democratic Republic of Congo*. Synthesis Report. Ohain, Belgium, June 2011. https://www.oecd.org/countries/congo/48859543.pdf.

DR Congo/Mbandaka: MONUC Finances a New Quick Impact Project in Iyonda – Democratic Republic of the Congo. ReliefWeb. Accessed 18 January 2019. https://reliefweb.int/report/democratic-republic-congo/dr-congombandaka-monuc-finances-new-quick-impact-project-iyonda.

DRC: MONUC Funds Two Quick Impact Projects in Kisangani – Democratic Republic of the Congo. ReliefWeb. Accessed 18 January 2019. https://reliefweb.int/report/democratic-republic-congo/drc-monuc-funds-two-quick-impact-projects-kisangani.

Fifth Pan-African Congress All-African People's Revolutionary Party. Accessed 5 March 2018. http://www.aaprp-intl.org/taxonomy/term/81.

George Shepperson, St. Clare Drake. *The Fifth Pan-African Conference, 1945 and The All African People's Congress, 1958*. Accessed 5 March 2018. https://scholarworks.umass.edu/cgi/viewcontent.cgi?article=1053&context=cibs.

Government of Canada, National Defence. *Civilian-Military Cooperation Influence Activities 5th Canadian Division Canadian Army*, 25 February 2013. http://www.army-armee.forces.gc.ca/en/5-cdn-div-ia/cimic.page.

Hammarskjold, Dag. *Address by Secretary-General Dag Hammarskjold at University of California Convocation*. California, USA, 13 May 1954. https://digitallibrary.un.org/record/1291161?ln=en.

Office of the Historian, Department of State, US. *The Yalta Conference, 1945*. Accessed 5 March 2018. https://history.state.gov/milestones/1937-1945/yalta-conf.

Office of the Historian, US Government. *Milestones: 1830–1860 – Office of the Historian*. Accessed 15 February 2018. https://history.state.gov/milestones/1830-1860/liberia.

Saunders, Richard. *Strengthening International Support for Peacekeeping in Sudan: Lessons from UNMIS*, 1–21, 2007. https://yorkspace.library.yorku.ca/xmlui/bitstream/handle/10315/7151/SAUNDERS%20-%20UNMIS%20in%20Sudan%20(Dec%202007)-2.pdf?sequence=1&isAllowed=y.

'Sudan: SAS on Heglig & Abyei'. *The Arabist*. Accessed 22 January 2019. https://arabist.net/blog/2012/4/30/sudan-sas-on-heglig-abyei.html.

'What Is River Blindness? NTDs Protecting Sight'. Sightsavers (blog). Accessed 10 March 2019. https://www.sightsavers.org/protecting-sight/ntds/what-is-river-blindness/.

Lectures and interviews

Berg, Michelle. 'UN Mandate to Protect-Meaning and Mission Considerations Regarding Civilian Population, UN Agencies, and Affected Personnel'. Lecture presented at the Seminar on UN Peace Support Operations, Inter American Defense College, Washington DC, USA, 3 April 2019.

Berg, Michelle, An independent consultant. NGOs: The way it functions and requirement of training. Oral, 3 April 2019.

Brigadier General Mahbubur Rahman, Bangladesh in UNAMIR, Oral, Dhaka, 8 July 2019.

Colonel Alexander Senchilin, Chief Current Military Operations Service, Department of Peace Operations, UN Headquarters. Civil-Military Coordination arrangements in UN Headquarters. One to one meeting, 30 August 2018.

Colonel Gonzalo Mila (Retired), Former Commander, Uruguay Infantry Battalion in MONUC. CIMIC Practice by Uruguayan Units in UN Peace Operations. Discussion on involvement of Uruguayan units in CIMIC activities, 5 April 2019.

Deputy Special Representative of the Secretary-General, MONUC. Deployment of Bangladeshi peacekeepers in the Eastern Congo. Discussion with Bangladesh Team, 22 April 2003.

Edgar, Alistair. 'UN Peacekeeping with "Chinese Characteristics"?' In *Operating in Asia and Africa*. Fredericton, Canada, 2019. http://www.army-armee.forces.gc.ca/en/events/gregg-centre-conference.page.

Elsamani, Yousif. 'Minerals Potential and Resources in Sudan'. UNCTAD, 23 November 2015. http://unctad.org/meetings/en/Presentation/17OILGASMINE%20Dr%20Yousif%20Elsamani%20S1.pdf.

Haque, S M Asadul. Discussion on CIMIC Cell at UN headquarters with Peacekeeping Affairs Officer, Current Military Operations Service, Department of Peace Operations, UN Headquarters. Telephone and email, 4 February 2019.

Jean-Pierre Lacroix, Under Secretary General Department of Peacekeeping Operation. CIMIC in State-Building. Oral, Dhaka, 24 May 2018.

Reza, Md Arifur. Discussion on CIMIC Cell at UN headquarters with Deputy Chief Current Military Operations Service, Department of Peace Operations, UN Headquarters. Telephone, 5 February 2019.

INDEX

Abyei, Abyei Boundaries Commission 106–111, 113, 117, 124–126, 134, 153–154, 175
African Centre for the Constructive Resolution of Disputes (ACCORD) 41, 169
Addis Ababa Agreement 102, 105
advisory services 76, 81
agriculture 2, 6, 8, 11, 29–30, 33, 53, 75, 81, 103, 110, 121, 138, 146, 149
Akol, Lam 25
Algerian War 31
Angola 5, 19, 22, 62–64, 84, 145
Annan, Kofi 5, 64
anthropology 1, 169
armed conflict 5, 7, 12, 18, 21, 25, 63, 65, 104, 127, 162
armed forces 67, 88–89, 91, 107–108, 113, 149
Arthur House 73, 83
Assistance to Child Survival Initiative Programme 118–119
Atlantic Conference 19
Autesserre, Séverine 18

Bangladesh 9, 34, 87–88, 90, 113, 115–117, 129, 146, 148, 151–153, 154, 156–157
Belgian 23, 25, 65, 68–72, 75, 77–78, 81, 83, 93, 137
Best Practices 149
Betts, Raymond 3
Black UN 44–45, 155
Blue Nile 106, 110, 113, 117

Blue UN 44–45, 155
bottom-up 2, 8, 13, 41, 66, 115, 138, 145–147, 162
Brahimi, Lakhdar 6, 64, 65
Brahimi Report 6, 46, 64
Building Resources Across Communities (BRAC) 128–129, 132–134, 153

Capstone Doctrine 46–48, 64, 146
Chapter IX 3, 61, 67
Chapter VII 3, 65, 67, 85, 107, 111
Chief of CIMIC section 13, 112, 117–124, 127, 129, 133–138, 153–159
civil assistance 47, 51, 56, 114, 162
Civil Military Operations 7, 49
civil war 5, 12, 19, 25–26, 62–65, 70–71, 89, 103–105, 120, 124, 127, 130, 132, 134, 137, 150, 156
civilian operations 4, 6, 20, 72, 74, 79, 145
civil-military relations 12, 30, 39–40, 44, 156
CMCoord 7, 40, 49–51, 55, 159, 167–168
Cold War 1–6, 19–24, 28, 31, 34, 39–40, 46, 52, 63, 69, 75, 83, 110, 145
Communism 19, 21, 34
community support 51, 56, 152, 162
community-level 2, 8, 10–11, 33, 40, 56, 90–91, 103, 117, 146, 149, 158
complex emergencies 46,50
Comprehensive Peace Agreement 33, 102, 104–105, 113–114, 124, 134, 149
conflict-ridden 8, 20, 30–31, 34, 39–40, 42, 44–45, 50–51, 87, 134, 146, 152–153, 159

INDEX 193

consent-based operation 7, 49
country-level 40, 45, 149
Current Military Operations Service 160

Dag Hammarskjold 4, 62, 69, 72, 93
De Coning, Cedric 31, 39, 45, 49, 52, 160
Demobilization, Disarmament, and
   Reintegration (DDR) and Disarmament,
   Demobilization, Repatriation,
   Resettlement, and Reintegration
   (DDRRR) 2, 55, 65, 85, 87, 89–90, 149
Department of Peace Operations 2, 8, 156,
   160–161
Department of Peacekeeping Operations 5
Department of Political and Peacebuilding
   Affairs 2, 161
Doctors Without Borders 151

Economic and Social Council (ECOSOC) 67
Emergency Relief Coordinator 10, 54–55,
   160–161
energy 8–9, 11, 33, 103, 121–122, 124–125,
   138, 146, 149, 153
European Union 7, 49

Fanon, Frantz 68
female peacekeepers 53
First World War 2, 19, 24, 29
Food and Agricultural Organization (FAO)
   81, 132–133, 155
food supply 6, 75, 81
football 91, 116, 127
force commander 8, 42, 55, 75–76
Force Intervention Brigade 7
Force Publique 68
Forces Armées de la République
   Démocratique du Congo (FARDC) 34,
   88, 91
foreign trade 6, 75
forestry 29
Former Yugoslavia 7, 30, 35, 46

Garang, John 107
gender mainstreaming 53
General Assembly 3, 23, 61, 73
Genocide 5, 64, 83–84
Goldstein, Joshua S. 62
good governance 1, 24
Great Lakes 65, 84
guerilla warfare 89, 102, 105

Haskin, Jeanne 22
healthcare 5, 8, 25–26, 109
High-Level Independent Panel on Peace
   Operations (HIPPO) 10, 41, 121, 147, 169

hospitals 86, 91, 109, 115–117
host government 1, 19, 41, 49, 51, 63,
   118–119, 146, 148–149, 152, 156
Howard, Michael 21
human rights 6, 39, 52, 55, 88, 89, 168
humanitarian agencies 6, 54, 91
Humanitarian Coordinator 40, 47, 54–55,
   114, 137, 160
Humanitarian Country Team (HCT) 6, 44,
   47, 54–55, 64, 150, 159, 168
humanitarian partners 6, 40, 44
humanitarian space 42, 51, 53, 151
Huq, Ameerah 137
Hutus 5, 64

ideological warfare 19, 21
Internally Displaced PersonI (DPs) 8, 33,
   116, 120, 127, 130
in aid to civil administration 7, 20, 30,
   32, 40
indigenous 18, 24, 105, 147, 150
information-sharing 7, 51, 90, 150
integrated mission 6, 31, 146
Inter Agency Standing Committee 44–45
Inter-Governmental Authority on
   Development (IGAD) 105
international development 1, 169
international relations 1, 5, 28, 63, 167, 169
ivory 25, 104

Johnson, Hilde 105, 110, 112
Juba 109, 115, 122, 129, 133

Kabila, Joseph 86
Kabila, Laurent 84, 86, 89
Kasavubu, Joseph 68, 83
King Leopold II 45

Lacroix, Jean-Pierre 156
League of Nations 2, 3, 19, 23, 34
Lessons learnt 151
local ownership 11, 29, 49, 82, 92, 146,
   149, 155–156
local populations 2, 7, 8–12, 30, 56, 91,
   103, 108, 119, 121, 130, 151, 162
Luard, Evan 61
Lumumba, Patrice 4, 22, 62, 68
Lusaka Peace Agreement 33, 65

Macmillan, Margaret 2
Macqueen, Norrie 3–4, 63, 67–68, 84
Major-General Romeo Dallaire 42
Mamdani, Mahmoud 23
mandate gap 124, 156
Marshall Plan 28

194 INDEX

Mau Mau 31–32
Military and Civil Defence Assets (MCDA) 47
Military Government 6, 20, 28–30, 35, 105
military observers 43, 118, 151
Mobutu, Joseph 26, 65, 83, 147
Muglad 109, 134–135, 150, 155

National Liberation Front (*Front de libération nationale*) (FLN) 31–32
New Horizon 48
Non-Aligned Movement 23

Operation Husky 29
Oslo Guidelines 47
O'Sullivan, Christopher D. 62
outreach programmes 90

pacification 7, 20, 29–32, 40, 48, 151
peace dividend measures 86, 146
peace enforcement 5, 7, 12, 49, 63, 65–66, 85, 103–104
Peacebuilding Commission 7
people-centric 10, 41, 52, 56, 121, 147, 162
Permanent Court of Arbitration 109
post-conflict 2, 9–10, 13, 66, 158
President Nasser 72
protection of civilians 2, 5, 11, 31, 45, 48, 63–64, 88, 90–91, 107, 110, 120
public administration 1, 6, 30, 75–77
public information 6, 39, 55, 168
public works 6, 29, 75, 78, 80

recommendations 6, 23, 46, 52, 64, 153, 159
reconstruction 6, 39, 41, 46, 106, 168
resolution 3, 23, 25, 32, 41, 53, 63–66, 70, 88, 170

river blindness 122–123
roots of conflict 2–3, 8, 13, 19, 34, 86, 122, 145
rule of law 1, 6, 11, 39, 52, 55, 88, 169

Saikal, Amin 24
Sayward, Amy 5, 64
SDGs 10, 41, 49, 52, 147, 159, 170–171
Second World War 3, 4, 19–21, 26–28, 37, 104, 145
Security Sector Reform 2, 65–66, 88, 90, 149
Shipway, Martin 19
social welfare services 79
socio-economic development 26, 28, 49, 73, 125–126, 134, 147, 149, 154
source of conflict 19, 21, 24, 33, 126–127, 147
sports for peace 126–127
stabilization 5, 49, 63, 66, 89, 93, 145, 155
Sudan Model, the 149
Suez Canal 62

Thomson, Alex 24, 84
top-down 1, 4, 12, 14, 62–63, 73, 82, 93, 145
Tutsis 64

U Thant 72
UN Archives 66, 75
UN Charter 3–4, 61, 63, 66–67, 69, 107

veterinary services 29

Williams, Paul D. 25, 63
win the hearts and minds 10, 20, 30

Printed in the United States
by Baker & Taylor Publisher Services